For COLIN McMULLEN

RCC PILOTAGE FOUNDATION

THE ATLANTIC CROSSING GUIDE SECOND EDITION

Edited by PHILIP ALLEN

ADLARD COLES
8 Grafton Street, London W1

Adlard Coles
William Collins Sons & Co. Ltd
8 Grafton Street, London W1X 3LA

First published in Great Britain by
Adlard Coles 1983
Reprinted with amendments 1984, 1985
Second edition 1988
Revised reprint 1989

Copyright © RCC Pilotage Foundation 1983, 1988

British Library Cataloguing in Publication Data

Atlantic crossing guide.—2nd ed.
  1. Pilot guides—Atlantic Ocean
  I. Allen, Philip
  623.89′223 VK810

ISBN 0 229 11828 3

Typeset by CG Graphic Services, Tring, Herts
Printed and bound in Great Britain by
Butler & Tanner Ltd, Frome, Somerset

THE RCC PILOTAGE FOUNDATION

In 1976 an American member of the Royal Cruising Club, Dr Fred Ellis, indicated that he wished to make a gift to the Club in memory of his father, the late Robert H Ellis MD, of his friends Peter Pye and John Ives who were both prominent members; and as a mark of esteem for Roger Pinckney, a past Commodore of the Club. An independent charity known as the RCC Pilotage Foundation was formed and, with the approval of Dr Ellis, the funds provided by him were transferred to the Foundation.

At the request of K Adlard Coles, the Foundation undertook the 1980 revision of the *North Brittany Pilot* and was then asked by Professor A N Black to revise the *North Biscay Pilot*. The RCC Pilotage Foundation gratefully acknowledges to these authors the gift of the copyright of their two famous books. It is the intention of the Foundation and the publishers to revise them at appropriate intervals so that the valuable work of the original authors will be kept up-to-date for the benefit of cruising yachtsmen.

The Atlantic Crossing Guide is the first new book to be produced by the RCC Pilotage Foundation; it is intended to fill a gap in cruising literature by providing a basic guide to the sailing routes, islands and ports of the North Atlantic that are used by an ever increasing number of yachtsmen. The Foundation is deeply indebted to Philip Allen for the enormous amount of thought and work that has gone into the compilation of this book.

Contents

Introduction by Eric Hiscock   xi
Preface to the First Edition   xiii
Preface to the Second Edition   xv
Acknowledgements   xvi

Part I – Preparations

Chapter   1   THE PHILOSOPHY OF OCEAN CRUISING   3

2   ATLANTIC STRATEGY   5
Winds and Weather – Currents – Planning the Voyage

3   NAVIGATION   12
Background – Chart Table – Time – Barometers and
Thermometers – Books – Sextant – Charts and Plotting
Diagrams – Dead Reckoning – Great Circle Sailing – Checking
Compass Deviation – Landfall and Pilotage – Stars and Planets –
Modern Position Fixing Methods

4   THE MECHANICS OF CRUISING   22
Paperwork – Money – Books – Keeping the Log Book –
Watchkeeping – Maintenance – Docking Plan – Heavy Weather
– Clothing – Fishing – The Law – Landfall – Pests – Insurance

5   THE BOAT AND HER GEAR   34
The Hull – The Rig – Ground Tackle – Below Decks

6   THE CREW   47
Recruitment – Replacements en Route – Training – The Skipper

7   RADIO AND ELECTRONICS   52
Radio – Electronics

8   PROVISIONING   57
A Formula – A Test Run – Hints when Buying – A Spartan Diet

9   SPECIAL EQUIPMENT   60
Downwind Rig – Vane Steering – Extra Gear – Trysail –
Awnings

10 SAFETY WHEN OCEAN CRUISING — 64
Avoidable Risks and Prevention – Personal Safety Gear – Life
Saving Equipment – Man Overboard Drill – Fire – Gear Failure
– Illness – Radio – Security – Firearms

Part II – Ocean Passages
Chapter 11 EASTWARD — 77
General Description – Routes 1 and 1A – Routes 2 and 2A –
Routes 3, 3A and 3B – Currents – Winds and Weather – Special
Considerations – Ports – Passage Times and Distances – Charts
and Sailing Directions

12 LANDFALL ON EUROPEAN COASTS — 83
Formalities – The Approach – Scottish Coast – Irish Coast –
English Coast – French Coast – Oil Rigs

13 WESTWARD IN HIGH LATITUDES — 88
General Description – Route 1 – Route 2 – Route 3 – Route 4 –
Currents – Winds and Weather – Special Considerations – Ports
– Passage Times and Distances – Charts and Sailing Directions

14 LANDFALL ON THE CANADIAN AND AMERICAN
COASTS — 94
Formalities – Coast Guard – Cruising Licence – Sewage Disposal
– The Approach – Newfoundland – Nova Scotia – USA

15 THE TRADE-WIND ROUTE — 98
General Description – Part 1 (English Channel – Canary Is) –
Part 2 (Transatlantic Passage) – Provisioning – Watch Keeping –
Rythmic Rolling – Summary of Times and Distances – Charts,
Sailing Directions etc

16 INTERMEDIATE PASSAGES — 110
USA to Virgin Islands – Virgin Islands to USA – USA to
Bermuda – West Indies to Bermuda – Bermuda to Azores –
Azores to Gibraltar – English Channel to Azores – Azores to
English Channel

Part III – The Island Groups
Chapter 17   THE ISLAND GROUPS AND SOME PORTS — 129
Bermuda – Azores – Madeira – Canary Islands – Cape Verde
Islands – West Indies

Part IV — Port Information, Recommended Service Ports

30 recommended Entry and Departure Ports, and ports-of-call, with plans and tabulated details of the services available at each.   153

Bibliography   267

Index   273

List of Diagrams, Charts and Secondary Port Plans

Part I

Atlantic Currents	Fig. 1	7
Where to be and when	Fig. 2	9
Sextant – side error	Fig. 3	16
Seacock	Fig. 4	34
'Chum'	Fig. 5	38
Running-rig, boom	Fig. 6	61
Running-rig, halyard	Fig. 7	62

Part II

Gnomonic Projection (Routes Eastward)	Chart 1	79
Gnomonic Projection (Routes Westward)	Chart 2	89
Trade-wind Route	Chart 3	99
Iberian Peninsula	Chart 4	101
USA to Virgin Islands	Chart 5	111
Virgin Islands to USA	Chart 6	114
USA to Bermuda	Chart 7	116
W. Indies to Bermuda	Chart 8	120
Bermuda to Azores	Chart 9	122
Azores to Gibraltar and England	Chart 10	124

Part III

Bermuda Islands	Chart 11	132
Hamilton, Bermuda	Chart 12	133
Azores	Chart 13	134
Ponta Delgada, Azores	Chart 14	135
Madeiran Archipelago	Chart 15	137
Porto Santo	Chart 16	138

Baia da Abra, Madeira	Chart 17	139
Machico, Madeira	Chart 18	140
Deserta Grande, Madeira	Chart 19	141
Canary Islands	Chart 20	142
Pasito Blanco, G. Canary	Chart 21	143
Arrecife, Lanzarote	Chart 22	144
Los Cristianos	Chart 23	144
West Indies (Lesser Antilles) – Iolaire charts	Chart 24	146
Castries, St. Lucia	Chart 25	150
N. Atlantic ports	Chart 26	155

Part IV

Oban, Scotland	Port plan 1	157
Campbeltown, Scotland	Port plan 2	162
Cork Harbour and Crosshaven	Port plans 3a, 3b	167, 169
Falmouth, England	Port plan 4	172
Plymouth, England	Port plan 5	176
Cherbourg, France	Port plan 6	180
La Coruña, Spain	Port plan 7	183
Bayona, Spain	Port plan 8	186
Leixões, Portugal	Port plan 9	190
Lisboa, Portugal	Port plan 10	193
Vilamoura, Portugal	Port plan 11	197
Gibraltar	Port plan 12	200
Funchal, Madeira	Port plan 13	204
Los Cristianos, Tenerife	Port plan 14	208
Puerto Rico, Gran Canaria, Canary Is.	Port plan 15	211
Bridgetown, Barbados	Port plan 16	214
St George's, Grenada	Port plan 17	219
Prickly Bay, Grenada	Port plan 18	222
Fort de France, Martinique	Port plan 19	225
English Harbour, Antigua	Port plan 20	228
St Thomas, US Virgin Is.	Port plan 21	232
Road Harbour, Br Virgin Is.	Port plan 22	235
Miami, Florida, USA	Port plan 23	239
Fort Lauderdale, Florida, USA	Port plan 24	241
Charleston, S Carolina, USA	Port plan 25	243
Morehead City, N Carolina, USA	Port plan 26	245
Newport, Rhode Island, USA	Port plan 27	248
Halifax, Nova Scotia	Port plan 28	252
St John's, Newfoundland	Port plan 29	256
St George's Harbour, Bermuda	Port plan 30	261
Horta, Faial, Azores	Port plan 31	265

INTRODUCTION

I can think of few things more exciting (or at times more worrying) than preparing for the first ocean voyage, knowing as we do that anything forgotten, overlooked, omitted, or badly done may prove to be a matter of some consequence, and that, perhaps for the first time in our lives, we will be dependent entirely on our own resources for everything; when we get to sea there will be little chance of assistance, even if it occurs to us to seek it, should some disaster befall. As the months slip quickly by and the weeks then shrink to days, it seems as though those long lists of requirements which we have prepared with such care, have ticked off, added to, revised and redrafted again and again, will never be completed by the set sailing date. And the questions we ask ourselves (and others): Will the eggs really keep if smeared with Vaseline? Does the roll of new charts, clean and smelling enticingly of good paper and printer's ink, cover our requirements, with harbour plans of likely ports of arrival such as Crosshaven, Falmouth, Cherbourg in the east; or Barbados, mangrove-hedged English Harbour, Newport and St John's in the west? Is there a spanner aboard to fit that awkward little nut on the bilge pump, or to service the roller reefing gear and alternator? Have we sufficient sail needles and twine, shackles, screws, rope, Primus prickers? And, above all, are we carrying enough water (suppose it does not rain) and food so as to be independent of the land for at least twice as long as we expect the passage to take? Do we have all we need for navigation, and the ability to use it with confidence when, for weeks on end, our only trustworthy guides will be the sun, moon and stars?

Then there is the broad overall plan to consider: which way to go, where to put in, how long will it take, and what will the weather be like? In earlier days, and I am thinking back more than twenty-five years to my first Atlantic crossing, information about these important matters certainly was available, but we had to search for it. For a start we read as many as possible of the accounts written by earlier small-boat voyagers, a fascinating occupation which in the rush of today is often omitted, for not only did it reveal much of the character of each seaman/author, but told us which places he had found most suitable and enjoyable, which to avoid, and in general what kind of conditions he experienced. The big volume *Ocean Passages for the World*, first printed in 1923, was available with its lists of routes which experience had shown to be most beneficial to sailing vessels, and its pocket at the back bulging with route, current and rather sketchy wind diagrams. Most important of all there was that remarkable dogged collation of weather information provided by hundreds of thousands of ships . . . the US *Pilot Charts*, one for each month of the year for the North Atlantic.

To select the most advantageous route twenty-five years ago indeed took time and patience; but now, with the publication of this book, planning for an Atlantic crossing in either direction will be much quicker and simpler than it was in the day of Nutting, Long and Robinson, Mulhauser, O'Brien and Worth, for thanks to Philip Allen and his fellow members of the Royal Cruising Club, assisted by many others, including members of the Cruising Club of America, it will no longer be essential to do so much time-consuming research. In this one volume will be found most of the required information simply presented and enriched with a wealth of individual knowledge and experience, together with much good advice on preparing the vessel, on stores, navigation and radio. It has a certain something, difficult to define: a love, I think, of small vessels and the people who sail them, an aura of confidence, and – this is the essence of the deep-water community – a desire to assist.

How very much easier it would have been for Susan, my wife, and me and others of our day if such a comprehensive book had been available when we were preparing, a little apprehensively, to set out on our first Atlantic crossing.

Eric Hiscock

Preface to the First Edition

If you sail across the Atlantic, in either direction, you will find plenty of cruising guides and pilotage information on the other side. Northern Europe, the Mediterranean, the West Indies, Bahamas, and the east coast of America – they are all well written-up. But first you will want to know how best to sail your boat across the ocean, and what help is to be found on the way. The aim of this book is to answer those two questions.

Stowage space in a small vessel is precious, and to justify its place in a boat's bookshelf a work of this kind must fill a real need. By bringing together the know-how of several experienced small-boat sailors, we hope that we have provided in one handy volume, information that will help to fill some of the gaps in the knowledge of those who are about to make their first Atlantic voyage. Many first-time ocean voyagers will, of course, be experienced seamen, but it would be wrong of us to assume a level of knowledge which not all readers may yet have reached. If, therefore, you have already served your time in small boats, please bear with us if we seem occasionally to be spelling things out for the beginner.

We have tried to meet the needs of all: from the man who has sailed coastwise or in the narrow seas, and now wishes to make a really long voyage, to the one who is still only dreaming. Let me say now that here, and throughout the text, the word 'man' refers to the human animal, male and female.

When I began to plan this book, I set out to do two things. The first was to answer all the questions which had worried me when I was thinking about my own first transatlantic cruise; the second was to recall those things which I did wrongly, and the mistakes which I saw others make, and I attempted to help the reader to avoid the same errors. The book is divided into four parts. Part I covers thinking, planning, and preparations in general; Part II deals in detail with each of the main ocean passages; Part III discusses island groups; while Part IV is a factual guide to ports.

We have been careful not to overlap more than necessary those areas covered by existing cruising guides but, in order to keep essential information within the covers of one volume, we have included most of the ports habitually used by small-boat sailors when cruising in the Atlantic. With one exception, all are official entry-ports; and all of them offer reasonable service facilities.

In setting the limits of our coverage, some arbitrary decisions have been taken, based mainly on our estimate of what the average demand may be. Oban, in Scotland, is our most northerly port; the Cape Verde Islands are given a brief mention only, because they do not, at present, offer much for the small-boat sailor; and Trinidad and Tobago have been omitted because they are so rarely included in the itinerary of the average cruise in the West Indies.

This book is not intended to replace any existing official publication. The harbour-plans and chartlets are included merely to illustrate the text and must not be used for navigation, for which an official chart, corrected up to date should always be employed. While every effort has been made to achieve accuracy, neither the Publishers nor the

Editor can hold themselves responsible for any errors which may exist. Pilotage information is liable to become out of date in some particular almost before it is in print; and the value of future editions must depend on the goodwill of readers who draw attention to errors and report new developments. Your help in this way will be gratefully received by the publishers.

Philip Allen
January 1983

Preface to the Second Edition

The success of *The Atlantic Crossing Guide*, first published in 1983, reprinted with amendments in 1984 and again in 1985, has encouraged the production of this second edition, updated and revised to 1987.

Although still the Editor, I have taken but a minor part in the present revisions. Most of the work has affected Parts III and IV and has been handled by Mr O. H. Robinson, Director of the RCC Pilotage Foundation.

Since the Guide was first published the Pilotage Foundation has been equipped with a computer which has enabled it to collate port and other information as details were supplied. But the process is by no means automatic and I am much indebted to Oz Robinson not only for generating and marshalling the flow of information but also for supplying it to me edited and ready for typesetting.

There have been changes – additions and deletions – to the list of ports in Scotland, Spain and Portugal. We are indebted to Sandy Taggart for the new entry on Campbeltown on the Clyde, and to the Pilotage Foundation for the entries on Bayona in Spain and Leixōes in Portugal.

Developments in the fast moving area of radio and electronics have called for careful revision of Chapter 7 and this has been ably handled by Peter Price, working in collaboration with David Jolly who was responsible for the original work on this chapter in the first edition.

It remains for me to thank many readers, members of the Royal Cruising Club and others, who have supplied us with information. And this reminds me to mention the point that we have adopted the Admiralty practice of using local spelling of place names, instead of their anglicised equivalents.

Once more it is my duty to point out that a book of this type must rapidly become out of date, and despite every care it may contain errors for which neither Editor nor Publisher can accept responsibility. The accuracy of future editions must depend upon readers' goodwill and help. If you find a mistake or have new information which you think will be of value, the Publishers will be grateful to hear from you.

Philip Allen
March 1988

Acknowledgements

When the RCC Pilotage Foundation asked me to undertake the planning and editing of this book, my reaction was immediate: I screamed for help.

The most rewarding part of the task which has occupied most of my time for the past three years has been the friendships I have made with small-boat sailors, here and abroad, whom I might not otherwise have met – for the simple reason that we have, each one of us, been sailing and getting to know different parts of the Atlantic Ocean.

Looking back, it seems to me that this whole operation has resembled an Atlantic voyage. First came the planning; next, gathering together a crew; then, seemingly, a long period of preparation. And finally the voyage itself which, like other voyages, has had its plain sailing, its storms, its calms, and its moments of crisis – moments too, when one said to oneself: 'Why in hell did I ever start?'

As with other voyages, I look back with a deep sense of gratitude towards those who have shared it with me: recalling the problems we have faced and overcome together; the moments of excitement and of humour; and the tremendous exhilaration that comes from being part of a team, when all are fully stretched. It is impossible to make full acknowledgement of all the help I have been given, but some must be recorded.

The man who first saw the need for a book of this kind, and who began to do something about it, was Captain Colin W McMullen DSC RN. He not only generously handed over to me all his copious notes, but subsequently sent valuable and up-to-date sailing directions, based on his recent cruises to Spain, Portugal, and across the Atlantic. Both Mr John Power and his successor, the present Director of the RCC Pilotage Foundation, Mr C J H Thornhill, have given me their unfailing help and support. Among individual contributors, Major J K McLeod is outstanding. His knowledge of the routes in latitudes north of the Azores, and his ability to write clear sailing directions, have relieved me personally of a tremendous load. Grateful acknowledgement must also be made to Mr Forbes Perkins of the Cruising Club of America, and to Captain R C Clifford, Royal Marines, both of whom have provided valuable background material for the North Atlantic. Of the many who have helped with port information, special mention must be made of Sr and Sra Antonio Potier Godinho of Cascais, Portugal; Mr Noël Cossart, formerly of Madeira; Mr Marcel Geyer of Barbados; Mr Howland B Jones Jr of Harwich Port, Mass; Mr Robert R Miller Senior, of Bristol R I, and the Cruising Information Center, Salem, Mass. Many others who have helped are named in the list which appears below, and to some I must apologise for the fact that their contributions have had to be excluded owing to the need to limit the size of the book.

A special word of thanks is due to my three Assistant Editors, Richard Trafford,

Jonathan Virden, and Ian McLaren, who collected and collated much of the port information. I recall with affection and gratitude, the fact that the late Humphrey Barton was kind enough to read the trade-wind chapter and, to my great relief, to give it his blessing.

Where indicated, plans and diagrams have been based on British Admiralty charts and publications with the sanction of the Controller of HM Stationery Office and the Hydrographer of the Navy. Approval to use foreign and Commonwealth material occurring on the plans has kindly been given by the Hydrographic Services of France, Spain, Portugal, the United States of America, and Canada. The Bermuda Department of Tourism has supplied much useful pilotage and other information. Mr Frank B Rogers of Bermuda has been particularly kind and helpful.

I acknowledge Hutchinson Publishing Group Ltd, London, and David McKay Co Inc, New York, respectively the owners of the British and American copyrights in Commander Erroll Bruce's book *Deep Sea Sailing*, from which I have quoted; and Oxford University Press, former publishers of *Atlantic Cruise in Wanderer III* by Eric Hiscock; for their kind permission to allow me to make use of their material.

A special word of thanks is due to Mr W G Wilson of Imray, Laurie, Norie & Wilson Ltd, whose help with the cartography has been immeasurable, and far beyond the call of duty. Both the Foundation and I are indebted to Mr Tim Hall, without whose generous help our work would have been much harder and far less enjoyable; and I personally am grateful to Jennifer Bugg, who patiently and accurately waded through thousands of words, bringing order and neatness to my much scribbled-over manuscripts.

David Jolly has given valuable help on the subject of radio, but in fairness to him I must explain that the publisher asked me to convert his highly erudite technical chapter into my own layman's language. Commander Erroll Bruce RN (retd) has given me great help with the chapter on Safety, especially on the subject of the recovery of a man overboard. Perhaps I should add that the views expressed are not necessarily his, indeed he emphasised that nearly every experienced lifeboat skipper has his own special technique and that the more knowledgeable a man is the less inclined he is to be dogmatic on this subject.

I have reason to be especially grateful to the four who were kind enough to read the manuscript and to help me with their constructive criticism. All are experienced ocean-going small-boat sailors, three of them with transatlantic voyages to their credit. They are Major J K (Jock) McLeod, Dr R A Andrews, Mr John Power, and Mr Ralph Hammond Innes CBE. Quite apart from his help in reading the final manuscript, Hammond Innes has been a tower of strength. As Vice-Chairman of the RCC Pilotage Foundation, and as an experienced author, his professionalism has kept us all firmly on course, and his kindly and always helpful criticism of my work has been a constant source of encouragement and a spur to greater effort. Particular thanks are due to Captain R D Franks CBE, DSO, DSC, RN, who prepared the index.

To my wife, who has not only kept open house for contributors, but has seen little of me except at mealtimes for nearly four years, I have two things to say: first, thank you, darling; and second, I promise to stop bashing my typewriter at six in the morning from now onwards.

All those whose names appear below have made some contribution, and I hope they will forgive me for not specifying what each has done. To avoid any invidiousness, the names are in alphabetical order; any omission is entirely my fault and I can only apologise.

Mr G E Allen; Dr R A Andrews; Mrs Mary Barton; Maj Gen D A D J Bethell; Blandy Brothers & Co LDA; Capt G Borotra; Mr Edward Bourne; M Michel Briand; Mr Mark Brackenbury; Major H Bruce; Mr John Burnford; Mr Anthony Butler; Mr E H Butler; Mr H F P Clark; Dr J A Cochrane; Mr Basil D'Oliveira; Mr Brian Dyde; Group Capt D W B Farrar DFC AFC RAF (retd); Mr T H Fenwick; Mr M T Forshaw; Mr J C Foot; Mr Roger Fothergill; Mr W Arnott Fowler; Capt R D Franks CBE DSO DSC RN; Mr J H Hull; Mr J M Hunter; Mr Edward Kennerley; Mr Paul Kimber; Commander Bill King DSO DSC RN; Mr M D Lyne; Lady Rozelle Raynes; The Rt Hon Lord Riverdale DL; Mr F C Sarson; Mr David Simmonds; Major H Sjoberg; Mr D L H Smit; Mr Jonathan Trafford; Group Capt C A Vasey RAF; Mr W T Wilson; Thomas Walker & Sons Ltd; Dr F J Zino.

Philip Allen

Part I
Preparations

1 The Philosophy of Ocean Cruising

The essential quality which the ocean cruising man must develop in himself and in his vessel is that of self-sufficiency. Most of us begin as coastwise cruisers: day-sailors, depending on frequent calls in port for water, fuel, provisions and emergency repairs. Awareness of the need to become self-sufficient probably begins when, with growing experience, we venture further afield and then run short of something we badly need in a place where it cannot be bought.

Self-sufficiency implies many things. First, that the yacht herself should be sound and seaworthy; second, that her crew should be healthy and capable of sailing her, maintaining her and effecting all normal repairs both in port and at sea; and third, that she should be so equipped at all times that she will not run short of any essential item of gear or provisions at a place where a replacement cannot be found.

The sound and seaworthy ocean cruiser must be more than just a strongly built hull that does not leak, with an efficient rig and good gear. In addition to seaworthiness in the accepted sense, she needs to have a further quality, that of 'liveableness' when at sea. Whereas the average yacht spends most of her time at moorings or in a marina, the ocean-going cruiser will be many weeks at sea, continuously. The crew cannot live on snacks and the odd hot drink for that length of time. The galley is the power-house of an ocean cruiser, the source of energy for the whole ship's company, and its placing and planning must take priority over everything else below decks.

Next in importance are the berths. At sea, those below must be able to sleep without being disturbed by the watchkeepers. On the other hand they must not be in the way. This means that the watch on duty must be able to get at sails without turning a man out of his bunk in order to do so, that the cook must be able to cook and the navigator to navigate, unhampered by the sleepers. On deck, the aim must be threefold: first, to keep water from getting below; second, to keep the crew from falling overboard; and third, to keep the gear as simple as possible.

The relative smallness of the average ocean cruiser's crew demands that each member should have some special skill. Opinion is divided as to whether the chore of cooking should be shared or not, and the decision may depend on the size of the crew or upon whether one member is particularly skilled. If one person is able and willing to do all the cooking, the rest are lucky.

In addition to having special ability in one direction, each member of the crew should be able to stand in for at least one of the others, to however small an extent. A major sail repair might call for all hands to help, if the job were not to take several days; even the most gifted helmsman will add to his stature if he is found also to be a good ship's carpenter; and a navigator, however respected he may be for his prowess at shooting the stars, will, if he can shoot trouble in the heads, be loved.

The art (for it is an art) of ensuring that the ship never runs out of the things she needs, can be developed only through knowledge, experience and acquired skill. Self-sufficiency is of course a relative term, and a small community such as the crew of a yacht, cannot survive for ever without calling on outside help. The newcomer to ocean cruising tends to overstock at first, in his anxiety not to run short in far-off places. With growing experience he will learn that some things can be replaced easily, others with difficulty, and a few only at home. He will learn too, that a place that is good for one thing may be unexpectedly bad for others; that water does not always come conveniently piped, that when he sees something that he knows he is going to want later he'd better buy it because, especially among the islands, shopkeepers run out of stock.

Rope, canvas, blocks, shackles and many more items of chandlery which once were universal currency, interchangeable between yachts and fishing boats, are no longer so. It must be remembered that the yacht of today is a specialised piece of merchandise and that it is unreasonable to expect that a primitive fishing village in a foreign country will have a chandler able to supply much that is suitable for her. Wear and tear is likely to reach its peak when the boat is furthest from her starting point and, unless she happens then to be in an area well equipped to deal with the needs of yachtsmen, she had better carry plenty of spares and repair equipment.

To live aboard a well-found boat and to cruise in her over long distances for a year or more, is to experience the most wonderful elation of spirit, a sense of independence and of freedom that is almost beyond description. The petty annoyances of the land fall away, you live by the look of the sky, the feel of the wind and the run of the sea. As time goes on, your vessel becomes better and better conditioned to deal with any eventuality. Putting to sea becomes routine, and the prospect of an ocean passage no longer looms quite as large as it once did.

Your respect for the sea can only have increased, yet you feel better able to meet it, in all its moods. But to reach this happy state you must observe the rules. They are simple but exacting: careful planning; good seamanship; and vigilance.

4

Among the many things which go to make a successful ocean cruise, two are essential. One is to be in the right place at the right time: the other is to move in the right direction. On the Atlantic, for a little boat to be in latitude 60°N in December is wrong. Yet December, in 20°N, could be right – but only if you wished to sail westwards. It is an over-simplification – but a useful one – to think of the North Atlantic as a giant roundabout, revolving clockwise. The ocean currents revolve in a clockwise direction, and the weather systems (although not always the local winds) do so too. Both have their centre west of the Azores. Keeping within the limits of a favourable wind-system and following the tracks of helpful currents may involve you in more miles, but it makes life sweeter.

Winds and Weather
Winds and weather in this area are dominated by the permanent high pressure in mid-ocean and by the relatively low pressures surrounding it. Winds therefore tend to blow clockwise, and slightly outward, around the Azores High. This is true for the eastern side of the ocean, from Spain southward, and for the Trade-wind latitudes north of the equator and on towards the Bahamas and Florida. There are modifications elsewhere, for the land mass of North America, together with the warm Gulf Stream and its confluence with the cold Labrador Current, give birth to unstable conditions in that region. These result in the well-known North Atlantic weather pattern – a succession of lows which form in the west and chase each other eastward towards Europe. Each of these depressions creates its own wind-system in its immediate locality – anti-clockwise around the low. In spite of this, the whole area from west to east, in the forties and fifties of latitude, is known as 'the Westerlies'; indicating that the wind blows from that quarter more often than not. Gales are frequent in this area at all seasons.

Hurricanes
Tropical revolving storms, or hurricanes, are usually confined to the months of June to mid-November. They often begin between the Cape Verde Islands and the West Indies, and follow totally unpredictable courses. All of the West Indies, the Bahamas, Bermuda, and the eastern seaboard of America from Florida to 40°N may be affected. The US Coast Guard provides a monitoring and forecasting service, of which yachtsmen can take advantage.

In a well-planned Atlantic cruise there is no need to be in the hurricane zone during the hurricane season. You may, however, feel something of the effects of one, in terms of swell and some increase in wind force, even though you are in a part of the ocean two thousand miles away. If, for any reason you are cruising in the

5

area during the season when one might be encountered, make sure that you remain within a day's sail of a good 'hurricane hole'. Do not delay in getting there because they fill up rapidly. Talk to charter skippers, most of whom know the best places.

Fog
When a south or south-west wind takes warm moist air over the cold Labrador Current, fog becomes widespread on the coast of Maine and in the region of the Grand Banks. It is prevalent in spring and summer, and can be expected on about 10 days out of each month. The whole of the coastal areas on the eastern side of the North Atlantic, from Norway southward, are subject to a fog at times.

   Reed's Nautical Almanac (European or US Edition) gives details of weather forecasting services.

Ice
Icebergs occur in the North Atlantic in spring and summer between March and July. They arise from the melting of pack ice in the Arctic and from the breaking up of glaciers. Bergs are carried south by wind and currents. Boats crossing by the more northerly routes (see Chapters 11, 13 and 14) may encounter ice in the western part of the ocean. In general icebergs are not found east of 40°W, or south of 40°N. The International Ice Patrol locates the position of bergs and gives radio reports.

Currents
There is a close but complex relationship between ocean currents and prevailing winds. In areas such as the Trade-wind zone, and further north in the latitudes of the so-called 'Westerlies', surface water is blown towards the lee shore. The mound of water thus created naturally seeks a common level and flows along the line of least resistance in order to find it.

North Equatorial Current and Gulf Stream
The north-east Trade-wind pushes the North Equatorial Current before it, and creates a head of water in the Gulf of Mexico and the Caribbean Sea. This emerges through the Strait of Florida and, named the Gulf Stream, it flows in a general northerly direction until it meets the Labrador Current flowing south, around Newfoundland and Nova Scotia. The results of this encounter are that the Labrador current divides, one part forcing a passage down between the Gulf Stream and the American coast and the other turning eastward and combining with the Gulf Stream to form the North Atlantic Current. Wind, although it is usually a current's prime mover, is not always obviously so. A gale from the north, blowing over the Gulf Stream, will not halt its relentless flow towards the north-east. Yet the Stream's own power is derived from the NE Trade-wind, blowing thousands of miles away in exactly the opposite direction to the course of the Gulf Stream itself.

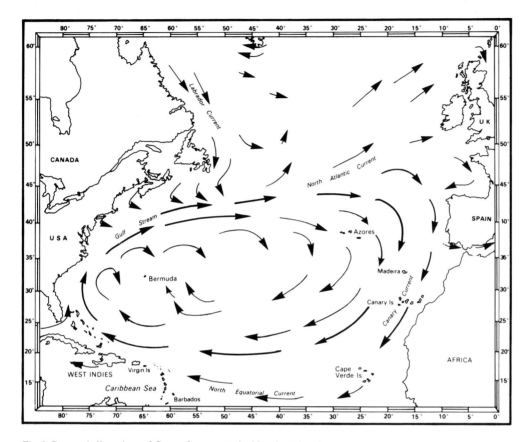

Fig 1 General direction of flow of currents in North Atlantic.

North Atlantic, Azores, Portugal, and Canary Currents

The North Atlantic Current, urged on by the prevailing westerly winds, eventually meets the obstruction of the British Isles and the continent of Europe, which together cause it to divide; part going north of Scotland and part turning south-east, and later south, to form the Azores Current, the Portugal Current, and finally the Canaries Current. This, apart from some minor features such as the Equatorial Counter Current and the currents flowing into the English Channel, the Bay of Biscay and the Mediterranean, is the general picture of what happens in the North Atlantic Ocean. (See fig. 1.)

When a current flows past a continental coastline its course tends to be more or less orderly, but if it encounters islands in its path, or is free to wander in mid-ocean, its track may split in two or become very ragged at the edges. In some places there are well-documented changes of course, due to land masses; and there are areas in which eddies or counter-currents occur predictably. The study of these can be important because parallel courses, only a few miles apart, may be in waters

7

moving in opposite directions. When this happens the choice of the right route could make a difference of thirty miles to the day's run.

There is no means of measuring in mid-ocean what a current is doing to you. You can measure only what it has done. It is, therefore, important for us to learn all we can from recorded information, so as to be able to get ourselves into a favourable current whenever possible, and to become reasonably good at guessing how much to allow when we think we are being set off course.

All currents are fickle; the Gulf Stream being no exception. The US Coast Guard constantly monitor its behaviour, and from their station NMN (2670 kHz) they send out reports giving the co-ordinates of the Cold Wall (i.e., the line of demarcation between the Gulf Stream and the Labrador Current flowing along the US coast) and they indicate the speed and position of the middle of the Gulf Stream at various latitudes. That this costly service is considered to be necessary, in an area where a lot of traffic crosses the Stream, emphasises the fact that its performance cannot be predicted; it has to be reported.

When dealing with currents always remember these rules:
1. If you think that a current may be setting you away from a danger, bear it in mind, but do not rely upon it.
2. If you think that a current might be setting you towards a danger, ACT.
3. If there are no obstructions, the quickest way to cross a current is to steer at right angles to its course and to let it take you where it will.
4. In ocean sailing generally, it pays to seek a route which affords a favourable current. Your chances of a fair wind would then be good. Wind against a strong current, such as sometimes occurs in parts of the Gulf Stream, and in the offshoot of the Portugal Current in the Strait of Gibraltar, can be both bumpy and dangerous; but these tend to be the exceptions which prove the rule.

Books and Charts
Perhaps the clearest and most explicit treatise on ocean currents generally is to be found in *Ocean Passages for the World* published by the British Admiralty. More specific information is given in *Sailing Directions*, both British and American. Most important of all, for the ocean sailor, are the so-called *Pilot Charts* (USA) and *Routeing Charts* (Admiralty). These charts, which are more or less identical in form, show both wind-strength and current-speed over the whole of the North Atlantic. There is one chart for each month of the year. The figures are derived from reports from merchant vessels, naval units, and from weather-ships; and they are averaged over a long period. Ignore them at your peril, but do not take them too literally.

Planning the Voyage
No matter where you begin your cruising, hop on to the roundabout and let it help you on your way. From America or Canada, head east; from northern Europe, head

8

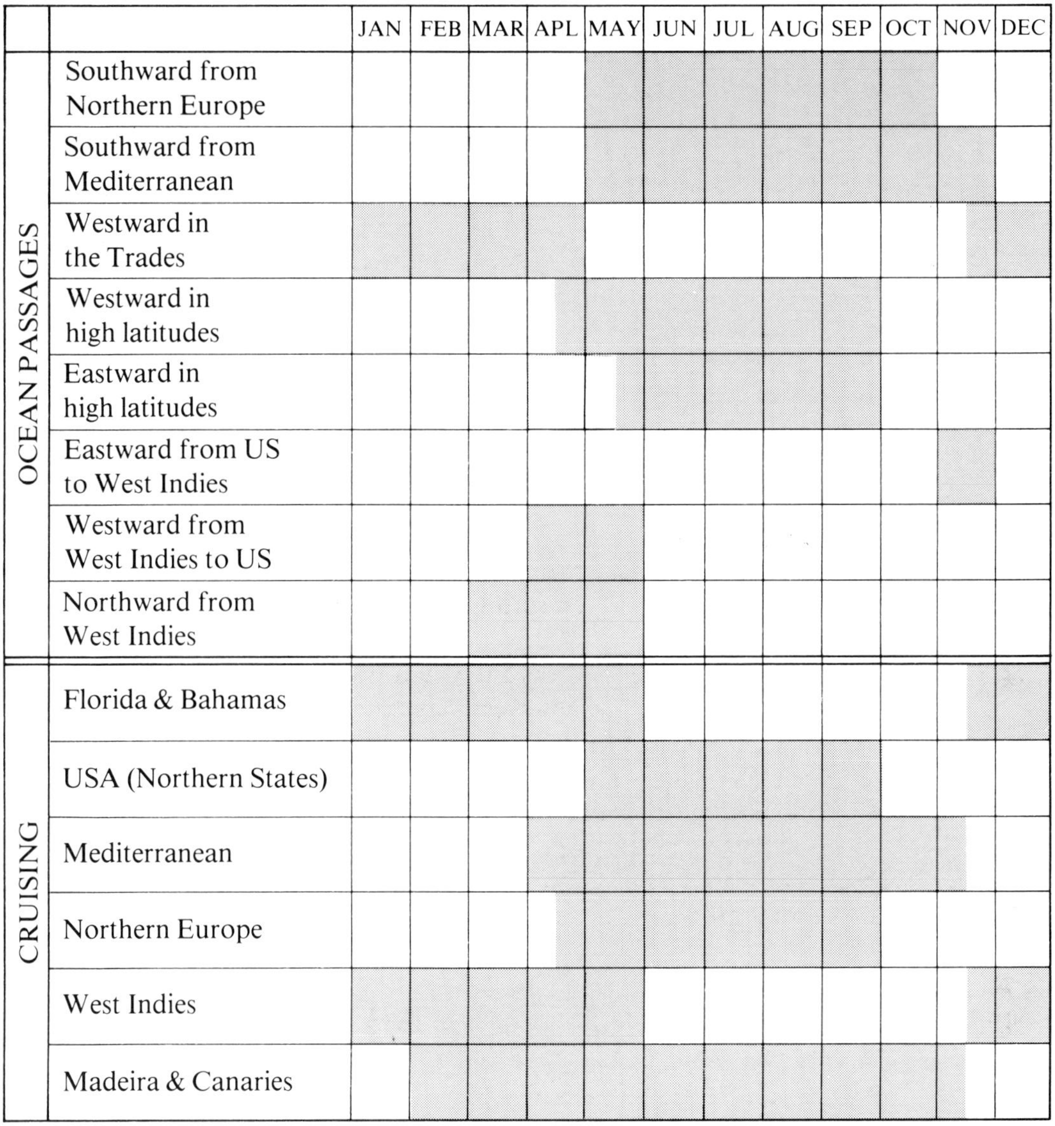

		JAN	FEB	MAR	APL	MAY	JUN	JUL	AUG	SEP	OCT	NOV	DEC
OCEAN PASSAGES	Southward from Northern Europe												
	Southward from Mediterranean												
	Westward in the Trades												
	Westward in high latitudes												
	Eastward in high latitudes												
	Eastward from US to West Indies												
	Westward from West Indies to US												
	Northward from West Indies												
CRUISING	Florida & Bahamas												
	USA (Northern States)												
	Mediterranean												
	Northern Europe												
	West Indies												
	Madeira & Canaries												

Fig 2 Where to be and when. Shaded areas indicate best times for cruising or passage-making.

south; from the Canary Islands, make for the Trade-wind zone and then head west. And from the West Indies, go north or north-west. Our simplified table (fig.2) shows the best times and seasons for each cruising area and for any ocean passage. For more detailed information make the fullest possible use of *Ocean Passages for the World* and the US *Pilot Charts* or their equivalent the British *Routeing Charts*.

Eastward (See Chapters 11 and 12)
In May or early June boats from America and Canada may begin their passages towards Europe, either sailing direct or, more likely, via Bermuda and the Azores.

Southward from Europe (See Chapter 15)
From northern Europe, there is a wide choice of starting times, according to what you want to do. If the object is to cruise your way down through Brittany, Spain, Portugal, Madeira and the Canary Islands, you could decide to leave the English Channel in May or even a little earlier. To minimise the chance of meeting an equinoctial gale, it would be well to leave the Channel before October. But a boat from the Mediterranean need not leave until November, unless her owner wished to do some cruising in Madeira and the Canaries before starting out on the Atlantic crossing.

Westward (See Chapter 15)
The factor which should decide your earliest date for beginning the Trade-wind voyage is the end of the hurricane season, which is mid-November. In fact, people do start before this, but there is no real point in doing so because the Trade-wind does not usually become strong enough to enable good passages to be made until later in the season.

The exact date is up to you – any time from mid-November until the spring; and the later you leave it the stronger the wind will be. Some like to reach the West Indies for Christmas and to have as long as possible cruising in the Caribbean, while others want to enjoy the exhilaration of the glorious downhill ride through the Trades, best done later.

Northward from the Caribbean (See Chapter 16)
The hurricane season officially begins in June, although the incidence of hurricanes in that month is very low. Nevertheless, most people leave the West Indies in April or May in order to reach their next cruising-ground at the best time of year. Starting at this time, some will be going towards America and others north, to Bermuda and on to the Azores and Europe. All will be aiming at higher latitudes in which summer cruising can be undertaken and tropical storms avoided.

Bucking the trend – eastward (See Chapter 16)
From the USA, a direct voyage towards the West Indies presents a problem for two reasons: headwinds and a foul current. In addition, the time for such a voyage has to be sandwiched between the end of the hurricane season and the onset of the winter gales.

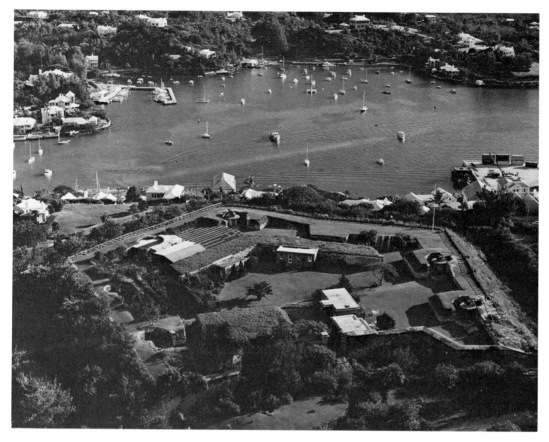

Bermuda The yacht anchorage at Hamilton. The Royal Hamilton Amateur Dinghy Club and its yacht basin can be seen in the top left-hand corner.

Bermuda News Bureau

Bucking the trend – westward in latitudes 40–60° (See Chapter 13)
In recent times, transatlantic races from England to the USA have become a regular part of the ocean racing programme, and even the cruising man cannot ignore the fact that his boat should be quite able to bash her way to windward against all that the ocean can throw at her, if he is willing to go that way. For those who want to try their hand at it, Chapter 13 will be of special interest. But Jock McLeod, an intrepid singlehander with many ocean races to his credit including OSTARS, has this to say about the northerly route: 'It could be described as a long thrash to windward with a permanently foul tide and should not be undertaken lightly.'

3 Navigation

It is not until our first real ocean voyage that many of us begin to take navigation, in all its aspects, seriously. Until then, however much we may have studied and practised and taken needless sights while the coast was still in view, we don't have confidence. We have to get out of our depth before we really believe that we can swim.

Background

About fifty years ago a set of tables was devised, which so simplified the working of a position-line sight that the navigator needed no more knowledge of mathematics than the ability to add and subtract. These sight-reduction tables, in their present form, are known in England as AP 3270 and in the USA as SRPUB249.

Nowadays, there are world-wide radio time signals and wrist watches whose accuracy exceeds that of many ship's chronometers. Equipped with these, together with a sextant and a nautical almanac, blindness is about the only thing to stop you from becoming a navigator. But satellite navigation and hyperbolic systems may consign to oblivion the time-honoured methods of position-finding at sea. In the field of navigational technology so much is changing that one hesitates to predict which system will eventually prevail.

Yet one thing is clear. For the man with limited funds, the sextant and the sun still work well enough. While not turning down lightly anything that will make navigation safer or more accurate, bear in mind the need to guard against relying entirely on highly technical apparatus, the repair of which might be beyond your own capacities at sea and beyond the resources of some ports of call. Make sure that you know how to use the sextant and the sun. They have, after all, served mariners faithfully for a long time.

In this book no attempt is made to teach the mechanics of taking and working out sights. You will find all you need to know about this in Conrad Dixon's *Basic Astro Navigation*, Mary Blewitt's *Celestial Navigation for Yachtsmen*, or Eric C Hiscock's *Cruising Under Sail*, and several other books published on both sides of the Atlantic. Here we shall talk more about the navigator's tools, the services on which he can call, and shall add what we hope will be a few helpful ideas which have not appeared elsewhere.

The Chart Table

In navigation, as in any other craft, order and method will help in producing the best results. First you need the right tools, and principal among these is the chart table. Ideally, it should be the size of a chart outspread; and this calls for a rectangle

42 in × 28 in, which may be too big for a small boat to accommodate. In this case an area measuring not less than 28 in × 21 in should be provided, which would allow most American charts and a full-sized British Admiralty chart to be used folded. Under the table there should be a ready-use locker large enough to take a set of charts folded once. Its internal measurements should, therefore, be just *over 28 in × 21 in*, with a depth sufficient to accommodate all the charts needed on the voyage currently being made. There is no point in making such a locker big enough to take all your charts, unless it has shelves. Charts are heavy, and a stack of more than about a dozen will make it difficult to extract those at the bottom; the excess can be stowed under bunk and settee cushions. A depth of two inches should accommodate a hundred charts folded once; this is the depth to have, even though you do not aim to keep that number for ready use.

Next, the navigator must be given a secure and comfortable seat where he will be safely wedged, with all his equipment in easy reach. Yacht designers, at last, have learned that the right place for the chart table is in an athwartships position, with the navigator facing either forward or aft. In even the smallest boat this can be done. Every single item of the navigator's tools must be to hand, and each must have a slot into which it can be put immediately after use: pencil, eraser, dividers, protractor, magnifying glass, books; they must all be there. Most important of all, the sextant must be ready for instant use, yet safely stowed.

Time

Accurate knowledge of the time is essential to the working of all sights except for a meridian altitude. Without it, everything else is wasted effort. There should be at least two good time-pieces aboard; and ideally one of them should be a clock with a quartz movement and a case designed to cope with humidity and condensation. The other should be a waterproof wristwatch, with a normal dial and a full-sweep second-hand, which the navigator can wear and will be able to use for the timing of sights. Both should be rated, independently of each other, checked daily against time signals, and the error recorded on a graph – one for each. If this is done it is a simple matter to project the line so as to show what the error will be at any time in the next 24 hours. A good quartz clock is likely to be accurate to within plus or minus 0.1 seconds per day, and will be powered by its own dry cell torch battery. Although a sophisticated radio-set or satellite navigator will have a built-in quartz clock, do not therefore assume that you need not have another. *Your source of time must not depend on the ship's main electrical supply, or be at risk if the radio or other equipment is struck by lightning.* Do not buy a cheap quartz digital watch offering numerous functions: it is all too easy to press the wrong button accidentally at sea, and the digits are difficult to read in bright sunlight. And do not go swimming with your watch on merely because it is marked 'waterproof'.

Time Checks

A radio receiver covering the whole high-frequency range, and with push-button tuning, will be needed to take full advantage of time-signals available on the Atlantic. There are five main sources of time signals, one or more of which can always be heard. Three of them are in plain language and the others in morse. On the western side of the ocean are WWV, at Fort Collins, Colorado; and CHU, in Ottawa, Canada. Both of these give time signals in plain English. WWV gives the time as UTC which for our purposes is the same as Greenwich Mean Time; while CHU gives Eastern Standard Time (GMT−5). Although both these stations have been heard as far as 15°W, they should not be relied upon east of 20°W.

On the eastern side, the BBC Overseas Service provides short-wave transmissions on various frequencies, and normally time-signals are given as six 'pips', the last being on the hour. This is usually given before the news bulletins. Occasionally the time-signal is suspended for reasons known only to the BBC.

Rugby, England (call-sign MSF) and Moscow (call-sign RWM) provide a 24-hour service, sending in morse on various frequencies, and one of them can always be heard anywhere on the North Atlantic. Experience will indicate which frequency gives best results, according to the yacht's position and the time of day. Full details are given in the Admiralty list of Radio Signals Volume V.

Barometers and Thermometers

Whether or not to have a barograph may depend on personal opinion and on cost, but in any case a normal aneroid barometer will be needed. On an Atlantic cruise a sea-water thermometer is of great importance, especially when crossing the Gulf Stream; an ordinary air thermometer is necessary for weather forecasting.

Books

The essential books for the navigator fall into four main groups:-

1. The work-books; including ship's log-book, navigator's work-book and possibly a book in which pilotage notes can be recorded for future use.
2. Permanent tables, such as AP3270 or HO249, to cover the latitudes in which you expect to sail.
3. Seasonal books such as almanacs and tide tables.
4. Standard books of reference; i.e. pilot books, light lists, lists of radio signals (for both time and direction finding).

For coastal waters, at the beginning and at the end of a transatlantic voyage from America to Europe, the appropriate volumes of *Reed's Nautical Almanac* will be needed. And for a voyage ending in the Caribbean one of the local cruising guides is essential. While most sight-reduction tables last forever (Volume 1 of AP3270 remains valid for a given epoch only; which should be noted when its tables are being used), the almanacs expire at the end of each year, so that their replacement should be arranged in advance if your cruise is likely to span two calendar years.

The log-book and navigator's work-book are important tools which should be used to the full. Accurate dead-reckoning depends to a great extent on a well-kept log and, if the navigator does his figuring in a book and not on loose bits of paper, he will have a permanent record of his work and be able to trace any error when necessary.

Notices to Mariners

Official pilot books, light lists and lists of radio signals have a longer life than almanacs, but do not last for ever. Up-dating is by means of *Notices to Mariners*, and it is wise to arrange for these to be sent to you at convenient stopping places during a long cruise. In Great Britain Admiralty *Notices to Mariners* can be obtained free of charge by applying personally at any Customs House. In the USA, *Notices to Mariners* may be obtained free of charge from the Defense Mapping Agency Hydrographic/Topographic Center, Washington D.C. 20315. With today's high postal charges, it may be best to arrange for crew-members who are joining the boat to bring the latest issues with them. If necessary, consult Table 4 in AP 3270 (SRPUB249).

Sextant

To be good, a sextant does not have to be elaborate. But it does have to be well made, mechanically sound and without backlash; and it should have a micrometer reading in minutes of arc (not a vernier). A rubber eye-piece aids vision when the sun is very bright. A good second-hand instrument may be excellent buy, but it should either be bought from a reputable firm or should have been tested and, if necessary, adjusted and approved by them.

Cheap plastic sextants have appeared on the market within the last decade. To the surprise of serious navigators, it has been found possible to take accurate sights with them, but care is needed. Being made from plastic they will distort and get out of adjustment unless treated kindly, and it would be wise to check for accuracy every time before taking a sight. Nevertheless, I have always kept one aboard and would not hesitate to use it if my regular sextant were to be lost or broken.

Adjusting the Sextant

The navigator must know how to correct the three basic errors to which his sextant is subject. They are as follows:

1. *Perpendicularity* (the index mirror must be perpendicular to the plane of the instrument. The index mirror is the one which is silvered all over.)
To test: place the sextant flat on a table, with the arc on the side remote from where you are. Move the index bar until you can see both the arc itself, and its reflected image, in the index mirror. If the arc and its reflection appear as one

continuous curve, all is well. If there is a break in the line, then the index mirror is out of perpendicularity.

To adjust: gently move the adjusting screw on the side of the index mirror and re-test. Continue to adjust and re-test until the arc and its reflection are in perfect alignment.

2. *Side Error* (the horizon glass must be perpendicular to the plane of the instrument. The horizon glass is half silvered, half plain.)

To test: set the index bar at zero and sight a star directly. Move the micrometer screw back and forth to split the image of the star vertically. When the images are in transit they should appear as one and not side by side. If side by side, error exists. A simple alternative test by day is shown in figure 3.

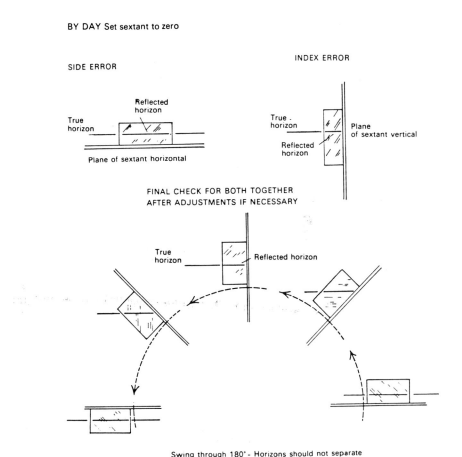

Fig 3 Testing for Side Error; day-time method.

16

To adjust: set both index bar and micrometer at zero and gently move the side-adjusting screw of the horizon glass (there are two adjusting screws at the back of this glass; the side adjusting screw is the one located on the side of the glass when the instrument is held vertically). Re-test and continue to adjust until the star images are in the same vertical plane and can be made exactly to coincide.

3. *Index Error* (the horizon glass must be parallel in both planes with the index glass when the index bar is set to zero).

To test: set the index bar and micrometer at zero and sight the sea horizon or some very distant horizontal line, or star. Hold the sextant vertically in the usual way. Move the micrometer screw until the lines coincide precisely. Read the arc and micrometer for any error on or off the arc.

To adjust: gently move the second adjusting screw of the horizon glass (the one which will be on its upper edge when the sextant is in normal use). Re-test and re-adjust until the error is eliminated.

Adjustments should be made in the above order. There may be some interaction between the second and third adjustments, therefore it may be best not to adjust fully for either of these errors until partial adjustment has been made for each. If any residual error is to be left, it should be index error because this can be allowed for in the calculation when working out a sight.

Learning to use the Sextant

It has often been said that the arithmetic and book-learning connected with modern astro-navigation is much easier to master than the actual taking of sights. This frequently accounts for a beginner's lack of confidence until he has really proved things to himself in deep water. Do not let this worry you unduly. Use your sextant as though you were sighting an object on the horizon with your binoculars. This is something you will have done many times and, although you know that it is more difficult in a big sea, you also know that it can be done. In a big sea, you know that it is useless to try to see anything on the horizon if there is a breaking crest in the way when the boat is in a trough. Wait until she reaches a crest herself and then try to bring the sun down so that its lower limb just touches the horizon. It will take you several attempts before you do this to your satisfaction. While you are using the sextant and turning the micrometer screw, try to form the habit of keeping it swinging from side to side like a pendulum, so that the sun just touches the horizon at the bottom of its swing.

If the watch you are wearing on your wrist is the ship's chronometer, then look at it immediately you are satisfied with a sight. This should take rather less than a second and is less productive of errors than a two-man operation using a stop watch.

Some advocate taking several sights, averaging them and averaging the times, and then working out a line of position or position-line from the averaged figures. This is a laborious affair, and one slip in the middle of the whole jumble of figuring can make nonsense of the final answer. If you want to convince yourself that the results you are getting are right, take three sights in fairly quick succession, work each one out and plot its position-line. Three position-lines almost coincident are unlikely to be wrong.

Charts and Plotting Diagrams

In pilotage waters, at the beginning and end of a voyage, you need a chart on the largest scale possible, but when crossing the ocean there is, in theory, no reason why you should have anything more than a school atlas. It is nevertheless more interesting to use a nice big chart, and to see the ship's track inching its way across it day by day. But however big a scale your ocean chart may have, it cannot be used for accurate plotting, when working out a sight. For this a plotting diagram is needed.

A plotting diagram (such as Baker's Position-line chart) is a specially designed sheet covering about two degrees of longitude, with a graduated latitude scale to enable the diagram to be adjusted for any latitude in which it is to be used. In use, the noon position of the boat is drawn as near as possible to one edge of the diagram, leaving space enough for the day's run by DR to be added to the plot. When the next day's noon position has been worked out, it can then be transferred back to the edge of the diagram again; and the whole of the previous day's plotting can be erased. The latitude and longitude will of course have to be re-numbered on the diagram each day. In this way, if a soft pencil is used, a single diagram-sheet can be made to last for a whole voyage.

Dead Reckoning

The importance of good dead reckoning should not be overlooked. Your noon fix depends for accuracy on measuring the distance run since the morning sight; a running-fix in fact. And dead reckoning becomes of great importance as land is approached, especially in thick weather. Throughout the voyage, the distance run should be logged at the end of each watch, and during the last day or so every opportunity of checking the vessel's position should be taken.

On a cloudy day, when you have to grab any chance you get of taking a sight, do not wait around in the hope that the sky may be clear when the meridian altitude is due. If you have been able to get a good morning sight, take any chance of snatching other position-line sights later in the day, and choose the one which is likely to produce the best cut with the line you already have.

By tradition, more than anything else, the ship's position is plotted each day at apparent noon. This dates from the time when mariners had to rely on the meridian altitude for their latitude. There is nothing sacrosanct about it and to some small extent it is misleading because, when sailing from east to west, there is slightly more than twenty-four hours from noon to noon, and slightly less than twenty-four when moving in the opposite direction. Although a Mer/Alt does not involve accurate timing or the reference to any tables, other than to look up the sun's declination, it

18

is more tedious than taking a sight using SR tables. You have to stay around, taking sight after sight, until the sun passes the zenith – a process which may take several minutes of concentration, and in rough going can be tiring and wet. Using SR tables, the instant you have a good contact, note the time, the log reading, and read the altitude; and there you have everything with which to start work.

Great Circle Sailing

The shortest distance between two points on the surface of a sphere is a *great circle*, i.e., one whose plane cuts the centre of the sphere. A straight line (rhumb-line) drawn on a Mercator chart is not a great circle course, unless it lies true north and south, or along the Equator. The simple method of arriving at a great circle course is to use a gnomonic chart (see Chart No 1, Chapter 11) on which a straight line can be ruled, and its points of intersection with lines of latitude and longitude then transferred to the Mercator chart. Rhumb-lines connecting these points will then approximate to a great circle course.

Great circle sailing is of limited use on the average Atlantic cruise, for various reasons. First, many skippers do island-to-island voyages whenever possible, and in consequence the distances are so comparatively short that the saving to be made by sailing a great circle course is rarely of any consequence. Secondly, the main concern is usually to get into a favourable wind or current, and this may or may not coincide with a great circle course. Thirdly, some of the routes used, such as sailing from the West Indies to Bermuda or from the English Channel to the Canaries, are so nearly great circle courses that no action is needed.

If making a direct voyage from USA to Europe, however, the possibility of exploiting a great circle route should be considered. Other passages where it might be of value would be from Bermuda to the English Channel or to Gibraltar. But in any case its value would have to be assessed in relation to the all-important matter of keeping within the most favourable wind and current systems, or avoiding ice.

Checking Compass Deviation

There are two methods of checking the deviation of the compass when at sea and out of sight of land. The rough and ready one, which is to take a bearing of the Pole Star, can give a quick indication and is accurate enough to confirm a suspected error or to set one's mind at rest.

The method of checking deviation by an amplitude is described by Eric Hiscock in *Cruising Under Sail*. Although useful, this has its limitations. One bearing only can be taken, at the instant when the sun is rising or setting and the boat is on course. Whatever the deviation is, will apply to that course only. This information might, however, be useful if the same course were to be held for several days, which could well be the case on an ocean passage. There is, however, another difficulty because, even on a clear evening, it is astonishing how often there is cloud on the horizon which prevents accurate judgement of the point of actual sunset. The same condition often applies at sunrise. Remember that amplitude tables are in N to S notation and beware of possible error when applying variation. The azimuth method calls for an azimuth mirror, shadow-pin, or pelorus.

Landfall and Pilotage

Nearly every landfall covered in this book is likely to have a conveniently situated DF beacon somewhere nearby, even if only on an airport. This might prove invaluable for homing or to furnish a useful position-line, crossing with one obtained from the sun. Unlike many marine beacons, most aero-beacons transmit continuously 24-hours a day. Ordinary broadcasting stations may give a useful DF bearing *provided that the exact location of the transmitting antenna is known. The antenna may be many miles away from the town from which the station gets its name.*

In areas with much traffic, more sophisticated methods of position-finding exist. In the English Channel there are several groups of stations, each group operating in a net on a common frequency. By tuning in to any one group and taking bearings on three or more stations in succession, a fix may be obtained. Although, in the past, the average slightly seasick radio operator in a small yacht might not always have great confidence in the results, the defect lay more at the receiving end than with the transmitters. Receivers are now available which are capable of indicating radio bearings automatically. But remember that freak conditions can affect all radio signals at times and that, while RDF should be taken seriously, it should not be used to the exclusion of all other methods of checking position; RDF is also subject to all the errors of any compass bearing in addition to its own electronic problems, and must be treated as suspect if coming over land.

When making a landfall the echo-sounder becomes important. Ideally it should have a range up to 200 metres or 100 fathoms. In thick weather it is often possible to find one's way confidently by the careful use of soundings. Since the echo-sounder will not have been used during an ocean crossing, perhaps for several weeks, make sure that its batteries are not flat and that the machine is in full working order, before soundings are reached.

Stars and Planets

In this chapter, so far, the sun has been suggested as the only body to be observed for celestial navigation. The objection to this is, of course, that two heavenly bodies need to be observed at the same time to obtain an absolute fix. Using the sun alone means relying on a running-fix every day, when plotting the noon position. In theory, this is perhaps a sloppy approach and as such unacceptable to the purist, but in practice it works very well.

While the planets and the stars can be observed with accuracy from the bridge of a large steamer, the result of doing so from the heaving deck of a small boat may be less reliable. The moon can be used, but the periods when it is available are limited. Nevertheless, anyone who becomes hooked on the fascinating job of taking and working out sights at sea will undoubtedly wish to do more than just use the sun, day after day. By all means spread your net wider but, if the starsights do not at first agree with the position in which the sunsights have put you, it is almost certain to be the starsights which are wrong. Do not ignore such a discrepancy: check all your workings again but if, after doing so, you can find no fault with your last fix using the sun, have confidence in that rather than in a possibly shaky starsight.

If you do decide to take starsights seriously, try this method – invert the sextant, having removed the telescope, and look through the ring directly at the star. Push the index bar away from you to bring the horizon up to the star (this avoids ever losing sight of the star you want). Then adjust the micrometer until the star seems just to be sitting on the horizon. Keep both eyes open while doing this.

Modern Position Fixing Methods

Satellite navigational systems are now commonplace among ocean cruisers although, in the North Atlantic, Omega, Loran and the more localised but highly accurate Decca have their adherents. For more details see page 55.

Conclusion

The more accurately we can navigate, the more fun it is and the better for us and those we meet at sea. But in adopting new methods do not throw overboard everything else. Modern electronic equipment is normally reliable but it can break down. Not long ago an OSTAR competitor was lost due to a navigational error almost at the finishing-line, because all the boat's electronics depended on batteries charged by an engine which failed in mid-ocean. Also, Eric Hiscock on his last cruise shortly before his death flattened his starter-battery so, with no power to run *Wanderer*'s satnav, it was sun and sextant which took them safely through dangerous coral waters.

And other things can happen. How do you set about repairing a calculator if it goes on the blink? And what happens if your boat is struck by lightning? There is a real risk of this and, unless you have experienced it, you may not be aware of what it can do to the vessel's electrical installations. I speak from personal experience. I was aboard with my family when it happened and, although none of us was harmed, nor was the yacht marked outwardly, the electrical and electronic equipment was all destroyed beyond repair. The main fuse-box was reduced to shattered fragments and little blobs of copper and brass, so that all wiring and light fittings had to be replaced; and the radio set, which was battery-operated with a loop antenna and totally unconnected to any of the ship's wiring, was reduced to scrap. The compass had an error of 45 degrees induced.

If this should happen in a thundersquall in the Atlantic, as it could, a yacht might suddenly find herself devoid of all her sophisticated electronic machines and dependent entirely on the navigator's ability to find his way by old-fashioned methods. With no radio set, he would need to have kept his watch-error faithfully recorded; with a useless calculator he would need to do his arithmetic on paper; and with probably a large deviation error he would have to navigate very carefully and accurately. And at the end of the passage there would be no DF set to help him into port – the sun, the stars, and dead reckoning would have to do it all. Don't throw your sextant away.

4 The Mechanics of Cruising

The master of any small vessel must be jack of several trades, especially if he is an ocean cruiser. This chapter contains a mixed bag of reminders about some of the many things with which the skipper has to deal.

Paperwork

Ship's Papers
Requirements vary from country to country, and a good principle to adopt is to have as many papers as you can lay hands on. These include:
1. Certificate of Registry. The principal ship's registration document should never be surrendered. It is wise to carry a couple of good full-size photostats to yield to particularly persistent officials.
2. Bill of Sale
3. Documentation (USA).
4. Bills of Health and all Pratiques acquired en route.
5. Cruising Permit (USA, Canada and some islands).
6. Sea Letter (from US Secretary of Commerce).
7. Complete crew list, with formal Crew Manifest if paid crew are carried. Normally all aboard should be listed as crew rather than passengers, as some countries levy high fees for passenger-carrying vessels.
8. Clearance papers, which show permission to sail from the port of departure.
9. Stores list, which should differentiate between opened and unopened items.
10. Charter documents, if applicable.
11. Insurance papers.
12. Ensign Warrant, if applicable.

Personal Documents
First, of course, passports. See that all passports are valid for all countries to which you might go, and make a separate list of their numbers. Be quite sure that no-one has a passport that will expire during the course of the cruise; renewal can be troublesome in a foreign country. Although the need for a visa does not often occur in the Atlantic, except for foreigners visiting the USA, it would be wise to check this before leaving home. Likewise few countries now demand a Bill of Health, but this should be checked and possibly re-checked from time to time. A sudden epidemic could alter the rules overnight (as it did in the Mediterranean in 1971).

Ship's Stamp
Before you start off, get yourself a rubber stamp with the ship's name printed boldly on it, your own name as owner, and a bit of fancy decoration if you have a friend

who can design it for you. Use it on any papers you are asked to complete for foreign port officials. They love it.

Money

Before sailing, make sure that you have some cash in the currency of the next country which you intend to visit. You may arrive at a weekend, and will need money for dues demanded on arrival. Exchange, spend or give away as tips, any balance of the currency of the country you are about to leave, unless you intend to return very soon.

Credit-worthiness of itinerant small-boat sailors is rated nil by most suppliers, who expect cash on the nail. Travellers' cheques and credit cards are the best means of obtaining cash when you need it. American Express and Barclays International are well represented in most of the places likely to be visited on a North Atlantic cruise.

Books

First, buy a notebook and label it DEFECTS. Pilot books, almanacs, sight-reduction tables, tide tables etc are covered in Chapter 3 and in Port Information. If your cruise is going to span two calendar years, you will need to arrange to be supplied with replacements for your nautical almanacs at the year's end; they are usually published from August onwards. Do not rely on being able to get what you want outside your own country. Although British Admiralty publications are obtainable in Gibraltar, US official publications are not always available outside America.

Unofficial Guides should be bought and studied before you actually reach any of the cruising areas which they cover. Details are given in the Bibliography at the end of this book.

The log-book and navigator's work-book can be plain books with horizontally ruled lines, which will allow you to put your own columns and headings at the top of each page, as may be required. They should have stiff covers, the log-book should measure about 13 in × 8 in and the navigator's work-book about 8 in × 6 in. You will need at least two log-books of about 100 pages each and about a dozen work-books. You should get three days per double page spread in the log-book, but every day will use up a double spread in the work-book. If you like to make plans and notes of the places you visit (and guides like this one can only be written if enough people do so) you will need some more books in which to do it.

Some people are avid readers when cruising, especially on long passages. A plentiful supply of paperbacks may be needed to keep them happy; in many ports of call there are book-swapping centres where you may give and take books on a one-for-one basis.

Letter-writing is a favourite occupation with some people, when nearing the end of a passage, so have a few writing pads and envelopes (preferably with latex self-sealing flaps which don't stick until you ask them to). And don't forget that paperwork must include a plentiful supply of the sort that comes in rolls, for use in the heads.

Keeping the Log-Book

Keeping a log-book is the basis of accurate navigation. It is also an important legal document. A simple system is more likely to be carried out, than one which makes great demands on the watchkeeper. The essential facts to be recorded are:

1. the time
2. the compass course steered
3. wind strength and direction at hourly intervals
4. the log-reading at hourly intervals
5. the barometer reading at the end of the watch (or at hourly intervals in bad weather).

Other useful and interesting detail may be recorded also, but the above items should always be covered; and the responsibility for recording them falls on the watchkeeper. Additionally, the navigator will make his own contribution, showing the time of each sight and the log reading at that time; and the ship's position at any time when he can fix it. It should go without saying that any change of course must be noted in the log-book, together with the time at which it was made. In tidal waters, one would also have to record the rate and direction of the tidal stream. It should be possible, at any given moment, for the skipper or navigator to have a look at the log-book, and from it to make a DR plot of the boat's position.

The mechanics of the operation involve three stages. The first is the slate or deck log, which in these days can be a sheet of matt white plastic laminate; headed if you like, in columns. Screw it to the underside of a locker lid in the cockpit, and tie a pencil to it so that the watchkeeper need not go below to do any writing. At the end of each watch it should be the duty of the oncoming watchkeeper to write up the rough log-book, at dictation from the man on deck (reading from the slate) and then to read the barometer and to record that also in the rough log. That is stage two. The third stage is when the skipper finally transfers the contents of the rough log into the main log-book. The object is not simply to copy out what is recorded in the rough log-book, but for the skipper to check the information and to query anything which fails to make sense. The rough log will be written in several different sets of handwriting of varying legibility and it is better that the final version should be in the skipper's own hand throughout. Nevertheless, the rough log-book and navigator's notebook contain the real meat and should not be thrown away.

Watchkeeping

The secret of a happy voyage depends to a great extent on establishing, from the beginning, a daily routine which not only ensures that all necessary work is done but that each crew member feels himself to be an important part of the ship and is seen to be pulling his weight. Many systems have been evolved for small boats, whose resources in manpower are more limited than those of the merchant services. The prime object of any watchkeeping system is to ensure the safe conduct of the ship. This entails – ideally at any rate – having on deck enough manpower to deal with

24

whatever needs to be done in each watch. In a small yacht on an ocean voyage and in reasonable weather, one man on watch – night or day – is normally enough. But bad weather, or a mishap of any kind, can ncessitate the call 'all hands on deck', however large the crew may be, when a sudden crisis has to be dealt with. In a storm, when perhaps it may be necessary to run before a big breaking sea, or in conditions of extreme cold, one hour on deck steering by hand may be as long as a strong fit person can stand. In such conditions the best of watchkeeping systems will have to be suspended for the time being.

With a crew of four there is no great problem, and the four different systems which follow have all been tried with success and recommended by their originators.

1. *The Iolaire System.* Devised by the late Robert Somerset, a well-known English yachtsman, one-time owner of *Jolie Brise* and also of *Iolaire* (which now belongs to Donald Street). This deserves careful study. The way in which the work-load is spread is well planned.

Day	1	2	3	4
Cook	D	A	B	C
0700–1100	A	B	C	D
1100–1500	B	C	D	A
1500–1900	C	D	A	B
1900–2200	A	B	C	D
2200–0100	B	C	D	A
0100–0400	C	D	A	B
0400–0700	D	A	B	C

2. *Samuel Pepys System.* Used by Commander Erroll Bruce when ocean racing in *Samuel Pepys*. It would be applicable for cruising in arduous conditions (i.e. extremely bad weather or heavy traffic) when there might be a need for a stand-by watchkeeper.

Day	1			2			3		
	Mate	*Standby*	*Cook*	*Mate*	*Standby*	*Cook*	*Mate*	*Standby*	*Cook*
0800–1200	A	B	C	B	C	A	C	A	B
1200–1600	B	C	—	C	A	—	A	B	—
1600–1800	C	A	—	A	B	—	B	C	—
1800–2000	A	B	C	B	C	A	C	A	B
2000–2400	B	S	—	C	S	—	A	S	—
0000–0400	C	S	—	A	S	—	B	S	—
0400–0800	A	S	C	B	S	A	C	S	B

(S=Skipper)

3. *Bluebird of Thorne System.* A method used by Lord Riverdale on two transatlantic crossings and a voyage to New Zealand. Designed to avoid monotony. It provides for a full day as cook for each hand; a three-man rota of watchkeepers, one each at a time on deck; and a full night off, in turn, for everyone.

Day	1		2		3		4	
	Deck	*Cook*	*Deck*	*Cook*	*Deck*	*Cook*	*Deck*	*Cook*
0000–0300	A	—	B	—	C	—	D	—
0300–0600	B	—	C	—	D	—	A	—
0600–0900	C	A	D	B	A	C	B	D
0900–1200	D	—	A	—	B	—	C	—
1200–1500	B	A	C	B	D	C	A	D
1500–1800	C	—	D	—	A	—	B	—
1800–2100	D	A	A	B	B	C	C	D
2100–2400	A	—	B	—	C	—	D	—

4. *Tallulah System.* Devised for a four man crew consisting of three watchkeepers and a full-time cook, where all concerned preferred to keep to the same hours throughout the voyage. It puts the skipper/navigator in the right watch to get his sights each morning, and enables him to take his noon sight when off watch just before lunch. I used this system on my last Atlantic cruise, when my wife was full-time cook and I had two good male companions to share the deck.

	Deck	Cook
0000–0300	A	—
0300–0600	B	—
0600–0900	S	C
0900–1200	A	—
1200–1500	B	C
1500–1700	S	—
1700–1900	A	—
1900–2100	B	C
2100–2400	S	—

(S=Skipper)

A Crew of Three or Less. It is impossible to lay down any hard and fast system when the crew is three or less. What must be said is that surely nobody is going to be silly enough to try to make an ocean cruise with only one or two companions, without first making sure of their abilities and stamina. The most demanding times on an ocean voyage are at the beginning and at the end, when accurate pilotage is essential and traffic is at its maximum. It is not uncommon for people to make coastal passages involving three days and two nights at sea, and a crew which can handle that kind of operation with confidence will be able to get their ship out of the traffic and away into the more relaxed conditions on the ocean, and vice versa at the end of the voyage.

The problem when short-handed is mainly due to people's varying needs for sleep. Some people can stand two hours on and two off – almost forever, while others if denied a solid six or eight hours sleep for a couple of days become useless. One can only try out such problems in advance, and remember that the smaller the crew the greater their individual abilities should be.

Maintenance

Every opportunity has to be taken, when on a long cruise, to catch up with repairs and maintenance. Some work can be done at sea, but most of it must be tackled when in harbour. Slipways are a bit scarce around the islands of the Atlantic and, the rise and fall of tide being so small, you cannot afford to pass a slipway without seriously considering whether or not to use it. At least every six months, the boat should be slipped and her bottom inspected and re-antifouled. As soon as she is out of the water remove every seacock for inspection, grinding-in, and greasing. If she is a wooden boat without sheathing, check carefully for any sign of worm. And if she is sheathed, look for any break in the continuity of the sheathing. In any boat, make careful checks to find out whether there is any sign of galvanic action or electrolysis and, if there is, try to find the reason. Look to the sacrificial anode and, if necessary, take expert advice.

Before going to sea, always go over the rigging meticulously. Check every turnbuckle. You may be surprised how many your boat has, so make a list, and mark each item off as you check it, just as the service station does when servicing your car. *Ready for Sea* by Basil Mosenthal and Dick Hewitt has excellent check-lists for most contingencies, or you can compose your own.

Turnbuckles may be secured, either with wire or split-pins; if one of these is missing, the turnbuckle will come undone and you might lose your mast. If a yard has been at work on the rigging do not assume that all is therefore well – make an even more careful check than usual. Innocently or in ignorance, somebody may have used a brass split-pin in one of your steel fittings, and if so it may disintegrate halfway across the ocean. Either go yourself, or hoist aloft a responsible crewman, to check that every shackle has been wired, to ensure that it cannot come undone. Be sure that all sheaves in the boxes at the masthead are running freely.

The evidence of chafe, on canvas and on lines, is usually quite obvious, but only the most careful scrutiny may disclose it elsewhere. I recall a splendid shipwright in Gibraltar who helped me to check our rigging on one occasion; and he removed the shackle of the topping-lift block, whose pin was worn away to wafer thickness. One

Frigatas of the Tagus beached at Seixal, near Lisboa.

does not associate a topping-lift with great wear and tear and yet, having seen what had happened, I realised that it was the very fact of its *not* having been under any stress that had caused the damage. It had been swinging freely, back and forth, back and forth, for two Atlantic crossings; putting no strain on the line, but grinding away the metal of the shackle-pin for six thousand miles.

There are some things which should be replaced with brand new items at the start of every long voyage. The belt of an alternator may look perfect but, unless it is new, it may have a weak place and give out suddenly; start your passage with a new one. Dry batteries for torches and other equipment should all be renewed; and wet batteries should be topped up and fully charged. Navigation lights – not used while in port – must be checked and made serviceable.

Check carefully your stocks of the many small items that become very much missed when they run out: WD40; Plus-Gas; distilled water; glass-paper; spare brushes for the alternator; spare light bulbs; spare fuses.

Docking Plan

If you have a full set of plans of the boat, take them with you. In case of a major repair they may be essential. Every time your boat has to be slipped in a strange

28

place, whoever does it will ask for a docking plan. It is useful, also, to make some small marks on deck to indicate the forward and after ends of the keel or fin, and the rudder/skeg appendage if any.

Heavy Weather

It is a fact that comparatively few who have crossed the Atlantic, especially by the more southerly routes, have experienced a storm of ultimate severity. But the possibility is ever-present, and only a fool would go unprepared to face a full gale. Before you reach the stage of starting out, it is to be hoped that you will have not only studied the handling of your boat in heavy weather but that, by accident or design, you will actually have experienced it and will know how you and your boat can be expected to behave when you meet it.

Having been through the whole routine of heaving-to, lying a-hull, turning tail and trailing warps – or whatever – there remains the overriding need to take precautions against a great mountain of green water falling aboard, to do everything possible to stop it from getting below, and to do all one can to minimise the damage which will result in the event of a knock-down.

Under bad conditions, canvas dodgers are a menace and should be unbent as soon as possible, otherwise the first big sea to come aboard will not only carry them away but may also remove half the lifelines and their stanchions. A cockpit filled with seawater can seriously affect a boat's trim and stability. If you can contrive to fill it with sails, in their bags and securely lashed down, do so. Also, if the main hatch, or doghouse, has doors make sure that you fit some kind of strong-back which will support them in the event of a heavy sea breaking against them.

Doghouse windows are an obvious source of weakness, and should be provided with plywood covers for use either as protective screens or as a temporary repair in the event of breakage.

It is impossible to foresee the results belowdecks, should a knock-down take place; but there are some obvious precautions to be taken. Avoid inside ballast like the plague, but if you have no option make sure that it is immovable. See that batteries are so fixed that, even if the boat is rolled right over, they cannot move. Make sure that lockers containing heavy tools, cutlery, or glass cannot empty their contents if capsized. You will not achieve complete success and, if the thing happens, you will certainly wonder how on earth some of the items managed to get where they did. But do your best; loose gear can cause serious trouble even though a complete knock-down does not occur.

An Atlantic gale is always an awe-inspiring spectacle but some of us can remember much worse moments in more confined waters. Try, if you can, to have your gale in deep water and as far as possible from a lee shore. This is not quite as silly as it sounds. Although we cannot choose what weather we shall have for our landfall, we can choose when to start the voyage. If you begin with a reasonable chance of three or four days' good weather, and use it to put a few hundred miles between you and the land, and if possible to get away from any continental shelf there may be in those parts, you will have done your best. From then onwards you'll take it in your stride.

Clothing

An Atlantic cruise calls for a variety of clothing. Some of the northern routes are in near-arctic temperatures while in the West Indies the climate is tropical.

If you are starting from a northern area, where waterproof clothing is used daily at sea, once you get into the tropics you may not use it for several months; but you will need it again when you return to home waters. So start with good new waterproofs and store them carefully when they are not being used. Don't just cram them into a locker and forget them.

In the tropics, few clothes are called for, but they will need washing each day so take plenty of changes. On board, trunks and bikinis are normal daywear, with a shirt or blouse for shore-going or protection at mid-day. But do not assume that a night at sea in the tropics will necessarily be warm. On deck you may be glad to have your watch coat.

Shoes are important. Although many people prefer bare feet on deck it is both slovenly and foolish to walk ashore without shoes; broken glass, sea urchins, and fallen fruit of the manchineel tree, can all cause painful injuries. Remember that you are not leaving civilisation, and that in many places you will be expected to wear a collar and tie, and possibly a jacket, when dining ashore.

Fishing

Do not depend on catching fish for food. If fish are needed for survival, the extremes available are plankton dredged up by trawling with a fine-mesh fabric, and catching sharks with heavy tackle, hauling them aboard and (with both danger and difficulty) slaughtering them, and eating the liver.

Although barracuda can be caught in the West Indies, they are poisonous when caught in certain areas. Local advice should be sought before eating them. On a trade-wind passage, flying fish will land on deck and may be encouraged to do so at night if a light is displayed. If this is arranged so that the fish hit a sail, some will fall on deck and may be collected for breakfast. There are rarely enough for more than one helping.

The Law

This book cannot attempt to provide an up to date treatise on the ever-changing laws in the many places visited by Atlantic cruisers. But a few guidelines can be laid down.

For a start, just try to put yourself in the shoes of an official whose task it is to check your credentials, when you arrive in his country. He has been told that vessels purporting to be yachts have been known to smuggle drugs and illegal immigrants. He has also been told that boats, which really are yachts, have been known to leave without paying. He has seen innumerable yachts arrive, some of them manned by crews who have looked and behaved like vagabonds. In England such an official used to be known as a preventive officer, and his whole training is based upon the need to be suspicious. To the extent that you give him cause for suspicion – whether by behaviour or appearance – you start out on the wrong foot. The fact of being clean and reasonably well clothed, and of having a smart boat, may prove nothing; but at least it gives no reason for suspecting that you may be a crook. The cruising yachtsman is in a vulnerable situation whenever he is in a foreign port, and only a fool would deliberately put himself more heavily at risk.

The authorities in most countries are concerned first with drugs and potential immigrants, and second with dutiable merchandise. Nearly every boat must carry some drugs (if only medicines); some human beings (who might jump ship); and some dutiable stores. We all must establish our bonafides wherever we go.

Avoid taking part in any shore-based activity even remotely connected with political affairs, and do not engage in work of any kind except on your own boat. Remember that some nations just do not understand or accept that human beings can give their services for charitable reasons. In such countries, where people expect to be paid for whatever they do, nearly every club or charity may be politically biased and anybody found to be giving his services may be labelled with a party tag, or considered to be depriving one of the local inhabitants of a job. Americans intending to visit British waters and Europeans planning to sail to the USA should enquire at the appropriate embassy to find out about the laws as they affect visiting yachts and their crews.

Wherever you go, be meticulous in declaring all dutiable or forbidden imports, and make sure that each member of your crew does likewise. Bearing in mind that we are all completely at the mercy of officialdom, it is to the bureaucrats' credit that they so rarely cause us serious trouble. The obligation of declaring everything correctly is always on the captain: a lapse of memory or the accidental writing of a wrong number is no defence, nor is it any excuse to say that the paper you signed was in a foreign language, which you did not understand, or that the customs officer filled it in and all that you did was to sign where he indicated. Whenever they like, they can throw the book at you, but if you are honest with them and are seen to be sailing for pleasure they will usually treat you fairly.

Landfall

Before making a landfall, wherever it may be, a few preparations should be made. Make a start on them two or three days in advance.

Gear which has not been used on the ocean should be checked and put in working order. First to be needed will be the radio direction-finder, which may or may not be part of the regular receiving set. It can be tested while you are still well outside its

31

normally useful range. In particular, if it relies on batteries of its own, make sure that they are not on the point of death. A similar check should be made on the batteries of the echo-sounder.

If your landfall is in an area which is subject to strong tidal streams, look up the details in a tidal atlas or the appropriate edition of *Reed's Nautical Almanac* (if it covers the area). The buoyage system in American waters is different from that used in Europe and in some of the West Indian islands, so make sure that you are familiar with the system into which you will be arriving. *Practical Pilotage* by Jeremy Howard-Williams has details of both systems, as well as the Collision Regulations, the international signalling code, R/T procedures, search and rescue organisations, and weather forecasting on both sides of the Atlantic.

Continental coasts are subject to fog or mist, and visibility may be worst just when you need to be able to find your way in strange waters. Take special care with your navigation during the last few days before landfall, and start to use radio beacons as soon as they come within range. Crossed with celestial lines of position they can give you fixes several times each day, until the moment comes when fog blots out the horizon and you cannot get a star or sunsight.

Check through entry procedures for the country to which you are going and prepare all necessary documents. Make out a crew-list with full names, dates and places of birth and passport numbers. Some people advocate having a supply of crew-lists pre-typed before the cruise begins, but not only may there be changes of crew, but some countries demand different kinds of information and some insist that the details shall be written on their own printed forms. Make a list of dutiable stores, especially wines and spirits. Be exact about this. Most authorities will turn a blind eye to a locker of half-used bottles provided it is displayed to the customs officer, but they expect to be given precise details of unopened dutiable stores. If you have drugs aboard, for medical reasons, there should be an accompanying certificate from a doctor, naming the patient and stating the quantity of each drug.

Next, check the ground-tackle, warps, fendoffs and anchor-winch. The winch, in particular, may need thoroughly lubricating. Finally, sort out the Q-flag, your national ensign, and the courtesy flag for the country in which you will be making your entry.

Pests

These fall into three categories: airborne, waterborne, and land-based. Unless one anchors close inshore, my experience (after living aboard and cruising in the Caribbean and Mediterranean for five years, continuously) suggests that flies are less of a problem afloat than ashore. In marinas, and inland waterways, mosquitoes and houseflies can be very troublesome unless screens are fitted to all openings. Of the waterborne pests, the teredo worm and gribble can be defeated by regular antifouling but the goose barnacle may be a small nuisance towards the end of a trade-wind crossing, but easily removed at the end of the passage. Of the land-based creatures, rats may come aboard if a boat is alongside and can be a great nuisance if they do. Among other things, they seem to like to eat plastics, and one yacht I met had her black plastic winch-handles chewed right off. Weevils will attack many dry foods, especially farinacious ones, and airtight packing seems to afford little protection although it must help. Cockroaches are the worst insect pest if they are allowed to gain a firm hold. Preventives include avoidance of lying alongside, careful examination of all food brought aboard; especially fruit, vegetables, and cartons which have been stored in a warehouse ashore. Cats may come aboard a boat which is alongside and unless there are rats on which they can feed they may try to steal your fresh meat. Cleanliness is the best protection against most pests.

Insurance

Marine policy

Whether or not to insure is optional, but if one stops to think of the kind of third party claim which might be made in the event of an accident involving others, some protection seems to be essential. A small boat, exploding in a marina, can do a lot of costly damage.

Some argue that it is not worth insuring for the actual voyage across the Atlantic, on the presumption that they may not live to collect the money if the boat is lost. In fact, if you insure at all, the extra cover for a transatlantic passage is not disproportionately high, although cruising cover may cost more in some areas than in others. The decision must be your own after taking the best advice you can get, not only from brokers but also from those with recent experience as boat owners who have had to deal with the problem.

Medical

Your existing medical insurance may or may not cover you while cruising. This should be checked and the policy amended if necessary. Private medical fees are high in the West Indies and the USA, compared with Europe.

Ship's Time

It is best to alter the saloon clock periodically, to conform to zone time, when the voyage involves a big change of longitude; otherwise mealtimes get out of step with hours of daylight. It need not necessarily upset the watchkeeping routine but the cook will grumble. But then, cooks do.

5 The Boat and Her Gear

There is no ideal type of ocean cruiser. Comparatively few boats have been designed specially for that purpose and most of the people who make long voyages do so in whatever they happen to own at the time. If you have owned your yacht for a long time it is almost certain that (unless she is totally unsuitable) you will trust her and will wish to use her for an Atlantic cruise. A vessel built for coastwise and holidays sailing will, however, need some modifications before she can be passed as fit for ocean work.

The Hull

Of whatever material it is constructed, the hull must be sound. This implies that a steel hull has not become dangerously corroded, that fibreglass has not succumbed to osmosis, and that wood has no worm, or rot, or sick seams. Do not take any of these for granted, but get hold of the best surveyor you can, and tell him to look critically at your boat in order to find out what needs to be done prior to making an ocean voyage.

Skin-fittings

Assuming a sound hull, the next thing to investigate is the condition of all skin-fittings. Every hole in the hull must be protected by a seacock. In many yachts, gate-valves are used instead of a lever-type cock, as illustrated in fig. 4. Gate-valves, which depend for their action upon two opposing screws one within the other, have proved to be unreliable after use in tropical seas, because the thinner of the two threads is apt to suffer early from electrolytic action and to fracture unexpectedly. At sea this could be highly inconvenient and might prove very dangerous. Seacocks of the lever-operated type, with an adjustable gland for water retention, will rarely let you down and will always operate if kept greased. Emergency wood bungs, shaped to fit all skin-fittings, are essential.

Fig 4 Lever-type seacock; more reliable than a gate-valve.

The stern-gland is the most frequent source of leakage in all vessels; access should be good and the means of adjustment made as simple as possible. Inspect the propeller shaft for wear, in way of the gland. If wear is evident, no adjustment of the gland will stop a leak. No matter what the pundits say, bronze bolts (such are used on the glands of stern tubes and seacocks) can degenerate under the action of salt water, especially if the stern tube or shaft is made of a metal well separated on the galvanic table; and these should be carefully examined and tested, replaced if defective, and a stock of spares held.

Decks

Having satisfied yourself that water cannot enter the hull from below, have a look at the state of things on deck. First of all, is the cockpit too big? The possibility of its being filled to the top of the coamings is a real one. Are the drains adequate in size, and able to get rid of water fast enough? Are the washboards or coaming of the main companionway high enough and strong enough? Washboards must not be loose planks simply dropped into slots. The Fastnet of 1979 demonstrated the folly of that. They must be so designed that they can be secured or released from on deck or below and that they cannot come adrift accidentally. Is the sail-locker hatch watertight? Unless you are satisfied with your answers to all these questions, the defects must be put right.

A bridge-deck between cockpit and main companionway, is a great source of structural strength. But even if there is no bridge deck, the companionway should be made watertight at least up to deck level and not, as so often is the case, open down to the cockpit sole. In a wooden yacht, which has spent her life in a cool damp climate, there will be the risk that her coachroof and perhaps her deck will open up if she makes a long cruise in the tropics. Put her into a warm dry shed for a few weeks, and have the whole of her upper-works re-stopped and covered with fibreglass, and thus be done with deck leaks for ever. Many owners needlessly endure leaky hatches. On a long ocean passage life can be miserable if, every time a sea comes aboard, what seems like half of it goes below. Most hatches can be altered to render them watertight, and it is worth the effort to make them so.

Pumps

Finally, check the bilge-pumps. There should be one on deck and another below deck, both hand-operated. Certainly have an electric one if you wish, but it should be additional to, and not instead of, the others. Spare parts for all pumps are essential.

The rig

Masts, Spars and Standing Rigging

If your mast has its heel sitting in a proper mast-step on top of the keel, rejoice. If not, remind yourself that a mast stepped on deck is utterly dependent on its rigging for support, and that if the rigging is not amply strong you may be heading for disaster. So many small cruising boats today have their masts stepped on deck that you may think me old-fashioned when I say that I would not willingly cross an ocean in a boat so rigged. If your mast is stepped on deck you may have had it long enough to have confidence in it. If so, all I would say is this: make sure that your feeling is one of real confidence based on knowledge, and not just a complacent attitude borne of familiarity.

It should not be necessary to stress the importance of ensuring that all standing rigging is above reproach. Nevertheless, many stock designs which of necessity are built to sell in a price-conscious market, have rigging that is no more than barely adequate. If you decide to have all your standing rigging replaced by the next larger size (and you might be wise to do so), remember that the size of its attachments is just as important as that of the rigging itself.

Examine the points of attachment of all standing and running rigging: fore and back-stays, chainplates, sheet tracks, eyebolts. Satisfy yourself that they are both strong enough in themselves and that their anchorage to the hull, and the way in which the loads are spread, is adequate also. Check also that there are toggles wherever they may be needed, to ensure that no unfair wringing strains are applied to the fittings to which the rigging is attached.

All stainless steel fittings, if old, may have almost invisible hairline cracks which will weaken them seriously. Your surveyor may or may not be an expert on this subject. Consult a man who is, and take his advice.

Running Rigging
My ideal for ocean cruising is to have all halyards of pre-stretched polyester, no internal halyards, and open barrel winches. If your boat is a modern one, and certainly if she has been rigged for racing, you may be stuck with your internal wire halyards and reel winches. Since going to the masthead in mid-ocean is not everybody's idea of fun, it is reasonable to have a spare halyard for each sail. This need not always call for anything extra. In an emergency the topping lift (if rove through a block at the masthead) can serve as a spare main halyard; and a spinnaker halyard can be used to hoist one of a pair of running sails, or may be used as a standby jib halyard.

Sails
If ordering new sails, give careful thought to their weight and design. It is a fallacy to think that cruising sails need to be heavier than racing sails. An ocean racer hangs on to the genoa after the main has been reefed, but the cruiser's genoa is usually the first sail to be handed. In a ketch there may be a good case for having a heavy mizzen and a comparatively light mainsail if, as is sometimes the case, the owner sails her under jib and mizzen when the going gets tough.

In a boat used solely for cruising, there can be no good reason for having a cross-cut mainsail with a roach to its leach, and battens. A vertical-cut main is not only less likely to split, but it can be taped along its leach which will give it even more strength in its most vulnerable part. A roach is nothing more than a rule-cheating device and a mainsail minus its roach has no need of battens, which are a constant source of trouble when cruising. It is also possible to do away with a headboard by the use of an extra-large thimble. A strong leach line should emerge from its sleeve at a point above that to which the sail will be reefed for Force 6. Headsails should be taped at leach and foot, and all sails triple-stitched with thread of contrasting colour, so that broken threads can more easily be spotted.

Your boat, especially if much used for racing, may have more sails than will be needed on an ocean cruise. For a sloop I would suggest the following:

Mainsail

Working jib

2 Genoas (together equal to the working area of the boat)

Trysail (with eyelets for parrels to back up the slides, if fitted)

Storm jib (fitted with shackles around the stay, at head and foot for extra security)
For a ketch or yawl, add mizzen and mizzen stay-sail. If you are a spinnaker man, take one along; it will occupy very little stowage space.

A major enemy of synthetic fibre sails is sunlight, and their casualty rate will be high unless great care is taken to protect them. Covers for main or mizzen are essential, and bags must be provided for all the rest. All coverings should be in a dark colour, and of an opaque material, that will really stop the sun's rays from reaching the sails. Unless sails are new, it would be well to have seams and tablings re-stitched. Pay particular attention to preventing chafe on sails and running rigging. Use proprietory anti-chafe guards, polythene tubing, or padding, and don't scorn baggywrinkle.

Sailmakers sometimes vary the size of hanks and clew-cringles, often using smaller sizes on big lightweight sails. The size of all hanks should relate to the thickness of the forestay on which they are required to work. They should be big enough to move easily and the size should not vary between one sail and another. Likewise the size of clew-cringles for all headsails should relate to the size of the sheets, which will be transferred from one sail to another, and need bear no relation to the weight of each sail. In a two-masted rig, it makes life simpler if track and slide sizes are the same on both masts. You may not get this, even on a custom-built boat, unless you insist.

Ground Tackle

Sailing folk today are so conditioned to berthing in marinas that a generation of cruising owners is springing up which has little experience of anchoring. On an ocean cruise there are many occasions when there is no alternative to riding at anchor, and the more experienced you become the more inclined you may be to prefer it to any other method of berthing. Different anchorages demand different gear: some are deep, and call for a lot of scope; others have coral bottoms, which cut through anything but chain; some anchors hold well in one place but not in others. We have to be ready for all conditions.

Anchors
Both the CQR and the genuine Danforth anchors, hold well in most situations, but be sure you buy the real thing. Both have their imitators, but the imitations may look right without having the essential qualities of strength and holding-power of the genuine articles. CQR and Danforth are trade names which their imitators cannot use.

There are certain types of bottom on which the traditional anchor still seems to be the best; and there are occasions when a light kedge-anchor is required. For the average boat, three hooks may be all that are needed: a CQR or a Danforth for general use, a good big fisherman or Herreshoff, and a smaller CQR or Danforth, as a kedge.

Anchor Rode
European yachtsmen find it difficult to understand why so many Americans use line instead of chain. It is safe to say that the more experience a man has, the more certain he is to use chain. As compared with line, it is virtually impervious to chafe, it is far easier to handle and to stow, it is easier to clean, and (perhaps most important of all) it demands far less swinging room. If you decide to use chain you will need a windlass with a chain-wheel of the correct size. If the chain falls straight down from the chain wheel into a large locker, without any pipe or chute to cause friction or a hang-up, it should stow itself.

Convention suggests that small yachts should have less chain than big ones, but this

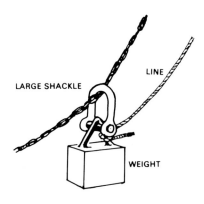

Fig 5 The 'Chum' helps to prevent snubbing the anchor-rode in a hard blow. Suitable for use with chain cable, but would chafe a nylon line.

38

is not true when on a long cruise. The theory is that small boats can lie in shallower water and therefore need less scope; but in fact we cannot always find shallow anchorages in which to lie. For an American boat aiming to sail in the Mediterranean, or a European boat planning a cruise in the West Indies, 100 metres or 50 fathoms should be regarded as the minimum.

Chain sizes and the weights of anchors can be obtained from most of the 'how-to' technical books and need not be repeated here, but for this word of warning: the strains and stresses applied to ground tackle, when at anchor, arise largely from wind pressure and swell. A boat which rides steadily, or can be made to do so, will apply a more even strain than one which is constantly sheering or pitching heavily. Displacement is not, therefore, necessarily the dominant factor in deciding on weights for anchor or cable; windage and liveliness of motion are to be taken into account. A 'chum' (fig. 5) with be found useful.

If you are doubtful about your ground tackle, in an open anchorage, you won't dare to take your sleeping pills. If you are happy about it, you won't need them.

Belowdecks
Comfort as well as safety demands that attention be paid to layout and gear down below.

Ventilation
If a yacht from temperate climes is being taken to the tropics, the problems of ventilation should be studied with great care. It is fairly simple to have hatches with hinges fitted both forward and aft, and for the hinge pins to be withdrawable so that the hatches may open either way. A wind-sail, which is a canvas scoop designed to funnel air down the forehatch, is also useful in strong enough breeze. Electric fans consume little current and, if battery charging is adequate, can be left going night and day. Extractor fans, in the galley and the heads, are a great advantage. Extractors or blowers which may, at times, have to deal with explosive gases must be fitted with flame-proof cowling, to ensure that sparks from a commutator cannot ignite any dangerous fumes. Apart from ventilation, comfort below is greatly improved by proper deck-insulation. The whole of the area under the deck and coach-roof should if possible be covered with one of the proprietory forms of expanded polyurethane, the thicker the better.

Dorade-type ventilators should have two holes in the top of the box, one over the water-trap and the other immediately over the deck inlet. In port the vent can be put directly over the inlet with a cover on the other opening. The reverse position is used at sea. There should also be an emergency cover for the deck inlet, in case the box is smashed.

Mosquito netting will be needed. This can be on a wire or light wooden frame to fit the washboard area, and on elastic to fit hatches, ventilators or scuttles. Anti-mosquito coils are obtainable in the West Indies and the Mediterranean.

Water tank capacity

In most boats it will be necessary to increase the capacity of fresh water tanks for an ocean voyage. With reasonable care consumption can be limited to 2.5 litres (half a gallon) per man/day. A more adequate figure is 4.5 litres (one gallon) per man/day; this would allow for washing-up in fresh water as well as a reasonable amount of personal washing and laundry. It would not provide for unlimited use of pressurized showers. An extra allowance of 50% should be carried for safety and thus for a 28-day passage with a four-man crew, you should ship about 200 gallons.

Unless the intention is to use the boat for ocean cruising for the rest of her life, it may be that the installation of special tanks is not worth the high cost. In that case neoprene bags or plastic jerrycans could be used. If possible, do not store all the water in one tank; and do not have tanks connected together unless cocks are fitted, to prevent a leak or contamination in one tank from causing loss of the whole supply.

The suction pipe for withdrawal of water should go through the top of the tank, reaching nearly to the bottom. This avoids total loss of water in case of a fracture at the joint.

A good method of metering water-consumption is to have service tanks, isolated from the main ones. In this way, usage may be measured by recording each refilling of a service tank, which is done by pumping (either elecrically or by hand) from the main tank. Service tanks may be of whatever size is most convenient and need call for no elaborate plumbing. In a small yacht, a one-gallon plastic can with flexible piping could be fitted at little cost.

A pressurized system is apt to increase the use of water: the mere fact of having to use a hand pump deters most people from being careless.

Collecting water   In some ports, it may not be easy to go alongside to collect water via a hose. In such cases it is useful to have aboard a supply of small plastic cans with screw caps and carrying handles. I emphasise small and plastic. Small, because they are easy to stow; and plastic because, even when full, they will still float. Collecting rainwater can be useful, but should not be relied upon in all areas. A sail cover or awning, inverted beneath the main boom is one method; and another is to have a hole cut in the awning with a canvas tube sewn into it.

The Galley

Cooking Fuel   The first and most important decision to be made about the galley is the choice of fuel for cooking. Alcohol (UK methylated spirits) which for many years has been popular in the USA is not advisable for any boat visiting Europe, where it is not always available and, even where it can be obtained, is usually costly. The choice may, therefore, be between LPG (liquid petroleum gas) and kerosene. Many a lifelong adherent to kerosene has at last been coverted to LPG; and not, be it noted, just because they have become convinced that it can be made safe, but for the further reason that it is now more generally available and that, in some areas, the quality of kerosene is so unreliable that gas is to be preferred.

Broadly speaking, propane is supplied for boats in the USA, Caribbean, and Scandinavia; while butane is more usual in England, France and the Mediterranean. French butane (Camping Gaz) is widely distributed and will be found in many ports of call on an Atlantic cruise. Camping Gaz terminal fittings are non-standard, and special adaptors will be needed.

Recommendations are:
1. Check that your cooking apparatus may be used on both butane and propane, and if so:-
2. Fit suitable piping and regulator for propane, mounted on the bulkhead (using a wall-block manifold, obtainable through Calor dealers) and connected to the cylinder with Calor Gas approved LPG high-pressure tubing, secured with stainless steel hose clips at each end. This rig will suit propane or butane supplies world-wide.
3. Obtain from Calor Gas Ltd, England, a Camping Gaz/Calor Gas adaptor, for use when necessary.
4. Use the fuel most readily obtainable wherever you are, as the main source of supply; with the other fuel as standby. Both butane and propane are available in England, in cylinders which are on hire and must be returned before departure. Foreign boats may apply to have their own cylinders re-filled before leaving, or alternatively buy Camping Gaz, also available in England, but much more expensive. In USA and Bermuda, cylinders must be fitted with safety-valves, otherwise service-stations will refuse to re-fill them.
5. Have a shut-off valve where it can be reached in case of fire.
6. It's not a bad idea to carry a Primus stove, just in case. Tucked away in a locker with a can of kerosene, a pint of alcohol and a pricker, you could be glad of it.

Galley Layout The general layout of the galley will probably not lend itself to major alterations but certain things will need to be done. Whereas the average boat's galley is mostly used in port, the ocean cruiser's must continue to work at its best when at sea. If lockers are to have doors at all, they should if possible be sliding and not hinged. The contents of a locker must never depend upon the door to keep them in place.

The cook will need plenty of places in which to stand various containers, sometimes with their lids off, while food is being prepared. There must be no risk of their going adrift. An open jar of jam thrown across the galley and ending, upside down, on the chart-table can be just as responsible for bad navigation as a bad sun-sight. Deep fiddles are not enough; they must be allied with narrow trough-like compartments which do not allow their contents to skate around and gain momentum. And remember, you will not always be sailing comfortably on one tack. Rhythmic rolling will produce effects of which neither you, nor your cook, will have dreamed.

An important feature of the layout, and one which can sometimes be improved with a little thought, is that of ensuring that the cook can work without interfering with (or being hampered by) those who need to get past the galley.

Berths

It is best, when on a long passage, to avoid if possible using the saloon settees as sleeping berths. This may prove difficult in a small boat, because berths forward of the mast are not likely to be very comfortable except when going down-wind. Quarter-berths, plus one or more pilot berths in the saloon, may solve the problem. Canvas lee-cloths, or portable plywood leeboards which can be slotted into position, are essential. But they must be amply strong. In the case of a pilot berth, part of the backrest of a saloon settee may be hinged up and bolted into such a position that its cushion can act as a padded leeboard.

Stowage

The ocean cruising boat will need more space devoted to stowage than will her coasting counterpart. Crew's clothes need more space; and so do food, water, charts, repair gear, spares and replacements. The modern stock boat, with more berths than are good for her, should have one or more of them pressed into use for stowage and suitably partitioned or adapted in whatever way seems best.

Food Stowage Every cubic inch of space under settees and bunks must be adapted for the stowage of food and other essentials. The purist, and certainly the owner of a very small yacht, will go to great lengths to keep weights as low as possible but tinned provisions need not necessarily be kept in the bilge.

Lockers – whatever they are to hold – should be lined or ceiled so that water sloshing up from the bilge cannot spoil their contents. This is easy to do in a wooden hull where battens or hardboard can be fixed over the timbers. It is less easy with steel or fibreglass, but nonetheless important. Never allow a locker shelf, or the cabin sole, to be close fitted to the side of the hull. If this is done, any water trickling down will collect on the shelf and soak the contents.

If the stowage of food is to be orderly, so that the cook will always know where to find what is needed, some kind of system must be laid down from the start. The galley itself should include a ready-use locker containing those items which are needed daily – such as coffee, tea, milk, sugar, salt etc. – plus enough other things to cater for the next few days' meals. Elsewhere, there should be lockers each containing the stock of a particular thing and, in a floating Utopia, the cook should keep a little book, marking each item off as it is used – a good resolution which will probably not last long. But if the basic stock is stowed in some sort of order, and transferred to the ready-use locker when needed, the cook will quickly begin to keep a mental tally of consumption and to adjust menus accordingly.

Stowage of Clothes The stowage space for crew's clothes must be more generous than is normal for weekend visitors in home waters. The owner's clothes should not overflow into every locker in the boat and, ideally, the only shared locker should be for oilskins. It is impossible to be specific, because yachts differ so widely in size and design, but the aim should be for each man to have locker space enough to keep his things in good shape and out of sight, and that he should not have to live, even partially, out of his luggage.

Sail Stowage Sails are, of course, the biggest items for which stowage has to be provided. The problem is to find a place, or places, which are not only big enough to contain bulky bags, but which have openings large enough to admit them. It may be that not all sails can be stowed below and it is not uncommon for at least one headsail to live, in its bag, on deck. Whatever stowage is provided below decks, try if possible to arrange access without having to disturb the sleeping watch.

Spares and Replacements

It has been said that, for the perfectionist, the only solution to this problem is to tow a replica of his boat. The man who has always done his own fitting out is more likely to know what to take than one who has relied entirely on a boatyard. The problem can be simplified if a policy of standardisaton is adopted. Many boats have, for example, six or eight different sizes of shackles in various locations. With a little thought, these might be reduced to three. The same reasoning can be applied to the sizes of sheets, halyards and mooring lines.

Sheets and halyards of polyester will last for several years if not subjected to chafe, but a few hours of careless use may destroy the strength of an important line. A replacement coil should be carried for each diameter in use. To suggest carrying enough steel wire to make a replacement of any rigging failure would perhaps be a counsel of perfection, but at least there should be a coil of wire, equal in strength to the strongest in use, and at least twice the length of the longest stay in the rig, together with a plentiful supply of bulldog grips (wire rope clamps) for emergency use. Sail repairs will be routine when ocean sailing, even if the sails are brand new at the start of the voyage. Palm, needles, sail hooks, beeswax, twine, and sailcloth in the weight and texture of each sail, will be needed. Needles must be stored in a tin containing plenty of grease.

All things mechanical are certain to need servicing, and partly or wholly replacing, during the course of a long cruise. Pumps will need new valves and gaskets; engines will need new oil seals, filters and injectors; alternators will need new brushes and belts. Do not imagine that if you have bought an engine maker's recommended package of spares and replacements, it will necessarily include everything you need. In six years, I used none of the main items included in the costly package which they sold me, yet it failed to contain such important things as a cylinder-head gasket, spare brushes for the alternator, and filter elements; all of which are certain to be needed for routine work on any engine. Think back, if you can, about those things which have failed in the past, and try to provide for possible recurrence.

In all departments, simplification and standardisation should be practised. To quote a simple example, if the boat has two heads, let them be identical. That way, spare parts will fit either and if the worst happens cannibalisation can be adopted, to make one out of two.

Some engine parts are difficult to repair, in areas where no service stations exist. Alternators are relatively cheap, and easy for anyone to take off and replace, and I would always carry a spare. Injector pumps are costly, but they cannot be repaired except by experts; so if embarking on a long cruise away from the maker's service depots, it would be wise to carry a spare. Carry also, at least one complete set of those funny-shaped moulded rubber hoses which fit to various parts of the engine. If they fail, there is no substitute.

When deciding what to take, and what not to take, make two lists: one consisting of those things which you can reasonably expect to be able to replace en route, and another of those which you think may not be obtainable. Ordinary paint, which is bulky to stow, can be bought in most seaport towns throughout the world. Specialised kinds, on the other hand, like antifouling and fibreglass paints are less likely to be found except in yachting centres. Spare parts for fittings such as the products of Gibb, Barient, Barlow and Lewmar, may be difficult or impossible to obtain in unsophisticated places. And a costly winch, whose only handle has gone overboard, is just a lump of misplaced ballast.

You alone can make these lists for your boat, and having made them, and bought all the items you think you will need, their stowage must be carefully arranged and recorded. Most of us, if asked whether we have a bulldog grip on board, will say 'Yes, I think I have one somewhere'. When a backstay parts with a sound like gunfire one dark and stormy night, you'll need to have a better answer than that.

The Toolbox
Tools are often needed in an emergency and should, therefore, be readily accessible and in known locations. The loss of an important tool could prove serious, and neither tools nor pieces of dismantled equipment should ever be left lying about on deck where they might slip, or be knocked overboard. A well-designed and well sited tool locker is an important aid, not only to the running of the ship but to the safety of all aboard her.

The Engine and Electrics
On an ocean cruise an engine is needed less for propulsion than for battery charging. But although few auxiliary yachts have fuel enough to give them much range under power, it can be useful on occasion to be able to motor for 500 miles or so. If, after several days of calm, drinking water were to be running low, or if one of the crew were to be seriously ill, use of the engine might avert worse trouble.

44

With electric pumps, electric windlasses, and all manner of minor gadgetry dependent on electric battery power, the need for a reliable engine to keep the batteries charged is obvious. It is best to have two quite separate sets of batteries; one for general service and the other solely for engine starting. If the circuitry is well designed, it will be possible to charge both sets together, to use either set for either purpose and, in an emergency, to switch the two in parallel. Except in a very large yacht, one engine will be used both for propulsion and to drive the generator or alternator. When excessive loads are being imposed on the battery (such as prolonged use of an anchor windlass) start the engine and run it while the load is being applied.

Modern wet batteries are designed to accept the high charging rates which alternators provide, possibly using a T.W.C. regulator which has been specifically designed for rapid charging, and they do not react well to prolonged trickle-charging; they like to be used, and respond best to reasonable exercise. Nevertheless, trickle-charging may solve an occasional problem and can be provided by means of a wind-generator or solar panels, neither being cheap. For use in a marina, a domestic-type mains-operated trickle-charger affords an inexpensive alternative. A battery used only for starting gets too little work, so make it earn its living occasionally by switching it over to supplying the lights, and use the lighting battery for starting. No battery likes to be left in an uncharged condition, so after a period of prolonged or heavy duty give it a quick re-charge to restore it to peak condition. A battery-state meter is most useful.

Because of high currents involved, circuit design and the work of installation must be of the highest quality. Batteries under simultaneous charge must be provided with suitable control-units, which will regulate the rates of charge to suit the individual needs of each.

Dry Batteries   If radios and other electronic equipment can be run off dry batteries as an alternative to the ship's mains, take spares as a reserve against loss of mains power. If using dry batteries only, take spares and if using rechargeable cells, keep a reserve set fully charged.

Shore Mains Equipment   When abroad, you may find that the shore mains differs from the supply you have at home in both voltage and frequency. If you have shore mains driven equipment aboard, find out the characteristic of the supply at your various destinations and take advice on the best way to convert it to your needs.

Corrosion   Any water-cooled engine is liable to be affected by galvanic or electrolytic action. A salt-water cooled installation should have sacrificial zincs somewhere in the water-jacket and these will need routine replacement. Take expert advice on where to place them, and be sure to carry enough spares. Even when fresh-water cooling is used, the heat exchanger is exposed to the corrosive action of hot salt water, so that zinc may be needed for its protection. The water-cooled exhaust and silencer are also potentially weak spots. After a few years' use a silencer may need replacing. Start any long cruise with a brand new one.

Dinghies   The choice is obviously between soft and hard. For the small yacht, a rubber boat may be all that can be stowed; and it will stand a lot of scuffing and squeezing without looking any uglier than when it was new. With care, a hard dinghy might last as long as the yacht but, in the tropics, a rubber boat may perish within a few years. Stowage for a wood or glass dinghy, on deck, must be securely and simply contrived: launching and hoisting aboard will be routine, morning and evening, in some ports. And at sea she will be subjected to some of the unkindest treatment ever.

Compass
Postpone swinging the ship until ready for sea *with everything stowed in its proper place*. Ensure that compass lighting is totally waterproof and fitted with a rheostat to dim the light. The rheostat should be just inside the companionway (out of the wet but near at hand). A hand-bearing compass is essential.

Log
Accurate dead reckoning demands a log, and if it is combined with a speedometer so much the better. Your existing log will serve, but should be checked and overhauled by the makers, unless brand new, and, if of the trailing type, spare rotators should be taken to replace those eaten by fish.

Echo sounder
Though not essential, this is very desirable, but it must be backed up with a lead-line.

Emergency tiller
A MUST. Equally important are its immediate accessibility and the ease with which it can be fitted if the normal tiller (or wheel steering) breaks down.

Radio   See Chapter 7

Special Equipment   See Chapter 9

Life-saving gear   See Chapter 10

6 The Crew

More cruises come apart because of crew trouble than for any other single reason. But with a happy ship's company consisting of people who know how to live afloat, and who enjoy each other's companionship, a long voyage can be an experience which all will remember with deep and lasting satisfaction. It is, therefore, worth taking a great deal of trouble in selecting and putting together the right people, and in planning the routine aboard.

Crew problems vary directly as the number of hands: the singlehander has none; the man-and-wife partnership has few beyond the odd domestic brawl. As the basis on which to discuss the subject in this chapter we are assuming a crew of four.

Recruitment

There are two aspects to this, (i) the recruiting of a crew before starting a cruise and (ii) replacements needed en route. The initial task can be done under relatively controlled conditions, possibly in home waters, while the whole project is being planned. There is a risk in attempting to do this too far in advance, because glib promises are sometimes made by people who are full of enthusiasm until you try to pin them down to a firm sailing date. Before approaching anybody, it is best to have the cruise clearly planned in broad outline and a sailing date, give or take a week, arranged.

A Package Deal

Prospective crewmen can then be offered a package deal. The offer should specify quite clearly what the commitments are to be, on each side, set forth in an exchange of letters.

(1) Starting date and possible duration.

(2) Who pays any travelling expenses, to or from the points of embarkation and disembarkation.

(3) What, if any, contribution the crewman is to make towards his keep.

(4) What, if any, liability the owner will accept in the event of accident or death involving the crewman.

(5) That the crewman shall bring with him a passport valid for the places likely to be visited and so dated that it will not expire during the possible duration of the cruise.

The owner of any vessel is obliged, by international law, to guarantee the cost of repatriating a crewman who may leave that vessel, for whatever reason, wherever she may be. Immigration laws are strictly enforced almost everywhere, and in many places tourists are not allowed to land unless they are in possession of a ticket which will enable them to return to their native country. An owner who could not afford to fly his crew back home in an emergency, would be well advised to insist on each man depositing the cost of flight from the furthest point of the cruise, to ensure that his premature departure would not bankrupt the project.

Choosing a Crew

Actually deciding whom to invite is of necessity a personal matter on which little advice can be given. Provided that the owner-skipper is competent in all aspects of seamanship and navigation, he may find it easier to make seamen out of a good novice crew than to cope with the *prima donna* attitudes of experienced hands, unwilling to adapt themselves to the customs of the ship. He should, therefore, concentrate first on finding, if he can, the right sort of people; taking account of character and temperament rather than technical knowledge or experience. He will, nevertheless, bear in mind that one of the crew will have to be second in command and whoever this is must, because of experience or age – preferably both – be acceptable to others without question.

The only reliable test as to whether two people can sail together in harmony is to go out and do it. If you have an old shipmate able and willing to join you in forming the nucleus of your crew, nothing could be better. Otherwise you can only shop around, meet people, talk with them, have them aboard, sailing, eating and living together until you feel reasonably sure that you'll get along.

Having settled for a mate, you may or may not wish to choose the other hands for some specially skilled job. In a crew of four, it has always seemed to me that, for an ocean cruise, it is worth having a full time cook. Good food, well prepared and served on time, is fundamental to the efficiency and well-being of the whole ship's company. There is no more difficult task than cooking, day in day out, at sea in a small yacht; and it takes a skilled and dedicated person, with total immunity from sea-sickness, to be able to do it. If such a one can be found, man or woman, welcome him or her aboard, provide the best galley you can, the best equipment, and let the cook play the leading part in choosing the provisions. It will go a long way towards ensuring the success of your cruise.

The fourth member of the crew may in fact be a complete novice, and this sometimes works very well indeed. Provided he is not so young as to be lonely, the boy who joins will probably walk ashore a man, despite the fact that the cook (if she is a woman) will have done her best to spoil him throughout the voyage.

Crew replacements en route

This may happen in two ways: (a) by pre-arranged changes of crew, whereby a new crewman joins the boat at some agreed point or, (b) if a vacancy occurs, necessitating the recruitment of one or more hands in a foreign country, perhaps far distant from one's home port.

The first case calls for no comment, but the second needs care. The seaports of the world all have, from time to time, itinerant bums who go from boat to boat,

48

trying to thumb a passage to some other place. Occasionally there may be a good crew among them but, unless you are lucky, you will probably ship a useless hand who will be sick and incapable until you land him at your next port of call (with perhaps the liability of paying the cost of his repatriation). At worst you may find that you have taken on board a junkie, or hi-jacker, whose presence will explode into serious trouble. So screen quayside applicants carefully. Always ask for references from previous skippers, and always take them up.

One's own countrymen are usually the best bet, provided one is satisfied on other counts: and next in line would be nationals of the country one is about to visit; because they would cause no immigration problem.

Training

It is not possible to simulate ocean sailing conditions except by making an ocean passage. Preliminary training of the crew will have to be limited to giving them a good working knowledge of handling the yacht at sea. All the usual sail drill should be gone through until each man is conversant with every operation. The simple routines, like putting about and heaving-to, will be quickly learnt; but handing and stowing the mainsail – a job which in coastal cruising is usually done in port – must be practised at sea, and finally perfected when conditions are tough. Bad-weather gear, harness, and life jackets, should be worn in appropiate conditions; and the crew must become accustomed to working in them whenever necessary.

Discipline

An important part of crew-training must of necessity take place during the early stages of the cruise itself. Its basis is discipline.

Discipline is an unattractive word, and to some people, anathema. Yet without it any community, ashore or afloat, degenerates into a disorderly rabble. If it is there, you may bet your last dollar that it has been taught – it does not just happen.

The ideal is for each crewman to be self-disciplined; but this again can come about only after some training. Every ship has her own routine – 'different ships, different long splices' – and it is up to the skipper to lay on his boat's routine as early as possible.

It begins with the simplest of things; which line goes to which cleat, exactly how to belay a sheet or halyard, where each item of gear is kept – and the importance of always keeping it in the same place. These are not just owner's fads – they could mean the difference between life and death on a dark night. It extends to the way in which each member stows his personal belongings and how well he washes his person; how he and the rest of the night-watch leave the galley after their coffee in the early hours. If the cook gets up to find a sink full of dirty mugs to be washed before he or she can begin to get breakfast, war will be declared. The skipper, on a long passage, will keep an eagle eye on the rate of using drinking water and cooking fuel; but it is less common to find that the crew have the same sense of urgency about these things unless it has been taught to them.

A new and willing hand will offer to make coffee and will begin by pumping water into the kettle until it is full. Although the water may not be wasted, his attention should be drawn to the fact that perhaps four times as much fuel as necessary will be used to heat it. These, and similar small matters, have to be gently but firmly laid on from the begining, ensuring that the skipper's routine is carried out and that any lapses are nipped in the bud. It would be ridiculous to suggest that the skipper should make a formal daily round in a small boat; yet in fact he should make an inspection and should let it be seen that he does so. This will not only ensure that essential work is done, and mistakes corrected as they arise, but it will give him the chance to acknowledge a job well done and to give each man a pride in his work.

A Happy Ship   The skipper has to deal not only with the relationship between himself and each of his crew, but must also try to prevent disputes arising between crew members. In doing so he must on no account take sides or become involved, unless the safety of the vessel should be at risk.

It is difficult to put matters of this kind on paper without seeming to be pedantic and stuffy, but a happy ship's company is so well worth attaining that no effort should be spared in the attempt. In a happy ship, we tend to accept the situation gratefully; without question. When the reverse happens we always conduct an inquest. The wise man enquires into the reason for success as well as failure.

In Port   Crew problems are more apt to arise in port than at sea. It has been said that for each day she's at sea, a boat needs three days in port – to be spent on maintenance. And every skipper knows that, for him, the real slogging work begins when the ship gets into port. A young crew, on the other hand will quite naturally want to see the town and to chat up the girls. A compromise has to be found; and a good one which usually works, is for the morning to belong to the ship, and for the crew to be free in the afternoon. This includes the cook.

The Skipper

Even more important than the training of his crew, is the skipper's own schooling of himself. He may have sailed for thirty years: he may have won a lot of cups: he may have been a flag officer of his club – but unless he has been in charge, on an ocean voyage, he still has something to learn. Those of us who have sailed much on our own, or with one regular sailing partner, are apt to get stuck in our ways. One of the most difficult things we have to learn is to be tolerant of those who have developed ways of doing things different from our own. While it is right for us to insist, in our own boat, that certain things shall always be done our way, and that the whole crew should learn a common drill for doing them, there are other things which afford the opportunity for experiment and the use of individual initiative. To quote only one

50

example, the watch on deck could be given freedom to try out new arrangements of sails, and the trimming of them, in an effort to improve the ship's performance.

The basis of a successful cruise depends very much on the skipper's ability not only to lay on an efficient watch-keeping system, which is not difficult, but also to apportion responsibility fairly, making the most of each man's abilities and giving to each a sense of purpose and the realisation that he is contributing adequately to the success of the project.

It is for the skipper to set the tenor of life aboard, and he can do this more by his reactions for events, and to people, than by any other means. If he has doubts or anxiety, he should not display them to his crew: like any good commander, he should exude confidence and cheerfulness, though he may not always feel either. Each crewman must be given pride in what he is doing and an incentive to do it well. The skipper who takes an obvious interest in the distances run in each watch, automatically sets up targets and stirs the competitive urge among his watchkeepers. A small celebration to mark some event – a birthday, the halfway mark, or the best day's run – not only creates a short spell of relaxation, but it gives the cook a chance of putting on a star turn. It is the skipper who must do the prompting.

The problem of incompatibility in a small ship's company is often the result of inexperience. Those of us who have sailed a lot and who recognise the warning signals, have a duty towards those who do not yet know the art of living at very close quarters. You and I know that for every cruise that has been spoiled by just one selfish individual, there have been many others so rewarding that the recollection of them binds us to those with whom we sailed, for the rest of our lives. When this happens a lot of things must go right. But if the skipper doesn't get his bit right, the rest can do little to help.

7 Radio and Electronics

Radio and electronics are highly technical subjects, the full treatment of which is far beyond the scope of this book. Your decision about what equipment to buy will depend on what you want it to do and how much you are willing to spend. First decide what your real needs are and then, before you spend your money, seek the best and most expert opinion you can find.

Radio

The purposes for which the ocean cruiser needs radio may be listed as follows:
1. Reception of time signals, weather, direction finding, news, entertainment
2. Two-way communications
3. Distress

Reception

Get a good, waterproof, set with a frequency range from 150 kilohertz to 30 megahertz and a digital frequency indicator. It should be able to receive both double sideband emissions, used for instance by the BBC and other broadcasters, and single sideband emissions, used where frequency crowding and power consumption have to be minimized – for instance long range communications. Such a set is probably the most useful single piece of radio equipment for an ocean voyage. Coupled with a direction-finding antenna (which may be built in) it will cope with all reception requirements outlined above. It is well worth spending money on this set. If, also, it can automatically record at pre-set times with the loudspeaker disconnected and double as the receiver for a weatherfax system (see below), so much the better.

La Coruña taken before the new Yacht Club was constructed.

Spanish National Tourist Office

52

Two-way Radio Communications

Two-way radio communications may be conveniently discussed in terms of frequencies:

Very High Frequency (VHF)	30 to 300 megahertz	Short range communications, usually line of sight between aerials
High Frequency (HF)	3 to 30 megahertz	Long range communications
Medium Frequency (MF)	300 to 3000 kilohertz	Medium range communications, say up to 500 miles at night

Both professionals and amateurs work in all the above bands at specified frequencies. A transmitter working professional marine frequencies aboard a yacht (called a mobile station) has to be licensed to the yacht, and the operator requires a separate licence (or, in the case of VHF, has to be under the supervision of a licensed operator). Courses for the limited licence required to work the VHF net are available through the RYA and other organizations. An amateur net in the HF band, often working between 14275 and 14295 kHz or between 21350 and 21450 kHz, geared to the needs of ocean passage makers has developed in the last decade. It is not only extremely useful in passing position and weather reports, port information and so forth but has sometimes proved to be the sole link in an emergency. Transmitters operated by amateurs are not required to be licensed, though the operator must be. Information on all aspects of amateur radio communications is available from the Radio Society of Great Britain, Lambda House, Cranborne Road, Potters Bar, London EN6 3JE, and licensing information is also contained in the booklet 'How to become a Radio Amateur' from the Radio Amateur Licensing Unit, Post Office Headquarters, Chetwynd House, Chesterfield S49 1PF, Derbyshire.

There are two bands, the Citizens' Bands, between 27.6 and 29 megahertz and between 934 and 935 megahertz in the UK (other countries have different standards) in which the operator does not require a licence to transmit. The transmitter, which can only work within the specified frequencies, has to be licensed. Although possibly of use on land, the Citizens' Band has no practical advantage offshore.

VHF Equipment

Besides being the preferred medium for short range communications, a VHF installation is rapidly becoming more than a convenience; some port authorities and marinas expect to be called before a yacht enters – many monitor channel 16 or another specified channel. A frequency modulated (FM) system is standard. The frequencies allocated to numbered channels vary between Europe and the USA (though 16 is common to both) and this must be taken into account when purchasing a set. There are many sets available at very competitive prices: robustness, the number of channels available and the possibility of duplex working are factors to consider. A masthead whip antenna will give the best range, but have a deck-mounted alternative in case of dismasting. A hand-held back up set will serve for this purpose besides being useful for dinghy work, towing or rescue.

MF Equipment

This is most useful in medium range ship-to-shore or, by prior arrangement, ship-to-ship communications but is generally of less interest to the ocean going yacht whose requirements lie either in short range VHF or the long range HF communications. Good sets are much the same price as HF sets and it may be better to direct resources towards HF or VHF.

HF Equipment

This equipment is at the more expensive end of the market but there are good amateur sets available, at reasonable prices, capable of working both professional and amateur nets. Sets built for professional use are more expensive and have special features such as automatic monitoring of distress frequencies. A wide range of frequencies is desirable. Precision in the selection of frequency is essential and is conveniently achieved by synthesized sets. A properly designed aerial (a backstay might be used) and a good ground are necessary; expert installation is advisable.

Distress

Use the standard procedure – alarm signal, distress call, and distress message – as laid down in publications supplied with any radio transmitter. If there is time to do so, include your boat's name, port of registry, and official number, to confirm your identity. Say if you will be turning on an Emergency Position Indicating Radio Beacon (EPIRB). When initiating a distress call, use the most appropriate frequency, according to where you are. In coastal waters use VHF Channel 16. In mid-ocean, away from shipping lanes, if you do not have professional HF communications, there remains only amateur radio, backed up with an EPIRB. Many boats carry a small amateur transceiver and portable aerial, solely for emergency use.

EPIRBs fall into two categories; the first type is essentially an air distress beacon, having great range to over-flying aircraft, whose crews monitor the appropriate channels – 121.5 MHz for civil, and 243 MHz for military aircraft. The frequency 121.5 MHz is also tracked by satellite but this needs 'line of sight' with the Ground Station to relay the information, which can lead to some hours of delay. Onward transmissions from aircraft would alert Search and Rescue organisations whose aircraft could home in directly on the beacon. These sets are small and relatively cheap, but there have been so many false alarms that their usefulness is suspect. The second type works at 406 MHz and is the system which has recently become mandatory for the OSTAR races. These sets are more sophisticated and are designed to avoid false alarms, and to identify your craft. They are monitored by the international SARSAT system, a continuous satellite system. The early sets may be bulky ($2'' \times 6'' \times 12''$). Authorities urge that an EPIRB, once started, should be left on continuously while batteries last, otherwise searchers may lose contact.

Electronics
The borderline between radio and electronics is not clearly defined, but for our purposes we can regard radio as covering normal types of communication, and electronics as covering such things as weather map reception, echo sounding, radar, and satellite navigation.

Weatherfax
This is the system for the reception of weather maps. Some may consider it a luxury but it can be of great value. If you already have a suitable receiver, this may considerably reduce the overall cost of the installation.

A complete installation is still relatively expensive, but prices are falling. It is a useful aid in the Atlantic where the forecasts are good, but of less use elsewhere.

Navigational Systems
The three main electronic systems are DF, landbased Hyperbolic systems, and Satellite based systems. DF is still the main international system. Unfortunately some stations, particularly in the US, are now reported to be out of service as most vessels are relying on Loran. All transatlantic voyagers, however, should still have a DF receiver as a back-up system for the foreseeable future.

Land-based systems of a practical nature now encompass Loran and Decca. Loran is extensively used in US waters and Decca in Northern Europe. Ideally you should have the set appropriate to your landfall. Land-based systems will survive until at least 1992 and it appears that Loran is likely to continue longer and to cover more areas. If you buy a Loran set make certain that it has good filters (to eliminate Decca and other interference). If on arrival in European waters Decca is in use it is essential to check by an independent fix that it is locked into the correct zone and is not 10 miles out.

Satellite systems fall into two categories: TRANSIT and Global Positioning System (GPS). The first is reliable, accurate (100 metres typical), and not affected by atmospheric conditions. When using TRANSIT and approaching coastal waters remember to take account of tidal set and drift, vessel speed and course or substantial errors can result. TRANSIT could be phased out when GPS is fully operational in about 1995. There is likely to be improved TRANSIT coverage over the next few years but there may still be some hours between fixes.

GPS (or NAVSTAR as it is sometimes called) should be operational by 1991 (subject to Shuttle performance). This has all the advantages of TRANSIT and gives continuous fixes as well. This is clearly the optimum system if cost is not an overruling factor. Other systems such as Geostar may well provide as good a service over the Atlantic, and with much cheaper receivers, by the same time – but would probably have user charges.

Radar
Like long-range HF equipment, Radar is costly and current-hungry; many users have to

run their charging plant whilst it is in use. The scanner unit is bulky top-hamper difficult to site on a single-masted yacht. Nevertheless it is without question useful in thick weather for both navigation and collision avoidance.

Power Systems
See page 45. But there must always be at least one receiving set, capable of obtaining world-wide time signals and RDF fixes, available for use on dry batteries independently of the ship's mains. A spare set of batteries in mint condition should be provided at the start of any ocean voyage.

Care and maintenance
All electronic apparatus must be kept dry: not all equipment is properly waterproofed. It is good practice to site most if not all such apparatus in a locker – well protected from any water which may come below and form condensation.

Costs
It can be misleading to quote prices, without qualification, in a book such as this which may be studied some time after the date of publication. The best we can do is to indicate costs at the time of writing (1987) with explanatory notes where needed.

Receiving sets   Communications receivers may be bought in the UK for anything between £150 and £1,000. For £1,000 you will get the best set obtainable for marine use; it will be strong, reliable and proof against dampness in whatever form. At the lower price you will get a set which will perform the same functions, although it is likely to be less robust, less reliable and almost certainly inferior in terms of waterproofing.

Long and medium range equipment   Either type would cost about £3,000 for transmitter and receiver fully installed.

Amateur radio equipment   About £1,500 installed.

Distress   The cheap EPIRB sets working on 121.5 MHz cost about £150 but the more sophisticated type working on 406 MHz and monitored by SARSAT cost more than three times as much.

Navigation equipment   Decca in the UK is available for £400. Loran in the UK costs about £900 but is much cheaper in the USA (but watch for lack of filters). TRANSIT is available in the UK for as little as £600. It is estimated that GPS, when available (possibly 1991), may cost £1,500 or less.

Weatherfax   About £2,000 installed.

Summary
If you are short of money, instrumentation is the best area in which to economise. An all-bands receiver, as suggested at the beginning of this chapter, will, if necessary, see you through.

8 Provisioning

A Formula

Most of us, when we first have to deal with the provisioning problem, tend to think that it is more difficult than it is. The formula is simple and can be expressed thus:

$$\frac{3PC}{2} \ (B+L+T+D)$$

where   P = Passage-time in days
           C = Number of hands·
           B = Food consumed at breakfast
           L = Food consumed at lunch
           T = Food consumed at tea
           D = Food consumed at dinner

A Test-run

Lying on your mooring, or better still doing a short local cruise with friends (equal in number to your proposed crew for the voyage), live aboard for a full week without going ashore to buy any food or drink other than that which you have taken with you at the start.

Take with you no fresh provisions, with the exception of new-laid eggs, onions and potatoes, of which take all you think you will need. Take ample supplies of canned, bottled and dried food; and staples such as flour, rice, pasta. De-hydrated products, foil-wrapped, keep well and cannot poison you, but you may have to adjust your usage of them to the size of your water-tanks because they will use up more water than their canned counterparts. Remember dried yeast if you intend to make bread; and remember also salt, pepper, mustard, sugar, cooking oil and baking powder. If you have the right sort of wife, forget everything and leave the whole job to her! At the end of the week, take careful note of exactly what has been consumed, item by item. The total quantities consumed divided by the number of days and again by the number of persons taking part in the test will give you the amount per man/day for each item. If you multiply each of these items by the factor $\frac{3PC}{2}$ it will give the total stores needed for the voyage. If, after the dummy run, all the meats are recorded as 'meat' and all the jams as 'jam' it will then be the cook's job to decide on how much of the meat shall be corned beef, bacon rashers, canned ham, or sausages; similarly to decide on the proportion of jam, marmalade, honey etc. The factor $\frac{3PC}{2}$ makes allowance for the possibility of the voyage taking half as long again as the estimated time.

Hints on Buying

Provisioning for a long passage is best done at a port of some size, for the obvious reason that it is likely to have the best resources. The ports listed in Part IV are capable of meeting most needs. If the last port of call is well chosen, it should be able to provide you with a sack of sound potatoes and of onions which, with careful weekly picking-over, will last for a month-long voyage even in tropical latitudes. Eggs, fresh from the farm on the day you sail, will last for a month without treatment, but not if at any time they have been in a refrigerator. Turn them over each week to prevent the yolks from settling. Fruit is less predictable. Green tomatoes will ripen gradually in a warm atmosphere, oranges will keep well but may go bad in tropical heat after a couple of weeks. A hand of green bananas will be uneatable for several days, but will then all ripen at once. Nevertheless, half a hand is well worth putting aboard if obtainable at your departure port, and even over-ripe bananas make a delicious sweet, cooked in rum.

Of the canned meats, corned beef is by far the best value and in moderately skilled hands is capable of many different end-products. Fish of various kinds, in cans, offers excellent food-value; and tomatoes retain their vitamins and their flavour, not to mention their versatility, almost as well canned as fresh.

In many places, it is possible to buy foodstuffs in cartons of a dozen or more at a slight discount, usually on a cash-and-carry basis, provided that no agent is taking a rake-off. When buying canned goods of all kinds avoid the 'giant economy pack'. It may not fit your boat's lockers and once opened, unless its contents can be used quickly, they may go bad. Cans containing enough for two people are easy to stow and, with four in the crew, may enable a choice to be offered. Butter is not always to be had in tins and, in the tropics, is liable to emerge in liquid form. Margarine, in plastic tubs, seems to keep forever and to retain its solid state even without refrigeration. For the boat with a deep-freeze, it is no problem to provide meat enough for a transatlantic passage.

Don't forget that the confines of a small boat, with attendant restriction on exercise, tend to promote constipation. See that the galley stores contain a supply of one of the bran-type breakfast foods.

Food, to the gourmet, cannot be considered without thinking about wine. And wine, to those of us who sail, is unthinkable unless it is bought duty-free. So whatever you do or don't do about the things mentioned in this chapter, remember this: somewhere you must have a great big lockable space, yet easily accessible, designed for the reception and accommodation of the bottled products of France and Spain and Portugal; of Italy, Madeira and the West Indies; of California and Mexico. And not, of course, forgetting Scotland.

Drinking Water
See Chapter 5 for advice on tank capacity and consumption.

A Spartan Diet

Commander Bill King on his classic voyage through the roaring forties in his tiny *Galway Blazer* devised a simple and healthy diet which needed no cooking. The ingredients were:

1. Dried fruit consisting of Australian sultanas and raisins, soaked overnight in fresh water.

2. A branded product called 'Notina' (made in Switzerland and bought from the Whole Food Store, Baker Street, London). This is a paste made from almonds, which was diluted with water, mixed to the consistency of cream, and one heaped dessert spoonful added to one cupful of the fruit.

3. Mung beans, sprouted and eaten raw. They can be bought from most garden shops or seedsmen, and can be sprouted in a screw-top glass jar, mixed daily with a little fresh water, the lid of the jar being perforated.

This provided all essential dietry needs, and Commander King reports that he kept completely fit during the voyage. He had less success with it as a means of entertaining friends. But do not treat this item lightly. If dismasted, or forced to abandon ship, a supply of this simple food, needing no cooking yet supplying all that the body needs, might mean the difference between life and death.

9 Special Equipment

Down-wind Rig

Originally, the development of twin running-sails was bound up with the demand that they should steer the boat on a down-wind course. Since the introduction of vane steering gears, they no longer have to do this. Before spending a lot of money on special sails, spars, and winches, which will be used for part of the time only, you should ask yourself if you really need them. One veteran of the Atlantic, who probably had more experience than most, thought not: Humphrey Barton recommended using the mainsail and a boomed-out genoa.

With the wind on the quarter, rhythmic rolling can be damped down to some extent if the main is in use, and certainly the worst rolling I have ever experienced was when running with a small staysail set across the deck. Nevertheless, on any future trade-wind passage, my own choice would be to stow the mainsail and use an assortment of headsails – jibs of varying sizes – boomed out with the wind astern, and the trysail ready to set if the wind should come abeam. In this way, the main would be saved from the risk of chafe, and from the harmful effects of strong sunlight; and the danger of an accidental gybe could be avoided.

Auto-Steering

Remember that self-steering mechanisms do not have the 'sixth sense' that a good helmsman has. They can react but they cannot anticipate what is likely to happen. They cannot see that great sea which is coming up on the quarter, which you or I would know is, in a second or two, going to cause the ship to take a violent sheer if something is not done before it begins. Nevertheless, some form of automatic steering is now standard practice for ocean sailing and the choice lies between a wind-vane and an electronic auto-pilot.

A wind-vane correctly trimmed with the sails will maintain a course relative to the wind direction, while an auto-pilot will hold doggedly to a compass course until everything is ashake.

Vane self-steering satisfies the purist because it is delightful to make the wind steer the boat. But there are times – and especially on a long down-wind passage like the Trades – when the vessel's speed so reduces the apparent strength of the wind as to make the vane ineffective. Today, there are reasonably priced electronic auto-pilots which consume very little current and are well worth having in addition to a vane gear.

Before using a robot, I like to sail the boat and get the feel of her and to know that she is happy. Only when she seems to be well balanced and easy on the helm is it fair to ask a machine to take it over.

Extra Gear

Whatever you decide to do, one or more spars will be needed for booming out headsails; a spinnaker-pole and its normal gear may serve if you already have it. Otherwise a stout scaffold-pole of light alloy with a gooseneck fitting at one end, and eyes into which the clew of a jib and its sheets can be shackled, will provide a spar at reasonable cost. For a complete rig, two such poles are needed and there should be two separate tracks on the foreside of the mast, long enough to allow the booms to be stowed up and down, with their outboard ends in chocks on deck. For the full rig, two stays will be needed. No guys are needed either fore or aft, but there should be an endless line attached to the gooseneck slide, and rove through a cheek-block on the mast above the limit of the track. This will enable the inboard end to be hauled up and down to the required position (see fig. 6).

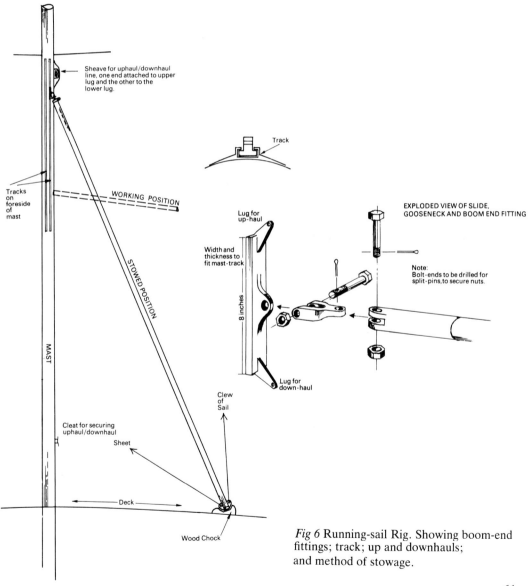

Sheave for uphaul/downhaul line, one end attached to upper lug and the other to the lower lug.

Tracks on foreside of mast

WORKING POSITION

STOWED POSITION

MAST

Cleat for securing uphaul/downhaul

Sheet

Deck

Wood Chock

Track

Lug for up-haul

Width and thickness to fit mast-track

8 inches

Lug for down-haul

Clew of Sail

EXPLODED VIEW OF SLIDE, GOOSENECK AND BOOM END FITTING

Note:
Bolt-ends to be drilled for split-pins, to secure nuts.

Fig 6 Running-sail Rig. Showing boom-end fittings; track; up and downhauls; and method of stowage.

61

When setting the sail, it is first hanked to the forestay, the tack made fast, and the halyard shackled on; next the sheets and clew are shackled to the outboard end of the boom. The sheet is then made fast to its cleat with enough slack to allow the sail to be hoisted under full control. After hoisting sail, the gooseneck should be adjusted for position (usually higher than the outboard end of the spar) and the sheet trimmed.

In a squall, all that is necessary is to let go the halyard and the sail will stow itself, hanging in a bight between the forestay and the outboard end of the boom. It may then either be left where it is until the squall is over, or unbent.

The twin forestays sometimes fitted to ocean racers are not wholly satisfactory, as their close proximity can cause a snarl-up. A simple way round this problem is to hoist to the masthead (using one of the two jib halyards) a wire jackstay and a single block through which another halyard is rove. The lower end of the jackstay is then made fast to an eyebolt 3 or 4 feet aft of the main forestay; one of the two running sails is hanked to it and hoisted by means of its own halyard. When not needed the whole contraption can be lowered and stowed below (See fig 7.)

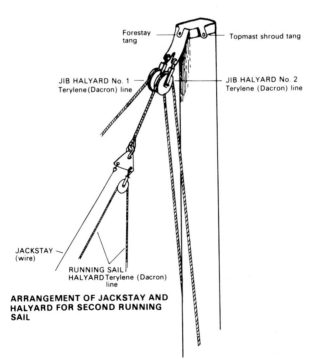

Forestay tang

Topmast shroud tang

JIB HALYARD No. 1 Terylene (Dacron) line

JIB HALYARD No. 2 Terylene (Dacron) line

JACKSTAY (wire)

RUNNING SAIL HALYARD Terylene (Dacron) line

ARRANGEMENT OF JACKSTAY AND HALYARD FOR SECOND RUNNING SAIL

Fig 7 Running-sail Rig. A method of rigging a jackstay and halyard for a second running foresail.

Trysail

In ocean sailing the trysail can be of great use, quite apart from the very occasional need for it under storm conditions. In a ketch or yawl-rigged boat, it can be set with advantage when the wind is such that a reef in the main might be needed. Under jib, trysail and mizzen, the sailplan will be kept low and spread out fore and aft; and the absence of a boom to bang about will make life easier for all. Some experienced ocean cruisers insist on having two tracks on the after side of the mainmast, one of them with a trysail permanently bent on, ready to hoist whenever it may be appropriate to use it.

Roller reefing and furling

The use of roller reefing and furling gear, for both jibs and mainsails, has become widespread in recent years among coastal cruisers. Among deep sea men opinion is divided: some, who have found the new gear to be successful, are enthusiasts and speak highly of it; others, who have experienced a bad snarl-up, have been put off. From my own experience, and from what others have told me, I am not happy to recommend roller furling gears generally as being suitable for an ocean going yacht. Some, including you, may disagree. If so, I would urge you to satisfy yourself that, if your biggest sail blows out and the thrashing mess can neither be rolled up nor brought down on deck, you will know what to do and be able to do it.

If you do opt for roller gear, the following points may be useful. It is possible to obtain gear with two luff grooves for twin running headsails. Unless a headsail is very high cut, the block will have to be moved forward as it is reduced, and easily adjustable sheet blocks should be provided. It is essential to provide either a permanent or temporary alternative forestay for a storm jib – a temporary stay might be a wire halyard to a strong point on deck – and the mast should have a short track for a trysail.

When making your own choice remember that, if anything goes wrong, the repairs may depend upon you alone, and perhaps in mid-ocean.

Awnings

Awnings should be made from a fairly heavy, limp, rotproof, synthetic material. Light nylon or polyester is not satisfactory; sunlight rots it and, because of its light weight, it rattles in the wind. Ask your sailmaker for his recommendation.

Awnings are most easily rigged in a ketch or yawl, where the corners can be lashed to the main and mizzen shrouds. A sloop or cutter will have to be provided with some means of spreading the after end of the awning. This could be a spar lashed across twin backstays, or attached to the boom gallows. Avoid, if possible, any stiffening battens on the awning itself. A separate cockpit awning, to protect the helmsman, will be needed in the tropics. If any of the crew sleep forward of the mast, a foredeck awning may be needed as well.

Detachable side curtains can be useful as a protection against the hot sun in late afternoon. Having said that, let me quickly add *keep it simple*. The simpler an awning is, both to rig and stow, the more you will use it. One that calls for a lot of work will not be used to the full.

Much has been written about safety, often in a coastal context, with the possibility of help from life-saving services in mind. On an ocean voyage, you are on your own.

The chance of meeting bad weather is always present, and must be faced as a fact of life. Falling overboard, fire, collision, and gear failure, are all avoidable, and must be prevented if possible, but you must know how to deal with them if they occur. The possibility of illness cannot be ignored, and both skipper and crew should be aware of any ailment to which one of them might be prone. It is to be hoped that, before you begin an Atlantic cruise, you and your boat will have become well acquainted, and will have faced some rough passages together. Anyone who has learned his sailing in northern waters, with strong tides, heavy traffic, and frequently bad visibility, should be well equipped to handle these problems which, although they may be met, are not everyday features except in higher latitudes of the Atlantic Ocean.

Avoidable Risks – Prevention

Design Features
Moving about the deck of a small boat at sea has been likened to trying to walk on a wet sloping roof in an earthquake. It is surprising how few of us fall off. Preventive measures should begin with the yacht designer. While high topsides may prevent some water coming aboard, excessive height (often in the interests of interior accommodation) can increase the danger to those working on deck when it is rough. We all know that the higher you go up the mast when at sea, the worse the motion. The same thinking should apply when deciding on the height of a boat's deck above the waterline – the lower it can be, consistent with keeping it out of the water, the safer it will be as a working platform.

The camber of the deck of a good ocean cruiser should be a compromise: too much camber makes the lee deck untenable, while making the weather deck more or less level, when the vessel is heeled. Ideally, one should be able to move all round the deck even in the worst conditions.

Deep bulwarks, such as grandfather's boat had, combined with low freeboard, were a mixed blessing; often scooping up a ton or so of water and holding it for far too long on deck. But a six-inch rail can be a very comfortable feature, and much safer than that little strip of perforated metal we often see today. Lifelines are helpful, but it is doubtful whether even the strongest could save a heavy man, thrown right across the deck. Stanchion sockets must be securely attached: bolted to a wood or fibreglass hull, or welded to a metal one. Plastic-covered wires look pretty, they are easy on the hands, and do not cause chafe. But you cannot tell what is happening to the wire underneath the plastic. After a year or two, it may suddenly give way. Pre-stretched polyester line, very little thicker than the covered wire, can be equally strong, and any defect will be obvious. Lanyards made from pre-stretched signal halyard are to be preferred to very small turnbuckles as fitted to lifelines. They are less subject to the ill-effects of distortion, and are easier to replace when necessary.

Pulpits must be strong, beyond all question. A man at the stemhead, handing a genoa, must feel and be completely safe. A good ocean sailing yacht should make it possible for a man to move about her deck from one handhold to another without ever having to let go with both hands. A raised coach-roof, which a few years ago was common to all small and medium-sized boats, is a good safety feature for those on deck at sea. It provides something against which to brace one's feet when moving fore and aft, and it forms an obstruction which prevents anyone from slipping across the whole width of the deck. And along its entire length on each side there should be grab-rails.

A good modern feature, coming into more frequent use, is a pair of strong stainless steel guardrails, placed abreast of the mast. These give valuable support to a man working at the foot of the mast. Among its many virtues, a ketch provides a comfortable cage of rigging around the cockpit. There is little excuse for falling out of the cockpit of a ketch.

Crew's harness is no stronger than its points of attachment. Modern practice is to have some form of jackstay running fore and aft, along the deck. It must be immensely strong and well secured at each end. In addition, there should be an eye-bolt immediately outside the main companionway, and another for the helmsman.

Personal Safety Gear

Harness
It is essential to wear harness when on deck in rough going. It takes a little time to get used to wearing it, and to avoid becoming snarled up around cleats and winches; so crew members should be trained to work in their harness before having to do so in anger. Use an officially approved type, which complies with the latest standards current in your country. There must be a set for each person aboard, fitted and adjusted before going to sea. Clips must be non-magnetic.

The safety-line on the harness should be strong, and as short as possible consistent with allowing freedom of movement. A clip in the middle of the line, to allow a choice of length, is an advantage. It should be seized on to the line and not knotted or spliced in; and must be used in addition to, and not instead of, the main clip.

The skipper should, by his example, encourage the wearing of harness; but he should also lay down positive rules about when it MUST be worn. The obvious times are when working on the foredeck, and when watchkeeping alone at night.

Lifejacket

A lifejacket does nothing to prevent your falling overboard, but it is better to have one on, if you do. The skipper must assume responsibility for deciding the time when lifejackets MUST be worn.

There must be an approved lifejacket for every crewman and each should be kept in a specified place. As with safety harness, each member of the crew should try on his lifejacket before going to sea, to ensure that he knows how it should be worn and secured, and how to operate it if it needs inflating or topping up by mouth. A good lifejacket should support a heavy man with his head out of water, even if unconscious, and should have a whistle, and also a light which will work automatically when immersed in water.

Rocket Pack

Personal rocket packs, small enough to go in the pocket, are available, and could prove invaluable at night or in high seas.

Life Saving Equipment

Liferaft

If you already own a liferaft, have it tested by the maker and professionally re-packed. Before doing this, you have a good opportunity of pulling the string (preferably in company with your crew) to familiarise yourself with how the thing behaves in use.

Lifebuoys

At least two fluorescent lifebuoys, one of them attached to a danbuoy, should be within reach of the helmsman, ready for throwing overboard. The danbuoy assembly must be carefully stowed, so that it and its lifebuoy and their line can be jettisoned instantly, and without fouling.

The danbuoy should have a long pole with an orange-coloured flag on top, and a counterweight to keep it upright. There should also be a light which will come on automatically when in use.

Danbuoy, lifebuoys, harnesses and lifejackets, should all have fluorescent reflective tape stuck on them, as this helps in locating them in the dark. Some materials do not hold their reflective quality indefinitely, so make sure that those in use at the start of the voyage are in good order.

Lifting gear

Gear for lifting an inert man out of the water and on deck, depends on whatever drill the skipper finds best for his own boat and crew. Some recommend a part-inflated rubber dinghy, others a triangular sail rigged as a parbuckle or, for a man who can to some extent help himself, a bathing ladder. Most, if not all, items which might be of use for this important task are ordinary boat's gear and,

66

depending on what you decide to use, all that is necessary in your daily routine is to check that the particular items are ready to hand. If it is a dinghy, try to keep it stowed on deck in a partly inflated condition; if it is a jib, let it be one of the right size (and preferably a spare), and stowed in a readily accessible place. Any gear may have to be rigged either to port or to starboard, so make sure that it can be handled both ways.

First-aid

First-aid equipment, the means of preparing a hot drink, blankets and a hot-water bottle, should be ready at hand at all times.

Man-overboard drill

This is the most widely-disputed question among those who know most about it. The skipper of a boat on an ocean cruise must, however, be on his guard when listening to advice which may be sound for inshore situations but unrealistic for application in mid-ocean.

The first thing to bear in mind is that it is rare to have more than two in a watch, in a small boat, when ocean cruising. More often it is only one. Also, the crew may include beginners who have had little training or experience. In planning his drill, the skipper must not only design it to fit the handling qualities of his vessel, but must adapt it to the abilities of the crew.

Any good drill must apply equally to all hands – both the skilled and the unskilled must abide by it – but it must make no demands which are beyond the ability of the least experienced, when alone on deck. The drill must be geared to two possibilities: first, that the man in the water may have been the only one on watch; second, that if another man remains on deck he may be a novice with little or no experience. A lone watchkeeper, who falls overboard while everyone else is asleep below, stands little chance of making his voice heard. But equipped with a shrill whistle he might possibly expect to rouse the sleepers, even were he to be in the water and astern. If one man remains on deck, he of course must sound the alarm.

Each member of the watch on deck should have a whistle; the whistles must be identical and their use must be confined to conveying one message only: 'ALL HANDS ON DECK'. To ensure that whistles are always carried by those on watch, each should be worn round the neck on a lanyard, and transferred from man to man, at the change of the watch.

Whatever the circumstances, the man left on deck must do two things immediately: (1) blow his whistle, (2) jettison the danbuoy/lifebuoy assembly. During the short interval between the whistle being blown and the arrival on deck of the skipper or mate, the watchkeeper must know what is expected of him and must act promptly and correctly. Authorities differ about what should be done, and the following are therefore put forward not as dogma, but as the considered opinion of a group of experienced ocean sailors. Others may disagree. You should listen to anyone who knows what he is talking about and then attempt to plan your own drill, suitable for your boat and your crew. The recommendations are:

If close-hauled – Heave-to at once
If reaching – Heave-to at once
If running – Keep on course

Close-hauled or reaching

If the boat is at once hove-to, she will be lying quite close to, and slightly to windward of, the spot where the man fell overboard. Also, even a novice can be taught to heave-to, and could do so singlehanded when close-hauled, or on a reach. Furthermore, the boat should be near enough to the victim for him to be in sight; and, once hove-to, the man on deck can devote his full attention to keeping his eye on the danbuoy or the man in the water.

Running

If a boat is running goose-winged, it is impossible to round up and heave-to immediately; and a novice who attempted to do so might make an already dangerous situation even worse. The skipper, when he arrives on deck, will want to have a bearing on the victim's position; and unless a steady course has been steered this cannot be given. If any type of automatic steering were in use at the time of the accident, it should be left untouched until the moment comes to round up and backtrack towards the man in the water.

Steering by hand, even an experienced helmsman would find it difficult to hold a good course while keeping an eye on a man in the water astern. Confronted with such a choice, a novice *must remember to concentrate on his steering*. If a steering vane or autopilot is in use the watchkeeper could, and should, try to keep the victim in sight. But it is no good pretending: if there is a big swell it may be impossible. It will certainly be impossible at night.

Action on hearing the whistle

Skipper or mate to go on deck first; last man to go on deck must note the time and enter it in the logbook. On reaching the deck, the skipper (or mate, if the skipper is the victim) must assess the situation and decide on what action to take. He should appoint the crew with the best eyesight to glue his eye on the man or danbuoy if within sight or, to search for them.

While preparations for rounding-up are being made, one man should be laying some kind of trail which will lead back to the scene of the accident. By day, this might be any dunnage that will float: empty beer cans, bottles, and if necessary cockpit cushions. Smoke canisters are recommended by some but not by everyone. Wrongly used they might hinder rather than help; but if thrown near to the victim (not to windward), smoke might be the best indicator in really rough weather. By night, lights will be needed, for example Cyalume sticks.

Backtracking

If hove-to promptly, having been close-hauled or on a reach up to the time of the accident, the boat will be lying somewhere up-wind of the man in the water. In that case the recommended drill of the Royal Yachting Association should be followed; i.e. go on to a reach (on the same tack as when hove-to). This might well take you very close past the victim, before the time came to turn (either by gybing or coming about) for the final course up to him.

From a position down-wind, much will depend on the way the boat is rigged, and the state of wind and sea. If under sail alone obviously any spinnaker would have to be handed and a jib set in its place, if so rigged; or if running under twins, both booms and one of the jibs would have to come in. In a sloop running under twins, the main would have to be set to make her perform under sail, but a ketch might handle well enough under jib and mizzen. Time being of first importance, it should be remembered that jib and engine, even without main or mizzen, usually form a very efficient windward combination. It might be the best means of getting back quickly, in conditions which would not permit the yacht to be motored straight back, directly into the wind and sea.

How best to get back to the rescue-point must be an on-the-spot decision by the skipper or mate; but certainly, as part of the preparations, the engine should be started and any trailing lines (such as a log-line), handed. The need to keep the engine in a state of instant readiness, so that it will respond immediately if needed, should rank equally in importance with all other life-saving precautions.

The final approach to a man in the water is a critical stage in the operation. Some very enterprising research, undertaken by two of the British yachting magazines, has stressed the difficulty of bringing a boat to a standstill alongside a helpless man, and of holding her there while the work of hauling him aboard is completed. Some boats, when hove-to under sail make headway; if you slow them down they drift bodily to leeward or, if you try to hold them head to wind by means of the engine, you risk seriously injuring the man in the water with the propeller. The consensus seems to be that a man can most easily be picked up on the lee side. A man who can, to some extent, help himself is obviously at a great advantage over one whose whole waterlogged weight has to be lifted by his companions; but it would be dangerous to count on getting any help from the victim. Most authorities recommend trying to get a rope round the man and this would suggest that the wearing of harness, even if it had failed to prevent the accident, might help in the rescue.

The single-hander

The risk of falling overboard should be foreseen by the single-handed sailor, and precautions taken against it. One recommendation is that a line be trailed astern, so that he might grab hold of it and haul himself back aboard. Easier said than done. With the helm lashed, or the yacht being steered by some mechanical means and sailing relentlessly on course, the chance of survival would be slim, unless the line were to be attached to some device which would trip the self-steering gear and bring her head to wind, hove-to. To avoid an unacceptable degree of drag, the line would have to be of thinnish nylon, but drag or no drag, there would have to be some knots in it for hand-holds. The knots might be more closely spaced along the piece nearest the boat, which would always be clear of the water, and a rope ladder might be attached to the taffrail ready to be pulled overside when needed.

Fire

The most obvious places in which a fire might start are the galley and the engine compartment.

Galley fire

With stoves which burn paraffin/kerosene or alcohol, fuel spillage is a possible cause. Although neither of these fuels is volatile, wood or fabric soaked in either of them will burn vigorously. It is not enough just to mop up any spillage; the area should be washed with detergent to emulsify paraffin or to dilute and render alcohol harmless. Many galley fires have been started by the ignition of hot fat or cooking oil. Deep frying should never be done at sea.

A fire arising from bottled gas is more likely to be the by-product of an explosion than anything else. Careful installation, cylinders sited so that any possible leakage must fall overboard, and meticulous attention to the tightening of unions and the condition of their washers and piping should guard against the risk of explosion. Always turn off at the cylinder when cooking gas is not in use.

Engine room fire

A likely cause of a fire in the engine room is the electrical system. Alternators and electric anchor-windlasses generate or consume very high currents, and they call for wiring and circuitry of the highest standard, professionally designed and installed. This should ensure that fuses are put wherever necessary, but it cannot guard against your replacing a blown fuse with one that is too large. Have the fuse-amperage written against each one so that there can be no such mistake.

Sparks from electrical equipment, or loose connections, can ignite gas or fuel vapours. If you have the least doubt about the wiring, have it checked by an expert. All electrical equipment should be properly maintained and all wiring checked regularly to ensure that no faults are developing.

A fire in the engine compartment, depending on its nature, may flare up if the engine hatch is opened. To combat this, a permanent installation, with extinguisher nozzles at all danger-points, is the best. It should be operable manually, by remote control and, since the operator will not be near the fire, CO_2 may be used safely.

70

Smoking

Smokers can be a fire hazard. On deck, when the sail-locker hatch is open, and there is a risk of a carelessly thrown cigarette-end falling into it, smoking should be forbidden. And smoking in one's bunk should be forbidden at all times.

Fire-fighting Equipment

The fire-blanket Effective for smothering a small fire; its use possibly being confined to the galley.

CO_2 Very effective in confined spaces because it denies the fire oxygen. Dangerous, for the same reason, to the operator unless remote control is possible.

Liquid chemicals Liable to produce toxic fumes when used on a fire, so generally unacceptable except in the very unlikely event of a fire actually on deck.

Dry powder Effective and safe belowdecks. Creates a lot of mess – but so does a fire.

You should consult a professional fireman before buying, and also find out your country's laws concerning fire-fighting equipment for maritime use. Not all manufacturers make the full range of apparatus and may therefore not give unbiased advice.

The Siting of Extinguishers

This is important. There must be extinguishers on both sides of any point at which a fire may start so that, wherever you or your crew are, it will be possible for you to approach the fire with the right equipment in your hands.

Boats are usually well ventilated, with a current of air moving in and out through open hatches – a condition conducive to the rapid spread of fire. To contain the blaze it may be necessary to fight the fire while below deck, without opening hatches. To do this, the use of dry powder extinguishers is indicated.

Gear Failure

Prevention is better than cure. Routine inspection for chafe should be made every day, and careful checks made before, during, and after each passage, to ensure that both standing and running rigging are in good order. All seacocks and pumps should be actuated periodically and all machinery given regular tests to make certain that it will work when needed.

Collision

Avoidance of collision depends on three things:

1. A good lookout
2. Good navigation lights
3. An effective radar reflector

The result of a bad collision with a steamer is likely to be beyond hope of survival, but a glancing blow might give time to size up the damage and, if beyond repair, to launch the liferaft.

Although one sees few vessels when making the trade-wind crossing, all the other routes are much busier. The risk of being run down is ever-present and vigilance should never be relaxed. See that the radar reflector is in the catch-rain attitude. Have a supply of white flares handy to the helmsman to draw attention to your presence when necessary.

The whale hazard

Worldwide, there have been alarming stories of encounters with whales.

Most of the reports in the Atlantic refer to accidental collisions at night, when little can be done to avoid collision, but in daylight steer clear and, if the whale seems interested, start the engine which tends to scare them off according to some people. The wrong coloured bottom-paint is said to be conducive to attack – red and white are thought to be bad.

Illness

The fact that we rarely hear of serious illness affecting the crews of small boats during ocean passages may be because the majority are young and healthy when they set out. It must be appreciated by all concerned that the illness of one man may deplete the crew-strength by two, if another hand has to nurse him.

Many people have to wait until late in life before they can spare time for an ocean cruise, and those of us who fall into that category should certainly have a medical check-up before sailing. People suffering from a chronic condition, such as heart disease, diabetes, or epilepsy should not only discuss the matter with their doctor, but must take all the crew into their confidence, and should have the agreement of all before taking part in a transatlantic passage.

The commonest illness, which can affect most people at some time or other, is seasickness. Fortunately, this is usually a passing phase only and after a couple of days most of us recover and become immune for the rest of the voyage. Of the many remedies on the market, Stugeron seems to suit most sufferers and to be the most effective. It is unlikely that a would-be crew-member for a long voyage will have done so little sailing that he will not know how he is going to react in a rough sea. If he is one of those rare individuals who never get over seasickness, he had better stay ashore.

The medical check should extend to visiting your dentist, and he should be asked to remove any tooth which cannot be guaranteed to last the voyage. Many years ago William Albert Robinson, a famous American sailing man, was struck down with appendicitis in the Pacific while aboard his boat. His dramatic rescue and survival set off a trend for the routine removal of the appendix before any ocean voyage. We hear less of this today, but for anyone with a grumbling appendix it would seem to be the right thing to do.

Although serious illness seems quite rare, accidents of one kind of another may occur and the knowledge of how to deal with them is essential. At least one crew member should be qualified in first aid. The skipper must make himself responsible for ensuring that this is done. A medicine chest should not just be bought over the counter in a yacht chandlery. Consult a doctor, and with his help buy not only a first-aid kit but the basic medicines capable of dealing with the whole spectrum of minor complaints from constipation to dysentery, from stomach-ache to sunburn. A first-aid box does not always contain a clinical thermometer nor does it have a hot water bottle, both of which should be aboard.

Radio

Those of us who sail small boats across oceans have no right to rely on air-sea rescue services if we meet trouble in mid-ocean, and would be foolish to do so. Radio can, nevertheless, provide not only the means of making a distress call in dire emergency, but also a channel for medical advice in case of need. For details see Chapter 7.

Security

Generally speaking, on an Atlantic cruise, thieving is less of a problem than it is in the Mediterranean or in England.

There are two kinds of thief: one, those who steal valuable articles for which there is always a ready sale; two, those who will pick up any trifle, if temptation is left in their way. The first will steal outboard engines and rubber dinghies, and has even been known to unscrew winches from yachts left unattended on moorings. The second will take the oars or rowlocks from a dinghy on the beach, or a coil of rope left on deck and within easy reach.

The obvious presence of people on board is the best deterrent. Neither the serious thief nor the petty larcener will normally risk stealing from a boat which can be seen to be fully manned. In some places (some ports in Spain and in the Canary Islands), do not leave an unattended dinghy anywhere ashore.

A dinghy which looks entirely different from the rest is less likely to be taken, than one identical to its neighbours.

People have been murdered in the West Indies. If single-handed, it would be wise to avoid anchorages totally devoid of other boats; and always haul the dinghy on deck at night. An experienced charter-boat skipper, Roger Fothergill, writing in the journal of the Ocean Cruising Club in 1978, recommended that those on board should have some means of switching on a bright light to illuminate the deck, without themselves having to go on deck, and that they should also be able to lock themselves in.

Piracy on the high seas has also taken place in parts of the Caribbean, notably off the coast of Venezuela. The defence against an attack by a vessel of markedly superior size and speed, whose crew might be armed with high-powered automatic weapons, could possibly come only by means of a radio call. The chances of suffering such an attack would be increased by sailing along a strange coast, devoid of harbours, other shipping, or habitation. It provides a good reason for trying to arrange to make one's landfall at right-angles to the coast, and as near to one's arrival-port as possible.

Firearms
Whether or not to carry personal firearms must be your own decision. The subject is too big and too controversial for discussion here, but two things must be said: first, that any weapon must be duly licensed in the country from which the boat comes; second, that it must be declared on arrival in a foreign country. In British waters, even a Very pistol needs to be licensed. It may well be asked of what value is a gun which, in many ports, will be impounded by the port authority on arrival, when the most likely place for an attack may be in some quiet anchorage. Some writers have suggested the use of such things as fire extinguishers or distress rockets fired directly at an intruder.

CAUTION – OIL RIGS

Oil rigs may be encountered working not only on soundings but in much deeper waters. You may also meet others which are being towed. Fixed rigs should be shown on up-to-date charts but very newly installed ones may appear in Notices to Mariners only. Until you have seen one, all rigs present a confusing sight at night – a mass of lights visible from far off in clear weather, although there will be many unlit buoys marking the ends of mooring cables.

Rigs on the move are attended by several tugs whose long tow-lines may be submerged and therefore invisible.

Night or day, fixed or moving, give all oil rigs a wide berth. International regulations require vessels to keep more than 500 m away from rigs except to save life, or if in distress or through stress of weather.

11   Eastward from USA or Canada to Europe

General Description

Time your voyage between mid-May and mid-August. There are several routes from which to choose, all of them offering passages with mainly fair winds and favourable currents. The first part of whichever route is taken will present three problems: the cold Labrador Current which flows SW down the coast of Nova Scotia; fog; and icebergs. The Labrador Current is a permanent feature with an average speed, in this area, of about half a knot: fogs and icebergs are seasonal, reaching a peak in midsummer. Icebergs are brought southward by the Labrador Current in early summer and affect an area lying roughly between 45°W and 55°W, with its southern limit at about 41°N; although they can be met well outside this area. There can be a concentration of bergs east of Cape Race, where the big ones go aground on the Grand Banks. As the season progresses and the icebergs begin to melt, they float off and move further south, finally reaching the northern edge of the Gulf Stream where they disperse and melt completely. Ice is therefore most prevalent in the northern and eastern parts of the Grand Banks early in the season, and at the southern end, and perhaps into the edge of the Gulf Stream, later. The American and Canadian Coast Guards maintain an Ice Patrol and broadcast daily reports of the locations and drift of bergs. A report can be obtained before sailing, by telephoning (902) 426-6030 or (709) 772-2083.

Fog, caused when a warm southerly wind blows off the Gulf Stream and meets the cold air over the Labrador Current, may be met anywhere between the American or Canadian coasts, and eastward of the Grand Banks. A northerly wind tends to clear the fog. It reaches its worst in mid-summer, and usually lessens after the end of July.

The choice of routes falls into three groups: 1, the Great Circle Route; 2, the Intermediate Route; and 3, the Azores Route. The first two may be further sub-divided according to whether the eventual destination in Europe is to be via the English Channel or round the north of Scotland. The Azores route would not be used by anyone intending to go round the north of Scotland, but might be used when making either for the English Channel or for the Mediterranean. (See Routes 1, 1A; 2, 2A; 3, 3A and 3B on Chart No 1.) The fact that fog lessens in August, and that most of the ice will by then have moved south, suggests that the Great Circle Route makes sense at the latter part of the season but that either the Intermediate or Azores Route should be used for an earlier voyage.

If leaving from any American port south of Cape Cod, it is worth considering passing through the Cape Cod Canal, instead of through, or south of, Nantucket Shoals. It will depend on which route you intend to sail.

Routes 1 and 1A

From anywhere in north-eastern USA, the Great Circle route to northern Europe passes close to Cape Sable on the southern point of Nova Scotia, thence to Cape Race on the SE corner of Newfoundland. Keep well west of Sable Island. The winds are likely to be fair but there can be a high incidence of fog and there will also be the weak adverse Labrador Current on this part of the route.

St John's Harbour (60 miles north of Cape Race) makes a good final port for provisions and stores, also an up to date ice report.

From Cape Race, or St John's, take the Great Circle course (i.e. Route 1 or 1A) to your destination. This will be north of the main shipping routes, except those making for the Gulf of St Lawrence, but is almost directly under a much-used air route. From the vicinity of Cape Race, and for about 500 miles eastwards, there may be icebergs and fog. Once clear of the ice zone, normal North Atlantic conditions can be expected with a predominance of fair winds and current.

Routes 2 and 2A

To reduce the time spent in possible fog, and to avoid icebergs, make for a point at about 40°N 50°W (see point X on Chart No 1). Between your departure port and point X you will converge with, and probably cross, the main shipping routes. Up-to-date weather and ice reports may make it possible to move this point X further north, and reduce the distance to be sailed, but your track could then coincide with the main shipping routes which you may prefer to avoid. Alternatively these reports may force you to move your point X further south, to avoid a strong southern drift of icebergs. From point X, sail the Great Circle course to your destination (i.e. either continue on Route 2 or alter course for Route 2A). When making for point X you may expect to join the Gulf Stream about 150 miles offshore and to get a lift of about ½ to 1 knot from it. The interface between the Labrador Current and the Gulf Stream, is known as the Cold Wall. Normally it is very noticeable by a change in water temperature and colour. The cold Labrador Current is pale green and the Gulf Stream deep blue. If starting from Nova Scotia, keep well clear SW of Sable Island.

Routes 3, 3A and 3B — Azores Route

The Azores Route should be warmer, and easier sailing (at the expense of much greater distance) but if the centre of the Azores High has moved north of its normal position there might be long periods of calm. Nevertheless, in the immediate vicinity of the Azores themselves, calms and squalls may alternate at any time. Make for about 39°N 60°W (see point Y on Chart No 1), thence sail east to the Azores. There is no special reason to use this route unless making a call in the islands, or going towards the Mediterranean. If, having called at one of the islands, you wish to proceed towards the English Channel, make as much northing as possible until

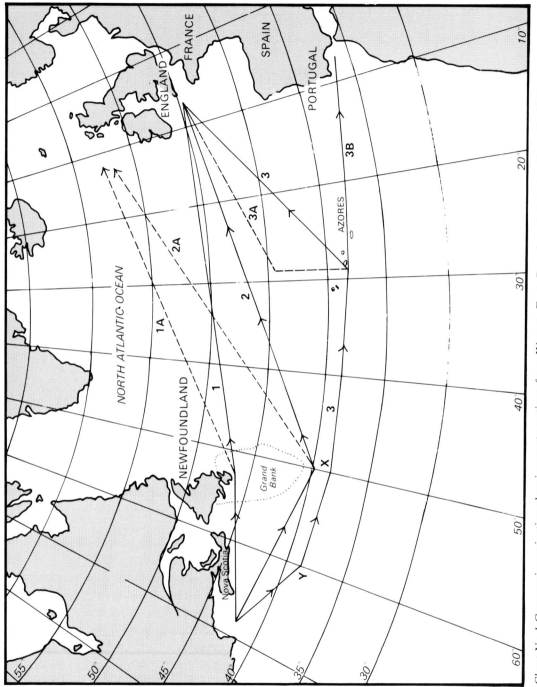

Chart No 1 Gnomonic projection showing route options from West to East. Based on Admiralty Chart No 5095.

about 45°N where more reliable westerly winds might be picked up. See Chapter 16 for more detail about Routes 3A and 3B.

Currents

Depending on the route to be followed, several currents may be encountered. All routes are affected by the weak adverse Labrador Current during the first stage of the voyage. Routes 1 and 2 will thereafter benefit from the influence of the Gulf Stream, while Routes 1A and 2A will later enter what is variously called the North Atlantic Current or North Atlantic Drift. Routes 3 and 3A demand that you shall keep north of latitude 39°N if you are to be sure of remaining well within the Gulf Stream. Eastward of Longitude 35°W you will, however, enter the Azores Current which sets SE towards and between the islands. Between the Azores and the English Channel, this same SE-going trend persists, setting towards Ushant and into the Bay of Biscay. On Route 3B the Portugal Current will be encountered between the Azores and Cape Vincent, setting in a general southerly direction. For details consult British Admiralty Routeing Chart or US Pilot Chart of the appropriate month.

Winds and Weather

Winds should be mainly fair. The pattern is low pressure to the north, a series of lows moving from Nova Scotia towards the British Isles, and the Azores High to the south.

If you keep north of the Azores you may expect winds from SW to NW most of the time, unless the Azores High swells or moves north, to produce calms; or if one or two of the lows track south, which could produce gale-force head winds. Air temperatures will probably be about 50°F on the Great Circle Route in summer, and as high as 75°F or more in the latitude of the Azores. On the intermediate routes temperature may be around 60°F. Although it is rare for a hurricane to track as far north as any of these routes, the possibility should be borne in mind and careful attention paid to weather forecasts.

Special Considerations

Although this may be expected to be a fair-wind passage, the weather may be very rough at times and frequent gales are to be expected. The boat's gear should therefore be in good order. The northerly routes can be cold, and a cabin heater will be desirable. On the other hand the Azores Route may be very warm at times and good ventilators, together with opening ports, will help to keep the boat cooler. But it must be possible to make these storm-proof. Your sea water thermometer will be useful, not only when moving from the Labrador Current into the Gulf Stream, but also when within the iceberg zone.

80

Ports

Departure

In addition to Newport, Rhode Island, listed in Part IV, there are several excellent ports on the American coast from which a start could be made.

Ports of Call

Halifax, Nova Scotia; and St John's, Newfoundland; are good ports of call, both of them listed in Part IV. If you intend to make a stop in the Azores, Horta in Faial is our recommended port of which details are given in Part IV. Note that if sailing Route 2, St John's, Newfoundland remains your nearest port for at least half the passage, in case of damage or sickness.

Arrival

Oban (Scotland), Cork (Republic of Ireland), Falmouth (England), Plymouth (England), Cherbourg (France). All are listed in Part IV.

Passage-Times and Distances

Distances from Cape Cod to the Bishop Rock are approximately as follows (all distances given are the shortest between points):

Great Circle route	2,700 miles (1,850 miles from Cape Race to Bishop Rock)
Intermediate route	(via point X at 40°N 50°W) 2,850 miles
Azores route	(via point Y at 39°N 60°W, and Faial) 3,250 miles Bishop Rock to Falmouth 70 miles

When calculating the probable duration of an ocean passage of this sort it will be found that a daily run of 100 miles a day is a good basis to use. This average will apply to boats of all sizes. It is a mistake to presume that a yacht will average anywhere near her top speed on a passage, and the apparently slow speed of about 4 knots will prove to be near the mark. The majority of cruising boats will make the crossing within 28–35 days.

Charts and Sailing Directions

NOTE. Charts essential for the ocean passages only are given here. For particulars of those necessary for your departure port, ports of call and arrival ports, see Part IV, Port Information. That section, in addition to giving the numbers of large scale harbour-plans, also gives the numbers of those charts needed for approach and departure.

The Sailing Directions listed hereunder cover the whole area referred to in the text, both ocean and inshore.

Charts		Sailing Directions	
Admiralty	US	Admiralty	US/Canada
4009	121	22	140
		27	
		37	141
5095 (Gnonomic)	5273 or	40	142
	5274	50	143
		52	145
		59	146
		65–70	191
			Eldridge
		Reed's Almanac	Reed's Almanac
		(UK & US eds)	(US and UK eds)
Routeing Charts	Pilot Chart	Admiralty Tidal	Canadian Tide
5124 (4–8)	13, 14	Atlas	and Current
			Tables Vol 1
		*List of Radio	*Radio Aids to
		Signals Vol 2	Navigation, Atlantic
			and Gt Lakes
		Light Lists	
		Vols A & H	

* The British Admiralty List of Radio Signals covers the world and is therefore the better buy.

Formalities

Customs regulations vary from country to country within Europe. Generally speaking Customs Officers treat yachtsmen benevolently, but this has only been built up over the years by honesty and good sense, and it is important not to break this tradition.

There is a universal ban on the import of hard drugs, and many countries look carefully at prescribed medicines; you should have a doctor's letter if you are taking drugs for your health. Import of fresh meat is often forbidden (it is not allowed into the UK), as are growing plants and some fresh vegetables. There are very strict regulations in the UK regarding bringing animals of any kind into the country (dogs taken ashore from a yacht even just for a walk are destroyed and the owners heavily fined).

Most countries make concessions regarding import of alcohol and tobacco for personal use; the amount varies.

The Approach

Approaching the European coastline, weather may be bad with strong onshore winds and poor visibility; there may have been overcast skies for some days, and your exact position may therefore be in doubt. If these conditions apply within twenty-fours hours of expected landfall, your best action may be to slow down or heave-to and await an improvement before closing the coast. This should certainly be done if you are in danger of making a bad landfall on a lee shore.

There is, however, a complete network of marine RDF beacons on the coasts, with ranges of 150–200 miles, which should enable you to establish your position 24 hours off, long before getting dangerously close to land. These are listed in the Admiralty *List of Radio Signals* (Volume 2) and similar publications from other countries, and also in some almanacs such as *Reed's Nautical Almanac*.

The coasts of Britain and France are tidal. The average spring range in Britain is about 3.6m or 11 ft 6 ins, and that of St Malo in France is one of the greatest in the world, with spring tides of 12.5m (about 40 ft). There can, therefore, be strong coastwise tidal streams which surge in and out of bays and estuaries.

Tidal streams can be particularly strong off headlands, with heavy overfalls. If these are marked on the chart it is important to keep clear of them, but tide rips and overfalls can occur off most headlands and you should always be prepared for this. Strong winds against the stream will aggravate the situation and can create dangerous conditions. Although headlands are often important landmarks and may have useful lighthouses and radio beacons, do not therefore home in on them too closely.

East of longitude 15°W you will be within the area covered by the BBC weather forecasts for shipping (1500m/200 kHz) and also the forecasts from coastal radio stations (156–162 MHz).

Once you are within the territorial waters of any country you should seek an entry-port and clearance from the Customs and Immigration as soon as possible, but most authorities will accept that, in stress of weather, a vessel may have to shelter in the nearest available haven, before moving to an official entry-port. In some places, where smuggling or gun-running are not unknown, you may be treated with suspicion if you enter a remote haven. To allay these suspicions, always contact the authorities, even if only the local police, by radio, telephone, or personally. Fly the Q-flag and your national colours during the whole of this period, until cleared.

Scottish Coast

Boats making direct for Scandinavia, and passing round the north of Scotland, should have no problems provided they are well clear of Rockall (57°37′N 13°41′W). The St Kilda Island group and the Flannan Islands, 40 miles and 20 miles off the west coast of the Outer Hebrides, should be well clear to starboard, but Sula Sgeir (59°06′N 6°11′W) and North Rona (59°08′N 5°50′W) could be close to your route and a hazard to be avoided in thick weather. They are now both marked with lights. The long-range radio beacons from Barra Head, round to the Orkney and Shetland Islands, should enable a vessel to be piloted clear of all dangers.

Do not pass through the Pentland Firth, between the north Scottish coast and the Orkney Isles, in conditions of strong winds or poor visibility. Shelter can be sought in the lee of Lewis by passing round the Butt of Lewis; and Stornoway Harbour on the east side is an official entry-port.

If making for Oban, see Part IV, Port Information. If the prevailing or forecast conditions make it inadvisable to approach the mainland coast, seek shelter on the east coast of the Outer Hebrides by making up to the north, passing east of Barra Head. The best haven would then be Loch Boisdale harbour on South Uist. Strong tidal streams and dangerous overfalls can exist off Barra Head. Keep at least three miles off. Bearings on the radio beacon on Oigh Sgeir in conjunction with Barra Head, will help locate Loch Boisdale in thick weather.

When anchoring in the Hebrides beware of kelp. A fisherman or Herreshoff anchor may prove best.

Irish Coast

If making for Crosshaven in Cork Harbour, on the south Irish coast, the radio beacon on Mizen Head, and subsequently the beacon on Round Island in the Scilly

84

Isles, both with a range of 200 miles, will help to fix your position before closing the coast.

Early shelter could be sought in Castletown in Bear Haven on the north side of Bantry Bay, but this would need good visibility as there are no suitable radio beacons to fix your position on that approach, and identifying the coast may be difficult in poor visibility. Approaching the wrong bay would be dangerous.

It would be best to stand off the southern Irish coast until Kinsale radio beacon is picked up (50 miles range) and shelter can be found in the lee of the Old Head of Kinsale and Kinsale Harbour entered, or continue to Crosshaven in Cork harbour.

English Coast

If making for Falmouth or Plymouth, the Bishop Rock Lighthouse marking the south-western extremity of the Scilly Isles, is the traditional first landfall in good visibility. But the radio beacon on Round Island in the Scilly Isles will be picked up 200 miles out, with Mizen Head to establish your position, and subsequently the radio beacon at Ushant off the French coast, with 100-mile range, and the radio beacon at Lizard Point with a 70-mile range, will enable you to run under the lee of the Lizard and then enter Falmouth.

There can be strong tidal streams off the Bishop Rock, and overfalls on the Pol Bank, 3 miles SSW of the Bishop. There can also be strong tidal streams off Lizard Point and heavy overfalls extending to the south for over three miles. Give these points a wide berth, and in thick weather make no attempt to sight the Bishop Rock Lighthouse, the Scilly Isles or the English coast until well round the Lizard and closing Falmouth after keeping clear of the Manacle Rocks.

Note that there are several Traffic Separation Lanes in the vicinity of Land's End, and the whole area is a form of crossroads and junctions. There can be heavy traffic in these lanes, proceeding at speed even in thick weather. This can be very confusing, especially at night, because ships proceeding to or from the Bristol Channel and the Irish Sea either cross the east-west lanes or alter course to join or leave them. In heavy or thick weather it is safer to keep clear to the south until you can turn north towards Falmouth and cross the traffic at right-angles.

French Coast

The north-west coast of France (the Brittany peninsula) is a particularly dangerous coast to approach in thick or heavy weather because of the many offlying rocks and strong tidal streams, and there is also heavy shipping traffic off Ushant which is a turning point with ships often altering course. A Traffic Separation Scheme extends for a lateral distance of 35–40 miles in a general north-westerly direction from Ushant, and it is essential to study an up-to-date chart or *Reed's Almanac* before approaching this area.

The many dangers are well marked but it is essential to have good visibility, a suitable chart, an awareness of the tidal streams, and an accurate position plot,

Falmouth, looking NW The fingers, at the entrance to Flushing Creek, from Falmouth's commercial docks. The Royal Cornwall YC is to port, below the bend in the Creek, and the marina is in the inlet on the same side, upstream.

Falmouth Harbour Commissioners

before closing this coast. If the weather is thick, and the marks cannot be seen and identified with certainty, it is far safer to stand well off the land, clear of the strongest tidal streams and shipping lanes, and either await fairer weather or proceed elsewhere.

If you are intending to make Cherbourg, or any port further east, it should be perfectly feasible to proceed up the English Channel in heavy weather, if the wind is fair, but conditions can become uncomfortable because Channel seas tend to be short and steep, particularly when there is a strong tidal stream against the wind. The tidal streams increase in strength as the Channel narrows towards the Cherbourg peninsula and can have a marked effect on your progress as they alternate from fair tide to foul. There is a Traffic Separation Scheme off the Casquets.

The Channel has a heavy concentration of shipping, and if visibility is poor you must proceed with great caution. The shipping traffic will be concentrated mostly on

Falmouth The entrance to the River Fal. St Anthony's Head in the foreground with Castle Point and St Mawes behind. Pendennis Point is on the left, with Flushing Creek to its right, and Falmouth town behind.

Falmouth Harbour Commissioners

two main routes. One route on the north side, rounding the Scilly Isles and Land's End and from there to the Dover Strait. The other route on the south side, rounding Ushant, then the Casquets and thence to Dover Strait. Each of these routes will have two-way traffic. There are also ferry routes crossing between England and France, and coastal trading vessels, fishing boats and yachts, which may be met anywhere.

There are strong tides off the Casquets and Channel Isles. The strongest tidal stream is in the Alderney Race between Alderney and Cap de la Hague (7 knots at springs). Keep well clear of this if the stream has any southerly component in it. You must have tidal information before navigating in this area.

When approaching Cherbourg, continue to make adequate allowance for the tides which can set you back towards Cap de la Hague or eastwards towards Cap Barfleur.

If at any time after entering the Channel, weather conditions or bad visibility make it advisable to seek shelter, close the English coast (not the French) and lie in a suitable English port to await improved conditions.

13 Westward in High Latitudes

General Description

Any route westward in high latitude involves a lot of windward sailing and adverse currents with, in the latter stages, the chance of meeting ice and the certainty of fog. Icebergs are brought southward by the Labrador Current in early summer and affect an area lying roughly between 45°W and 55°W, with its southern limit at about 41°N; although they may be met well outside this area. There can be a concentration of bergs east of Cape Race, where the big ones go aground on the Grand Banks. As the season progresses and the icebergs begin to melt, they float off and move further south, finally reaching the northern edge of the Gulf Stream where they disperse and melt completely. Ice is therefore most prevalent at the northern and eastern parts of the Grand Banks early in the season; and at the southern end, and perhaps into the edge of the Gulf Stream, later. The USA and Canada maintain Ice Patrols which issue daily radio reports of the locations and drift of bergs.

Fog will almost certainly be met on, and to the west of, the Grand Banks. It is caused when a warm southerly wind blows off the Gulf Stream and meets the cold air over the Labrador Current. A northerly wind tends to clear the fog. It reaches its worst at mid-summer, and usually lessens after the end of July. The best period within which to make an east-to-west passage is from mid-May to mid-August; but the exact time at which you start may influence your choice of route, so the two should be considered together.

There are four possible routes: 1, The Northern Route used by our forefathers can possibly (but by no means certainly) afford more favourable winds; 2, the Great Circle Route, shortest in distance, not always in time; 3, the Intermediate Route; and 4, the Azores Route. The Azores Route is normally the slowest. Route 1 can get better winds in early summer (April–June) because the lows tend often to track further south at that period; but this is the worst time for fog. Routes 1 and 2 will be clearer later in the season when the ice has moved south and the fog has become less. Route 3 is good early in the season, before the bergs have floated off the Grand Banks and into the Gulf Stream; and it can be taken any time between mid-April and mid-September. But remember that, being the most southerly, it is the one most likely to feel the effects of a hurricane, should one occur – as it might, late in the season.

Route 1

The object is to go north of the succession of lows which track across the Atlantic from west to east; hoping to get into easterly winds. From your departure-port, aim to reach Latitude 55°N, 30°W; thence sail a Great Circle course to Cape Race, Newfoundland; and onward down the coast of Nova Scotia, to your destination; giving Sable Island a wide berth. The gamble depends on being able to keep north of the centres of the lows. It is likely to be cold, and the weather heavier than on the

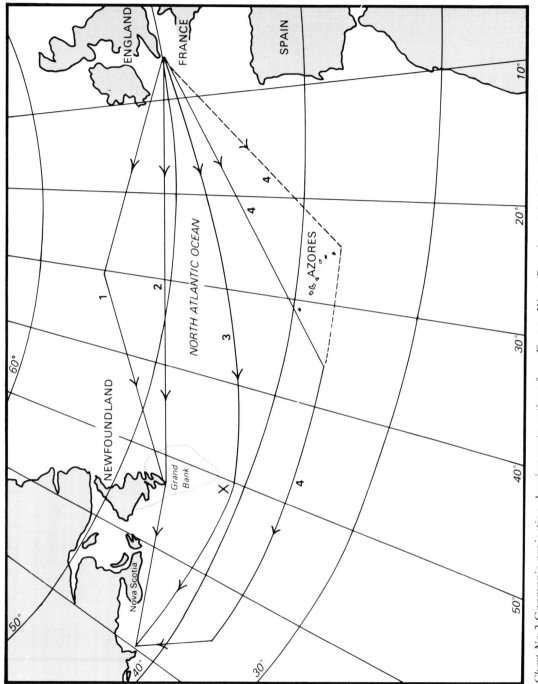

Chart No 2 Gnomonic projection showing route options from East to West. Based on Admiralty Chart No 5095.

more southerly routes; but it has been successfully sailed and fast passages have been made. The latter part of the voyage takes you straight through the fog and iceberg zone, but close to St John's, Newfoundland, where a stop could be made.

Route 2

From your departure-port, and as soon as possible, get on to a Great Circle course for Cape Race. In all other respects this route is the same as Route 1.

Route 3

The object is to make for the southern edge of the ice limit (see point X on Chart No 2) following the most direct course possible from your departure port; from then onwards proceed to your destination. A safe point to make for is generally considered to be 40°N 50°W, but this could be altered in the light of up-to-date ice reports. Main shipping routes make for a point between 42°N and 43°N at 50°W. If Halifax, or any port in Nova Scotia, is your destination, remember to give Sable Island a wide berth. In the latter part of this passage, if the ice situation permits, get out of the Gulf Stream and into the favourable Labrador Current as soon as you can.

Route 4

This is the most popular route for cruising boats; possibly making a call in the Azores and then proceeding westward along a rhumb line somewhere between 35°N and 38°N, later turning north-west for your destination, after passing 60°W. If you do not wish to call at the Azores, keep well to the north of them, in an effort to avoid the calms and light variable winds in their vicinity. Make for a point just north of Corvo at about 40°N 31°30′W; then south-west, to about 37°N, before turning west on to the rhumb line course mentioned above. If calling at the Azores, see also Chapter 17.

This route will be much warmer than any of the others and should have a high proportion of fair weather, though not necessarily fair winds. In latitude 37°N you can expect to be south of the main Gulf Stream, and may even benefit from a counter-current at times. The recommended north-westerly course, after passing 60°W, will take you at right angles to the course of the Gulf Stream when crossing it, thus minimising the time spent on it.

Currents

Routes 1, 2 and 3 are subject to the North Atlantic Current (also known as the North Atlantic Drift), the Gulf Stream, and the Labrador Current. The Gulf Stream and North Atlantic Current are merely names for different but ill-defined parts of the same circulatory movement which, in this area, runs almost exactly opposite to the Great Circle course between Britain and Cape Race. Its speed is likely to be just under half a knot. On Routes 1 and 2 you will eventually enter the cold Labrador Current with its south and south-westerly set, somewhere between 45°W and 50°W.

90

On Route 3 you are likely to remain in the contrary Gulf Stream which gradually gets stronger to the west of 50°W. From this longitude westwards the interface between the Gulf Stream and the Labrador Current is known as the Cold Wall and is normally very noticeable by the change in the water temperature and colour. The cold Labrador Current is light green and the warm Gulf Stream deep blue. At the Cold Wall they are both flowing eastward but the Labrador Current is weaker, and further north it will be flowing westward. If the ice situation allows, it is better to keep north of the Cold Wall, but do not expect a sharp unbroken line of division at all times; there will be bulges and eddies where the waters mix.

Route 4 will, after clearing the tidal waters of the English Channel, be subject to that nameless current which stems from the Gulf Stream and turns in a south, and south-easterly direction, setting into the Bay of Biscay. This and the Azores Current into which it blends imperceptibly, will make it best to sail on the port tack whenever the wind goes into the SW, thereby putting the current under your lee bow. The Azores Current sets south-east between the islands but after leaving them behind and reaching Latitude 37°N you may get occasional help from west-going eddies, south of the Gulf Stream. When you turn north-west, sometime after 60°W, you will have to cross the main core of the Gulf Stream but crossing it at right angles will minimise your time in it.

Winds and Weather

Whichever route you take, gale-force headwinds will be met repeatedly as the lows track past. The further north you choose to go, the more severe the weather is likely to be. On Route 1, if you are lucky, the lows will pass south of you and you will enjoy some fair easterly winds. On Routes 2 and 3, wind-direction may vary between NW and SW as the lows move past, north of your course, and the same may apply on Route 4 until south-west of the Azores, in Latitude 37° to 38°N, where SW winds may be more frequent. On Routes 3 and 4, apart from meeting the occasional depression, you will have calms and variable winds in the area of the Azores High. On the latter part of routes 1 & 2 (between Cape Race and Cape Cod) wind will be mostly light south-westerly, and the going may be slow. Air temperatures will probably be about 50°F on the Northern and Great Circle Routes, around 60°F on the Intermediate Route, and as high as 75°F or more on the Azores Route once down to Latitude 40°N. It is likely to be noticeably cooler when in the fog and iceberg zone of the Grand Banks. Although it is rare for a hurricane to track as far north as any of these routes, the possibility should be borne in mind and careful attention paid to weather forecasts.

Special Considerations

The boat's gear and rigging must be in good order and sufficiently strong to withstand hard windward sailing and big seas. Many people wisely increase the scantlings of standing rigging, turnbuckles, tangs and other fittings.

Consider your tactics and check your gear for heaving-to, lying a-hull or running before, and even give some thought to a jury rig. A cabin heater may be desirable on the more northerly routes; the iceberg zone can be particularly cold. The Azores route on the other hand can be warm; good ventilators and opening ports will help to keep the boat cooler, but it should be possible to make these storm-proof as well.

Remember that, unlike those who make this crossing from America or Canada towards Europe, you will not know, at the start of your voyage, what the ice situation will be by the time you reach the iceberg zone. Well before you reach 45°W, keep radio watch on the appropriate channel (*See Admiralty List of Radio Signals Volume V*, or US *Worldwide Marine Weather Broadcasts*) and log any ice reports affecting or likely to affect you. Also, make frequent use of your sea-water thermometer which will give an indication of the possible proximity of ice.

Ports

Departure
Departure may be made equally well from a Scottish port, sailing north of Ireland; from an Irish port, or from one in the English Channel or Gibraltar.

Ports of Call
On Route 4, Horta, on the island of Faial in the Azores, makes a good port of call; while on Routes 1 and 2, St John's, Newfoundland, affords the first possible stopping place, and one with good services. Both are listed in Part IV.

Arrival
The choice is a wide one, including Halifax, Nova Scotia; Camden, Maine; Gloucester, Mass; Manchester, Mass; Marblehead, Mass; and Newport, Rhode Island. All are well documented in pilot-books and local cruising guides. We give details of Halifax and Newport in Part IV.

Passage times and distances
    Route 1   3000 miles (2200 to St John's)
    Route 2   2700 miles (1900 to St John's)
    Route 3   2850 miles
    Route 4   3500 miles (1200 to Azores)
(All distances given are the shortest between points)

When calculating the probable duration of a windward crossing it will be found that a daily average of 90 miles made good is a good basis, regardless of boat size. The majority of cruising boats will make this crossing within the bracket of 30–40 days.

92

Charts and Sailing Directions

Charts, essential for the ocean passages only, are the same as those in Chapter 11. For particulars of those necessary for your departure port, ports of call and arrival ports, see Part IV, Port Information. That section, in addition to giving the numbers of large scale plans, also gives the numbers of charts needed for approach and departure. The whole of the US coast from Cape Henry to Key West is covered in the National Ocean Survey *Coast Pilot No 4*. The Intracoastal Waterway is fully dealt with in the *Waterway Guide* and also in Chapter 12 of the US *Coast Pilot No 4*.

The Sailing Directions listed hereunder cover the whole area referred to in the text, both ocean and inshore.

Charts		Sailing Directions	
Admiralty	*US*	*Admiralty*	*US/Canada*
4009	121	22	140
		27	
		37	141
5095 (Gnomic)	5273	40	142
	5274	50	143
		52	145
		59	146
		65–70	191
			Eldridge
		Reed's Almanac	Reed's Almanac
		(UK & US eds)	(US and UK eds)
Routeing Charts	Pilot Chart	Admiralty Tidal	Canadian Tide
5124 (4–8)	13,14	Atlas	and Current
			Tables Vol 1
		*List of Radio	*Radio Aids to
		Signals Vol 2	Navigation, Atlantic
			and Gt Lakes
		Light Lists	
		Vols A & H	

* The British Admiralty List of Radio Signals covers the world, and is therefore the better buy.

Formalities

European yachtsmen should be prepared for some sharp differences in regulations and procedures when they reach the USA. Compared with the somewhat easy-going attitudes displayed in Latin countries the reception in America may seem tough.

Certain things are forbidden imports. As well as drugs – fresh, frozen or dried meats, fresh vegetables of all kinds, and fresh fruit of all kinds may not be taken into the USA. If found to be aboard a boat on arrival, they will be confiscated by Customs.

There are strict rules about the possible import of animals and drugs and, if any are likely to be carried for whatever reason, it would be well to consult the US Embassy in your own country before setting sail. They will also give details of current regulations regarding duty free concessions for alcohol and tobacco, together with information on arrangements for sealing and bonding of stores while a yacht is in US waters.

Coast Guard

Unlike Britain, where lifeboats are the responsibility of the Royal National Lifeboat Institution, in the USA the Coast Guard runs its own search and rescue vessels and aircraft. It is a highly organised body whose task includes ensuring that all vessels proceed in an orderly manner, and its personnel are well accustomed to shepherding small boats. Those yachts equipped with radio should advise their approach to any harbour, by calling up on VHF channel 16 and being ready to shift to a working frequency; a skipper who blundered into trouble through not asking for advice would find little sympathy.

Cruising Licence

This may be applied for when being cleared inward on arrival and, if obtained, will absolve you from having to clear Customs at every subsequent port of call.

Sewage Disposal

The Federal Government has charged the US Coast Guard with the inspection of sewage disposal arrangements on yachts. The rules are an amalgam of Federal and State Laws, and are further complicated by local ordinances. The effect is that you will never know whether you will be subjected to the full force of the Law or not. The only way to cover yourself is to comply by installing a holding tank to receive sewage, which can be pumped out periodically at a shore establishment equipped to do this. An ocean-going boat may be fitted with a by-pass valve to allow sewage to be pumped directly overboard when out at sea. There are occasions when the bypass valve must either be disconnected or sealed.

Approach

The main problem is caused by high incidence of fog, and the fact that it can be prolonged. It is thus not practical to stand off and await improved conditions, and you must be prepared to continue, with caution, and enter port in bad visibility. It is therefore important to have an accurate fix before you run into fog.

Cape Race and the east coast of Newfoundland are within the iceberg zone in the early part of the season (April – June). This, combined with fog, will call for great caution when approaching this coast. The coasts of Nova Scotia and USA can generally be regarded as being to the west of the iceberg zone.

The Grand Banks, and the waters off Nova Scotia and USA, are popular fishing grounds for fleets of trawlers and coastal fishing boats. A sharp lookout should be maintained for them, and also for nets, and lines of pots marked by floats, which may be found well offshore. The prevailing wind is south-westerly, often veering to north-west when depressions pass over. The next most common wind is southerly. Gales are infrequent in summer and the wind is generally lighter off the coast than out in mid-ocean. Winds with a southerly component tend to create fog and winds with a northerly component to clear it.

There can be a strong northerly eddy off the south coast of Newfoundland. The currents near Sable Island are very irregular and this is a dangerous area.

The increasing reliance on radar by shipping means that merchant vessels seldom reduce speed much in poor visibility, even though small craft may not be spotted on the screen. The main concentrations of shipping may be expected off Cape Race, the approaches to Halifax, the Nantucket Light Vessel, and to the north of Cape Cod where the routes to Boston and the Cape Cod canal will be crossed.

Newfoundland

Cape Race (46°39' N 53°04' W)
Admiralty Chart No 2915 or Canadian Chart No 4016
St Johns is the nearest port to Europe and full details for approaching and entering are given in Part IV. Cape Race may be used as a landfall by those on the Northern or Great Circle Routes. The Grand Banks with its dangers must be crossed. The RDF beacon on Cape Race with a 100-mile range is particularly useful and may be coupled with the beacons on Cape St Francis and Cape Spear, each with a 100-mile range, to obtain fixes on approach. When approaching Cape Race from the east, sounding for Ballard Bank (about eight miles east of the Cape) gives an indication of position if visibility is poor. Offshore the current is southerly at about 1 knot; but westerly round the Cape. If close inshore beware of the tides and the possibility of being swept into the bays along the southern coast. Many wrecks have occurred in fog on the south-eastern and southern coasts of Newfoundland, owing to the indraught or to the current setting north-eastward.

Nova Scotia

There is an aero beacon on Sable Island with a range of 200 miles, which can be useful when approaching the Nova Scotia coast, but Sable Island must be given a wide berth as it is a graveyard of ships, with strong unpredictable currents and shoal water. A strong indraught has been reported off the S tip of Nova Scotia.

Other powerful radio beacons are situated at Scatarie Island NE Lt, Cranberry Island Lt, both with 100-mile range, and Sambro Island Lt with 125-mile range. These beacons can help to maintain a position plot, when approaching from the NE, and well offshore. There are also other beacons, with ranges of 50 miles or less, which are useful when closing the coast. There are no powerful beacons serving the southern part of Nova Scotia (i.e. more than 50 miles range).

Halifax is the recommended port for entering Nova Scotia and full details are given in Part IV.

United States of America

Nantucket Shoals Lanby
Admiralty Chart No 2492 or US Chart No 1107
For those who have crossed the Atlantic from Europe, and wish to visit Cape Cod, Rhode Island or New York areas, this makes the best landfall except for those who have approached from the north-east or east, and are making for the Cape Cod canal or ports in Massachusetts or Maine. The Lanby has a radio beacon (50 miles). Care must be taken in the area of the Lanby as it also acts as a separation zone for the sea routes in and out of New York.

The Nantucket Shoals, which stretch about 25 miles SE of Nantucket Island, have a shallowest depth of 1.25 metres (4 ft) and there are strong tide rips across them. They should be crossed in calm weather only and in good visibility.

The RDF beacons on Nantucket Lanby and in the Cape Cod area give little indication of one's distance offshore when in the vicinity of the shoals. From the area of the Lanby, course should be steered to avoid the shoals. If Newport, Rhode Island, is to be the entry-port, see Part IV.

Cape Cod (42°04′N 70°15′W)
Admiralty Chart No 3096 or US Chart No 15246
For those making for the Cape Cod canal, the Cape Cod peninsula will be the first landfall. Landfall should be made on the Hook of the Cape, which terminates at Race Point. The Hook is composed mainly of sand dunes of varying heights, and few natural landmarks can be distinguished but a number of lighthouses, towers and church spires can be useful if they can be positively identified on the chart and if visibility is good enough.

Cape Cod lighthouse has a powerful (150-mile) RDF beacon, and landfall should be made 8 miles to the west at Race Point. The RDF beacon (50 miles range) at

Chatham Lighthouse can assist in establishing your position as you close the coast.

It is safe to approach the shore of the Hook if visibility is poor, using the depth sounder and chart, as the bottom is clear of rocks and obstructions but this would be inadvisable in strong onshore winds or heavy swell. Note that deep water is close inshore at Race Point. In certain conditions there can be overfalls about two miles west and one mile south-west of Race Point. It is better to keep outside these unless you wish to identify Race Point positively in thick weather.

From Race Point lay a course across the bay to the eastern entrance of the Cape Cod canal. If weather conditions make a temporary stop desirable, you can enter Provincetown Harbour where there is good holding and shelter from all winds. (See page 247 for details of the canal.)

Oil Rigs

For those who have not met one before, an oil rig presents a puzzling sight – it also presents a danger to all. Oil rigs are normally very large structures, sometimes forming part of a group, and they can be seen from far off in clear weather, by day or night, as they are well lit. They are commonly surrounded by unlit buoys marking anchor cables, and have a number of vessels in attendance.

Fixed oil rigs should be shown on up-to-date charts, but those under tow may be met anywhere, and at night their lights can be confusing. There is also, of course, the danger from very long, submerged, tow-lines from a large number of tugs.

Oil rigs and their attendant vessels must be given a wide berth.

15 The Trade-Wind Route

General Description
This is the traditional sailing ship route from Europe to the West Indies, some of it pioneered by Columbus on his second voyage, and made use of ever since 1493. It allows a good deal of freedom in the choice of time, the winds are mostly fair; the main part of the voyage will be in warm latitudes and there are good cruising grounds to visit on the way to the Canary Islands, before you actually start on the Atlantic passage itself.

The Route
First, across the Bay of Biscay to Cape Finisterre, thence towards Madeira and the Canaries and from there steer SW until in latitude 18°–20°N after which you can follow a more or less direct course to your destination in the West Indies.

Timing
The trade-wind season may be said to be from mid-November to late March. The hurricane season, which affects the area between the Cape Verde Islands and the West Indies, is from June to mid November and a transatlantic passage should be avoided during this period.

Part 1 – From the English Channel to the Canary Islands
If you are starting from the English Channel and are not in a hurry, you will probably wish to sail in June or July. This would give ample opportunity for a cruise in Brittany, Spain, Portugal, Madeira and the Canaries, before beginning the Trade-wind passage across to the West Indies.

If time is limited, two choices are open. One is to leave the English Channel late in the year – say in October – and run the gauntlet of the autumn gales in the Bay of Biscay. The other is to sail south in the summer and leave the yacht in some safe port until the time comes to start the transatlantic leg from mid-November onwards. Gibraltar, Vilamoura, or the more recently established Puerto Sherry just N. of Cadiz would be good places to leave the boat. Gibraltar, although a slight diversion from your route towards Madeira or the Canaries, offers advantages to those who speak English and it also affords very easy importation on boat's gear duty-free for vessels in transit.

Winds and Currents – English Channel to Canaries
Conditions at the mouth of the English Channel cannot be forecast with any certainty except to say that the climate is less cold and gales are less frequent in summer than in winter. It pays to avoid starting across the Bay of Biscay if SW winds are forecast. Wait until a depression has passed, then a NW wind will help you on your way. June and July generally afford the best chance of good weather for

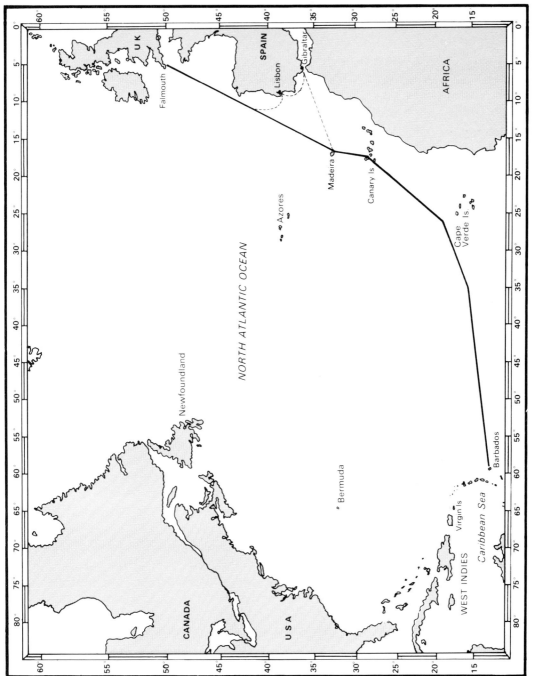

Chart No 3 The trade-wind route from East to West. Based on Admiralty Chart No 2059.

Vilamoura An aerial view from seaward, looking N. The arrival and fuelling berths can be seen to port in the entrance channel leading to the marina.

Marina de Vilamoura.

a passage across the Bay and at that time of year the Portuguese Trades have usually set in. These blow from a northerly quarter, down the Spanish and Portuguese coasts and often will be found as far as Madeira.

The Portugal current, which is part of the vast circulation of water in a clockwise direction in the North Atlantic, runs in a general southerly direction from Cape Finisterre to the Canary Islands, where it becomes known as the Canary Current.

If making a diversion into Gibraltar, you may find that the wind is more variable in both strength and direction after you have passed Cape St Vincent and, by the time the Strait of Gibraltar is reached, that the breeze is blowing either straight in or straight out. There is a constant flow of current from the Atlantic into the Mediterranean, due to the high rate of evaporation in the confined area of the Mediterranean Sea. The speed of this current is affected partly by the tide, which retards or accelerates it and partly by the wind. In moderate weather there is no difficulty in beating into Gibraltar, but against the Levanter (the local name for a strong easterly wind) it may be impossible for a small yacht to make much progress, due to the steep sea kicked up by wind-against-current. In that case, shelter may be sought in one of the Spanish ports westward of the Strait. A strong westerly or south-westerly wind which reinforces the current can make it virtually impossible for a yacht to get out from Gibraltar and into the Atlantic. Even a very slight easing of

100

Chart No 4 The west coast of the Iberian peninsula. Based on Admiralty Chart No 87.

the wind-strength does, however, make an immediate and remarkable difference and as soon as this happens good progress may be made by hugging the Spanish coast as far as Tarifa, after which the strength of the current falls off rapidly.

Once clear of the coasts of Spain and Portugal, the chances are that a breeze from a northerly quarter may be found to take the yacht towards the Madeiran Archipelago or the Canaries.

Sailing Directions – English Channel to Canaries

As there are in existence some very good cruising guides for Brittany and the northern coast of Spain (see Bibliography for details) this chapter will pass over that area and be confined to the direct course across the Bay of Biscay from the English Channel to Finisterre and onward from there.

The greatest concentrations of traffic will be encountered off Ushant and again off Cape Finisterre. There is no point in keeping close to Ushant if you start from Falmouth because the direct course to Finisterre lies well to the west of the island. When crossing the Bay of Biscay French fishing vessels are very likely to be met and when approaching the northern coast of Spain there may be some shipping heading to and from such ports as Bordeaux and Brest. If a SW gale is imminent just before you reach C. Vilano, La Coruña offers good shelter. Otherwise get well offshore before proceeding down the Iberian peninsula unless the weather is reasonably fair. Beyond Finisterre, other possible ports of call or stopovers are Corcubion Inlet, Bayona, Leixões, Cascais and Lisboa (for further details, see Part IV). Cascais may be impossible if the wind is SW, but this does not often happen in the summer months.

A yacht sailing westwards out of Gibraltar will encounter a high concentration of traffic in the Strait. This fans out as soon as the narrowest part is passed, the merchant shipping dividing into three main streams, one going westward to St Vincent, one coastwise to the south, and one in the general direction of Madeira and the Canaries. There will, in addition, be large numbers of fishing craft. In twenty-four hours most of this will be left behind and little more will then be seen until the main north-south Atlantic shipping lane is crossed, west of the longitude of Cape St Vincent.

If sailing from anywhere north of the Canary Islands and making a direct passage to them without calling at Madeira, your course is likely to lie close to the Selvagem Islands. These islands, which are badly lit, are in two groups; about 135 miles from Ilha Bugio, at the southern tip of the Madeiran archipelago, on a bearing of about 165° True.

The only port on the Moroccan coast which is used by yachts is Casablanca. The British *Admiralty Pilot* warns of a heavy swell which sets into the harbour, even in fine weather. The coast is also subject to rollers which can be dangerous for small craft.

Your first sight of the Madeiras is likely to be the conical peak of Porto Santo. This a most satisfying landfall, rising as it does in solitary grandeur, visible in daylight at a distance of forty miles or more. The islands are well-lit, and there are

102

aero beacons on both Madeira and Porto Santo, so that Funchal may be approached and entered at any hour of day or night, without difficulty. It is, however, a busy harbour and in addition to the normal commercial traffic and fishing craft, there is a great deal of coming and going of large cruise-ships. See also Chapter 17.

Those who have used Funchal nearly all agree that, although not the safest or most comfortable of anchorages, it is one of the best places from which to start on a transatlantic voyage. All basic supplies can be bought and you will find no better fruit and vegetables, however far your cruise leads you. The shopping area and market are both within walking distance of the harbour. The island itself is delightful and should not be missed. See Part IV for Port Information.

For a long time the Canary Islands were in disfavour with small-boat sailors, due to oil pollution in La Luz, Gran Canaria, and in Santa Cruz de Tenerife which were the two ports most often used by small craft. Conditions have improved recently, and there is now a wider choice of places at which to stop, some of them with marina services. See Chapter 17 for more details.

Part 2 – The Transatlantic Passage

On leaving Madeira or one of the Canary Islands, whichever is your final departure point, the first objective is to get into the Trade-wind belt as soon as you can. The northern limit of this belt varies with the seasons of the year, being nearest to the equator in the winter and at its most northerly in mid-summer. The winter latitudes are from about 2°N to 25°N and in summer from about 10°N to 30°N.

The best advice one can give is not to start too early and do not turn west too soon. In other words give the winter season a chance to establish itself before you start and make sure that you are well into the wind-system before turning west. The position 25°N 25°W is often quoted as being the point to make for and, to the extent that one should not turn west until reaching the winter latitude of the Trade-wind zone, it is right. Nevertheless, one often has to go a lot further south before picking up the true wind. In general it pays to sail SW for 1,000 miles from the Canaries to a point 100 miles NW of the Cape Verdes before turning west.

The trade-wind, contrary to popular belief, does not always blow from the same quarter or at the same strength. Sometimes it does not blow at all. It is, however, less fickle than winds in many other parts of the world and, in general, it is stronger and more reliable as the season progresses. Its strength rarely exceeds Force 6 Beaufort Scale and according to Ocean Passages for the World its average is Force 4.

Wind, Current and Ocean Swell

When the trade-wind is fully established the sky is usually speckled with small clouds, round, like puffs of steam from an old-time railway engine. Any large mass of cloud, lower and darker than the rest and coming up astern, is apt to denote a squall which at best may give the ship a welcome burst of extra speed or, at worst, might make it necessary to shorten sail. Sometimes these squalls bring a sharp downpour of rain, occasionally with thunder, although the worst of the thunderstorms seem to take place to the north of the Trade-wind route and one is often a spectator (and thankfully only that) at an impressive display.

The Canary Current, as it approaches the Cape Verde Islands, changes its course and changes its name; it turns increasingly to the westward and becomes known as the North Equatorial Current. Unpredictable as ever, it will give you a welcome push of perhaps about a dozen miles on some days and then, unaccountably, little or nothing on others.

Swell is apt to appear for no reason which is immediately apparent. Usually it arises from a storm many thousands of miles away and in itself a swell, however majestic it appears to be, is quite harmless. Whatever sea there is will superimpose itself on the swell and may be running in quite a different direction. When this happens, and if the trade-wind becomes strong for a sustained period, a big sea running contrary to the swell can cause troublesome crests some of which may come aboard. But in general, even a small boat will do most of the voyage with a dry deck.

Landfall

Few of the islands in the West Indies are well lit. But both Barbados and the French island of Martinique make easy landfalls day or night. Barbados apart, all the islands are high and will be in sight long before you are likely to hit them. Usually the weather is clear and heavy rain, which is the only thing likely to cut down visibility, will normally be in the form of short-lived squalls which soon move away. The islands which have major airports also have aeronautical radio beacons. See Part IV for details of main entry ports, and Bibliography for further cruising guides.

As you approach land, give yourself enough time to brush up your knowledge of entry procedure for the particular island to which you are going. They are all different. Each island has one or more official entry ports and it is important that these be used. Since the advent of independence the former British colonies have become fiercely independent of one another and are on the alert for illegal immigrants, the smuggling of drugs and the possession of firearms. They deserve our help and we should not complain if, in order to do their job, the local officials have to put us to some slight inconvenience.

Provisioning

The best places for provisioning for a trade-wind crossing are Gibraltar, Madeira or one of the Canary Island ports. Gibraltar, although it involves a considerable diversion from the direct route for anyone sailing from the English Channel, is good for a number of reasons. There is a marina, a slipway, shipwright, engineer, rigger and sailmaker. There are well-stocked chandleries and a British Admiralty chart depot holding complete stocks of all Amdiralty publications. All provisions can be obtained and also bonded stores at advantageous prices. What cannot be bought

Martinique Diamond Rock, scene of a famous British landing in Napoleonic times, lies to the south of Martinique.

Philip Allen

locally can be flown out from England and will be cleared through Customs with little delay. Gear for a yacht in transit is duty-free. There is the added bonus that in Gibraltar they speak English. If visiting Gibraltar, the opportunity should be taken of replenishing medical supplies, if necessary, and of stocking up with everyday needs from a chemist's shop as these are more expensive in the West Indies.

Madeira is far enough on the way to be the last port of call, and is a more sophisticated island than most of the Canaries. It affords an excellent choice of high quality merchandise, including really new-laid eggs. Perhaps most important of all, excellent fresh fruit and vegetables can be bought just before sailing. Some experienced ocean voyagers consider that Santa Cruz de La Palma is a good place at which to provision for the crossing.

While the recommendations given in Chapter 8 can be applied in a general way to this voyage, remember that it is in the tropics and in consequence some things will not keep well. The temptation is to take a bit too much, especially on a first voyage. The majority of small boats take from 22 to 28 days to make the crossing but a passage lasting over 40 days is by no means rare. When using the provisioning formula suggested in Chapter 8 give the factor 'P' a value of 30.

There is no need to worry much about what you may not be able to get in the West Indies. In most of the islands, and certainly any you will be likely to use for your landfall, there are supermarkets and in all islands fresh vegetables are easy to find. Fruit is good and plentiful in some but not in others: good in Barbados, excellent (but expensive) in Martinique.

Bread, if well-baked, can be made to last nearly a fortnight but if the boat is big enough to have an oven it is well worth arranging to make bread at sea. When buying tinned foods use your imagination and if there is to be a full-time cook let him or her play a leading role in choosing what is to be bought. The trade-wind voyage is a long one, and one on which time can be devoted to the preparation of interesting meals (which is not always possible on an eastward passage in higher latitudes) so bear in mind that part of the pleasure of this voyage is likely to come out of the galley.

Watchkeeping

The secret of a happy trade-wind voyage depends to a great extent on establishing, from the beginning, a daily routine which not only ensures that all necessary work is done but that each crew member feels himself to be an important part of the ship and is pulling his weight. The relatively undemanding nature of the trade-wind voyage can be a demoralising influence on a crew that is not given some sense of purpose by the skipper. When one meets an unhappy ship that has just arrived after an east-to-west passage it nearly always turns out that the skipper has failed to lay on a proper system of watchkeeping.

With the advent of singlehanded ocean-racing and the development of various forms of automatic steering, the practice of regular watchkeeping seems to be considered by some to be 'old hat'. Once clear of the islands and coastal traffic, there is so little shipping to be seen that the need for a full time lookout perhaps does not exist and with a crew of only two, even a careful skipper seems willing to turn in at night and to leave the ship to sail herself. With a crew of three or more, I would certainly set watches covering the full 24 hours of each day. I would do this partly to keep everyone on his or her toes but also because unless you have stood your watches in the dark hours in the tropics you have no idea of what goes on in the heavens at night. The man who would forego this, or deny it to his crew, would go blindfold through Venice or sit through Beethoven's 5th Symphony wearing earplugs.

Rhythmic rolling

This can take place on any vessel when running, but certain conditions are conducive to its happening. Twin keel enthusiasts will tell you that their boats are

106

less prone to rolling: and I am sure this is true. Those who do not believe in the use of special running sails argue that, if the main is set, rhythmic rolling will be diminished. This must depend to some extent on the direction of the wind relative to the boat's course and whether there were to be a steady heeling force applied to the sail.

In most yachts rhythmic rolling seems to be a fact of life which, from time to time, will occur and all aboard must learn to live with it. Whatever is being done – cooking, navigating, maintenance, repairs, eating or sleeping – the careful chocking-off of everything moveable is essential. This makes for an orderly method of tackling every job because any piece of gear not in immediate use has to be stowed away safely. The crunch comes when, unaccountably, the rolling stops and we all forget about it and begin to leave things lying around: and then, without warning, it suddenly begins again. It has been worked out that, on a trade-wind passage you may roll as many as half a million times. You'll get used to it.

Summary of times and distances
The Bay of Biscay can usually be crossed in four or five days unless headwinds are encountered. When coasting down the Spanish and Portuguese coasts, plan on 50 miles per day, plus time spent in harbour. (You should do better than this but it is a safe planning figure.) From Cascais to the Canaries allow 7 to 10 days and the same from Gibraltar. From Gibraltar to Madeira allow 5 to 7 days. The voyage from Madeira or the Canaries to Barbados usually takes from three to four weeks. Plan on 100 miles per day and you will not go far wrong unless your yacht is very small or slow, or you strike an exceptionally bad season for calms.

All the above figures are necessarily approximations, based on the experiences of the owners of vessels of different sizes and in varying conditions of weather.

Falmouth to Finisterre	450 miles
Finisterre to Cascais	280
Cascais to Gibraltar	280
Cascais to Madeira	500
Cascais to Canaries	750
Gibraltar to Madeira	625
Madeira to Canaries	240
Canaries to Barbados	2700

Charts and sailing directions
The amount of magnetic variation differs greatly as you cross the Atlantic Ocean. It is therefore important to remember that the chart you are using will most likely show nothing but the True compass rose. According to where you are, you will have to find the amount of magnetic variation from the isogonic lines which are drawn on most ocean charts, linking the places which have a common amount of variation.

Charts essential for the ocean passages only are given here. For particulars of those necessary for your departure port, ports of call, and arrival port, see Part IV Port Information. The Sailing Directions listed hereunder cover the whole area referred to in the text, both ocean and inshore.

Charts		Sailing Directions	
Admiralty	US	Admiralty	US
Ocean 2059	121	1, 22, 27, 67, 71	191 143 142 140 147

Unofficial Publications

Title	Author(s)	Publisher
North Biscay Pilot	RCC Pilotage Foundation	Adlard Coles, London
South Biscay Pilot	Brandon	Adlard Coles, London
Cruising Association Handbook	Brackenbury & others	Cruising Association, London

108

Santa Cruz de la Palma, looking N. The yachts' berth can be seen on the left of the picture.

USA to the Virgin Islands

This passage can be classed as a delivery trip, because it has to be made against predictably adverse conditions of wind direction and current, and it must be sandwiched between the hurricane season and the winter gales.

Route

Assuming that the yacht has been got as far as Florida, a start may be made from Fort Lauderdale or Miami, crossing the Florida Strait towards Nassau or Spanish Wells. The Gulf Stream runs strongly through the Strait, 4 knots in mid-stream but less at the edges. Departure from Miami enables advantage to be taken of the Stream when making for NW Providence Channel. The passage from Nassau to the Virgins has been described by Eric Hiscock in his book *Atlantic Cruise in Wanderer III*. With that clarity and economy of words which are characteristic of him, he says:

'I would stand out to sea from Nassau on the starboard tack until I thought I could fetch the Virgins on the other tack, and then go about. Bermuda might even be a convenient stop'.

This advice perhaps needs qualification to the extent that in the event of a NE wind, it may pay to go on to the port tack in order to make easting.

Timing

The object is to get the yacht to the West Indies by December. The month of November affords the best opportunity of doing this; the chances of encountering a hurricane are slight and the winter gale-force winds known as 'northers' will not yet have started in earnest. Nevertheless, enquiries should be made and a reliable weather report obtained before starting.

Wind and Currents

Pilot charts show that the wind will almost certainly have an easterly component, with a high percentage tending towards NE. Wind strength is likely to be 4–6 Beaufort with a chance of a gale; there is a 5 percent possibility of calms. In the NW Providence Channel currents are unpredictable and much influenced by the wind, but watch the tides which set on and off the banks to the south. Consult the appropriate tide tables for full details. On the ocean, the North Equatorial Current sets NW at about ½ knot.

Times and Distances

It is nearly 200 miles from Miami to Nassau and if stopping there it would be wise to allow 72 hours for the passage. There is deep water through NW Providence

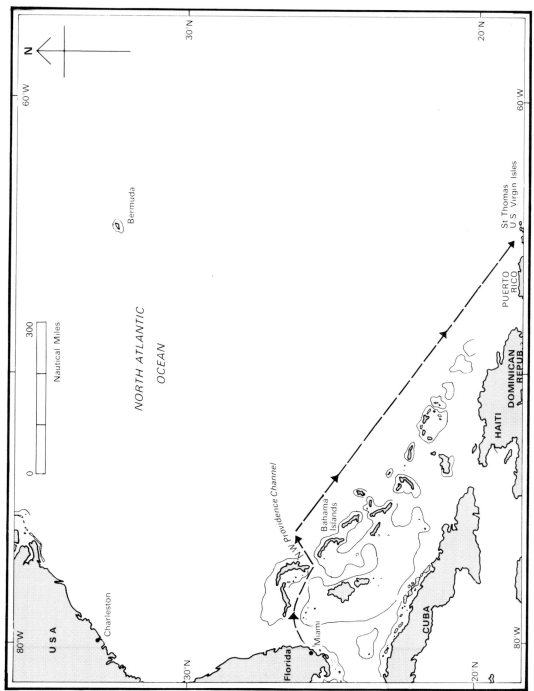

Chart No 5 From USA to the Virgin Islands, via the North West Providence Channel. Based on Admiralty Chart No 2059.

111

Channel but shipping traffic will be encountered. From Nassau to the Virgins is about 900 miles direct but you might have to sail twice this distance. Every opportunity of making easting should be taken, and it is well to carry as much fuel as possible and to use it motoring east if there are any periods of calm. Given reasonable conditions, 10 to 14 days should be long enough, but it would be wise to ship provisions for three weeks unless you plan to restock at St Thomas, or another good centre in the Virgins, immediately on arrival.

Although replacements of all kinds can be made at St Thomas, and with varying degrees of success elsewhere in the West Indies, this will usually be more costly than at home, so stock up before you set sail and aim to be as nearly self-supporting as possible by way of ship's gear.

Charts and Sailing Directions

Charts			*Sailing Directions*	
	Admiralty	*US*	*Admiralty*	*US*
Ocean	4403	145	69	140
Providence Channels	399, 2077	26320	70	147
Nassau	1452	26309, 26310		
Florida Harbours	3684	11468, 11470		
Virgin Islands	130	25641		
St Thomas	2183, 2452	25647, 25649		

Virgin Islands to USA
This passage will normally be undertaken at the end of a period of cruising in the West Indies. The object will be to reach the coast of the USA without the risk of meeting winter gales en route, and before the onset of the hurricane season. April and May suggest themselves as the best months.

Possible Routes
There are several possible routes:

1. A cruising passage may be made through the Bahamas by a yacht whose draft does not exceed 5 feet. Before undertaking this, study carefully *The Yachtsman's Guide to the Bahamas* and make sure that you have all the necessary charts.

2. An ocean passage, leaving the Bahamas to port until the island of Eleuthera is abeam, thence through the NW Providence Channel and across the Strait of Florida to Miami or Fort Lauderdale.

3. A more northerly ocean passage towards Charleston, Morehead City, or Newport, Rhode Island.

Since *The Yachtsman's Guide to the Bahamas* gives full information for those wishing to cruise through the islands, we shall deal here with the ocean passages only. See Chapter 17 for navigational warning on the Bahamas.

Winds and Currents

Whichever route is taken, winds are likely to be fair and of moderate strength. The outside chance of encountering a hard blow is greater in the case of the more northerly passages.

A current of about ½ knot NW-going follows the trend of the islands until it merges with the Gulf Stream north of the Bahamas. In the NW Providence Channel currents are unpredictable and much influenced by the wind. But watch the tides which set on and off the banks to the south. Consult the appropriate tide tables for full details. In Florida Strait the Gulf Stream has a rate of from 3½ to 4 knots in the middle, less at the edges. If making for Miami or Fort Lauderdale, due allowance must be made.

When making for Charleston or Morehead City, aim to cross the Gulf Stream at a point which will enable you to sail straight across, at right angles to the current, and to come out the other side at the place where you wish to be. By doing this you will spend less time actually in the Stream than if you have to head into it to counteract its effect on your course.

Times and Distances

To Florida, the distance is about 1100 miles and to Charleston and Morehead City about 1200. Given the fair conditions which are probable for any of these passages, one could expect to take from 10 to 15 days.

Climate

Coming from the West Indies, you will notice a marked drop in air temperature, especially if the destination is one of the northern ports and the voyage is made in April, when the mean air temperature in latitude 15°N is listed as 70°F, while in 33°N it is shown as 60°F. Warm clothes – the existence of which may have been almost forgotten in the West Indies – will need to be rummaged from a locker and given an airing.

Formalities

It has been said that US citizens who have entered at St Thomas, or elsewhere in the US Virgins, do not need to clear customs on arrival in USA. If this is true, it can apply only to US citizens and certainly not to those of other nationalities. All foreigners must report to customs on arrival at any port in the USA; see Chapter 13.

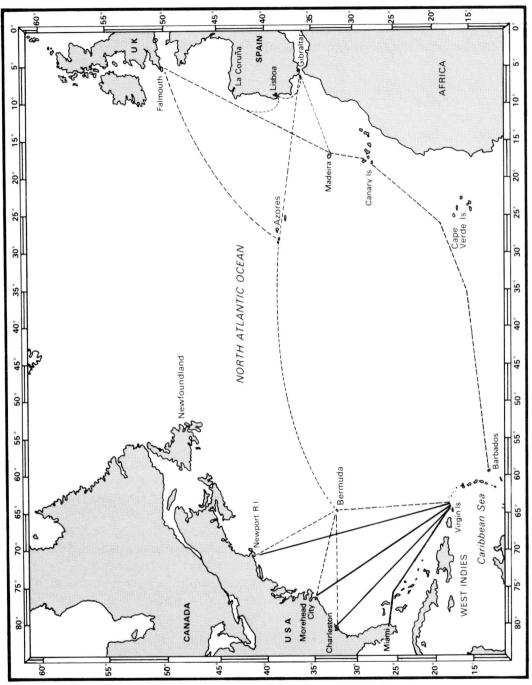

Chart N . (From the Virgin Islands to the USA. Based on Admiralty Chart No. 2059.

114

Charts			Sailing Directions	
	Admiralty	*US*	*Admiralty*	*US*
Ocean	4403	145	69	140
Providence Channels	399, 2077	26320	70	147
Nassau	1452	26309, 26310		
Florida Harbours	3684	11468, 11470		
Charleston	2806	11524		
Morehead City	2864	11547		
Virgin Islands	130	25641		
St Thomas	2183, 2452	25647, 25649		

USA to Bermuda

This passage may form part of a voyage to the West Indies or to Europe, if starting from south of Cape Hatteras.

Route

The most direct route is likely to prove best, except that it may pay to enter the Gulf Stream at a point which will enable the boat to be sailed straight across it, so as to emerge in the right position on the far side, without having to head into the stream. This will minimize the time spent within the Gulf Stream itself.

Timing

A passage which is to be part of a voyage towards Europe is likely to be timed for late spring or early summer. May would be a reasonable month to start.

The important thing is to make one's offing as rapidly as possible and get into deep water before there is any chance of meeting heavy weather. In 1964 *Bluebird of Thorne* encountered a severe gale in early May, between Charleston and Bermuda. She rode it out safely in deep water but in the same storm, *Doubloon*, a fine yacht, found herself in the more confused seas where the ocean bed rises towards the east coast of America and was dismasted and seriously damaged.

The timing of a passage forming part of a voyage to the West Indies is a little more difficult. One would want to reach the West Indies in late November or December but to do this, making only a brief stay in Bermuda, would mean starting from the USA in late October or early November. While the risk of a hurricane at this time might be acceptable, the passage would be a mighty cold one. An alternative would be to do the run from America to Bermuda in June, and to

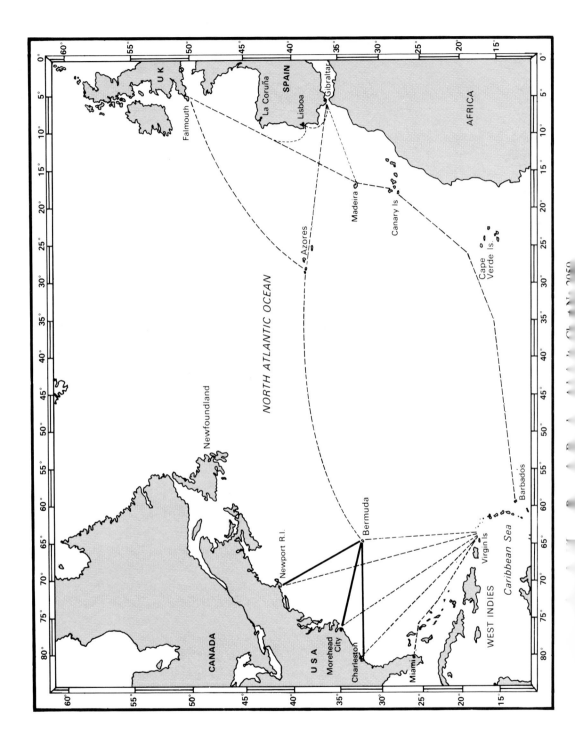

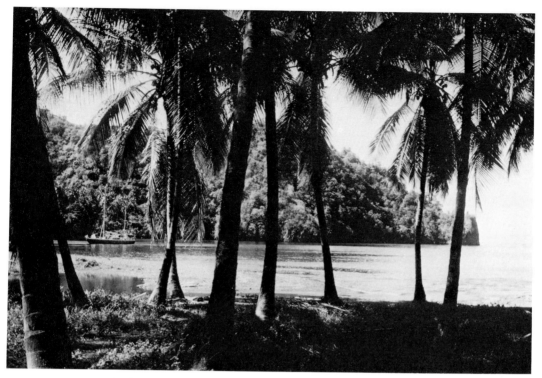

A tropic anchorage in the West Indies. Thoughts of an anchorage like this are what spur some of us on to make an ocean voyage.

Philip Allen

postpone the second leg of the voyage until November. Although June falls within the hurricane season, the risk is acceptable to those who compete in the Bermuda Race.

Hurricane forecasting has become a fine art and expert opinion suggests that, if you leave the US coast with a favourable forecast, although you may not reach Bermuda without the need to take evasive action, the weathermen will give enough warning to enable you to keep out of trouble.

Although a hurricane can occur any time between June and mid-November, the worst period is from July to September inclusive. To that extent it would seem reasonable to sail to Bermuda in June and stay there until November when the rest of the voyage to the West Indies could be completed.

Winds and Currents

In May, on the US coast between Maine and Cape Hatteras, the strongest winds are likely to come from a northerly or north easterly sector. On the other hand the percentage of winds having a southerly component is about equal and their strength is likely to be F4–6. The Pilot Chart for June shows that SW winds of Force 4–6 predominate over the whole area, which is favourable for anybody sailing from ports anywhere between Cape Cod and Charleston.

While the Pilot Charts show the Gulf Stream in this area as having an innocuous 1–1½ knots, many observers have experienced much higher rates, together with eddies and offshoots totally uncharted and inexplicable. There are no doubt expert navigators, who help to gain winning places in the Bermuda Race and who understand what is going on, but for the novice crossing the Gulf Stream for the first time, intelligent guesswork, combined with accurate position-finding must suffice.

For comfort (if not also for safety) avoid crossing the Stream in a strong northerly wind. And remember that the quickest way across any flowing stream is at right angles to its course.

Landfall

Bermuda is totally encompassed by coral reefs and can be approached with safety only from the east of St David's Head. Gibbs Hill lighthouse has a radio beacon, as has St David's Head; both of which operate continuously and provide excellent bearings for the approach. The fairway is well buoyed, but it is very narrow and tortuous and the new-comer is advised to heave-to outside and await daylight. St Georges, which is entered via a narrow channel lying on the port hand just inside the main fairway, is the official entry port and must be used on entry. For fuller details see Part IV Port Information.

Time and Distance

The distance to Bermuda from harbours on the E coast of the USA varies from about 670 to 700 miles. Allow about 6 days for the passage from US under reasonable conditions.

Charts and Sailing Directions

Charts		Sailing Directions	
Admiralty	*US*	*Admiralty*	*US*
4403	145	69	140
		70	147

West Indies to Bermuda

Route
The course is almost due north from the most northerly islands in the West Indies.

Timing
This passage is likely to take place in late spring or early summer, at the conclusion of the sailing season in the West Indies, when boats are heading towards Europe for the summer season there.

Winds and Currents
Although she will enjoy the trade-wind at the start, a vessel is sure to run into the variables and calms of the Horse Latitudes and to encounter great patches of Sargasso weed. Use of the engine may be the only means of ensuring regular progress. A trailing log is of little use in this area.

A current, NW-going of about ½ knot, is to be expected until within a hundred miles of Bermuda, after which it will vary in both speed and direction.

Landfall
Although Bermuda is reputedly difficult to find and the approach has a bad name because of extensive coral reefs which surround the islands, those coming from the south have the least difficult landfall. Gibbs Hill light and St David's Head light are both easily identified, by day or night, provided visibility is reasonable. Each has a radio beacon working continuously. See Part IV Port Information for details of approach and entry procedure.

Time and Distance
Bermuda lies about 800 miles from the Virgin Islands. If you are lucky with the wind this passage could take a week, but if you run into calms progress will depend on how much use you make of the engine. Unless you are a purist and are going to find your way through the light and fluky airs in these parts under sail alone, you can plan on seven to ten days.

Charts and Sailing Directions

| | Charts | | Sailing Directions | |
	Admiralty	US	Admiralty	US
W Indies	130	25001		
Ocean	4403	145	70, 71	147
Bermuda	334	26341		

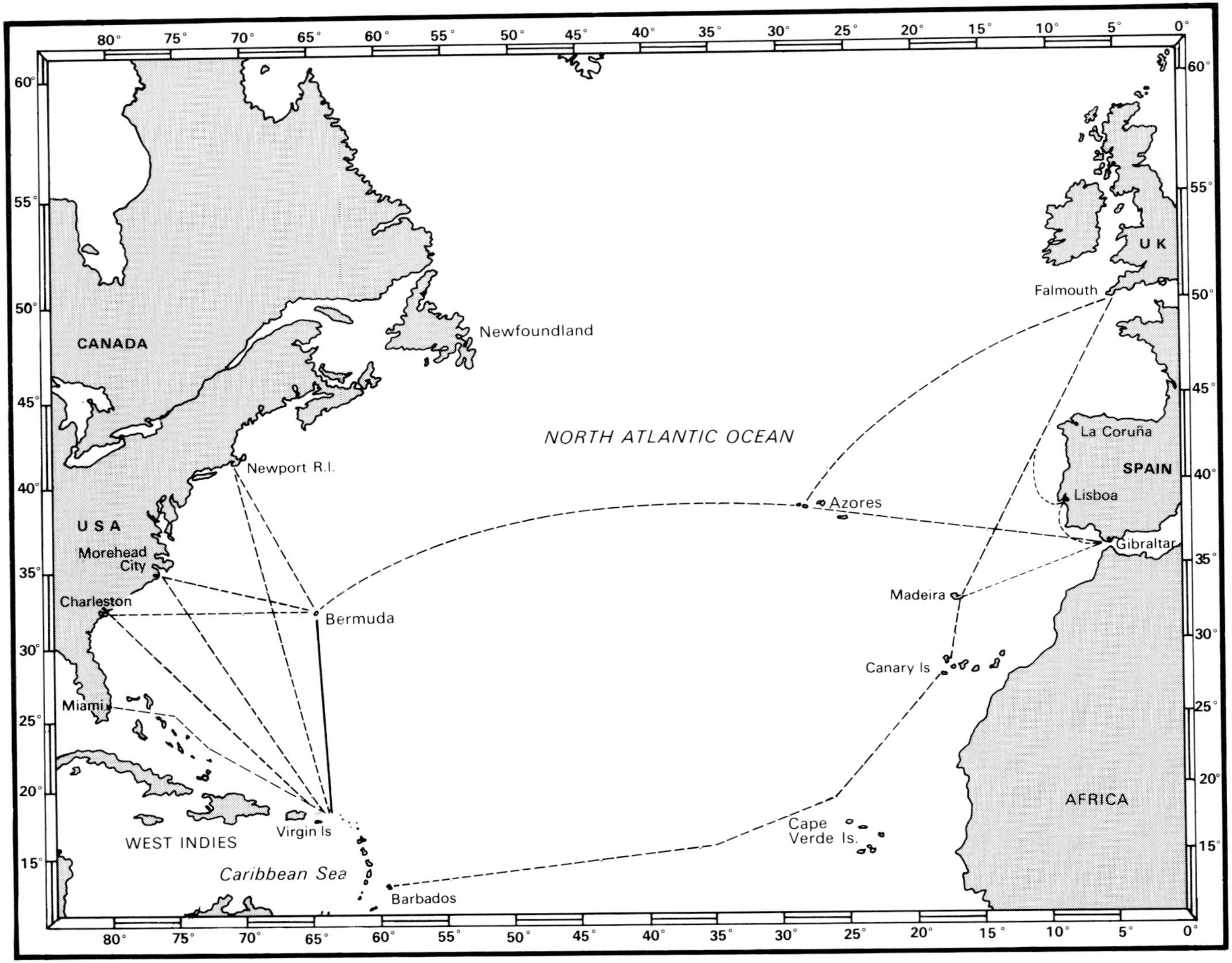

Chart No. 8 From the West Indies to Bermuda, Based on Admiralty Chart No 2059.

Bermuda to Azores

Route
Bermuda lies near to the northern limit of the Horse Latitudes and, when sailing towards the Azores, it is wise to make some northing in an effort to find the fringe of the westerlies which prevail in higher latitudes, and possibly a fair current.

Timing
This passage will normally be made in early summer, as part of a voyage from the West Indies or the USA, to some port in Europe.

Winds and Currents
At this season it is unlikely that the wind will prove reliable in either strength or direction, and almost certainly by the time you get near to the Azores you will run into the summer high, which is a big almost stationary anti-cyclone and an area of calm. Predictable progress through this can be made only by using the engine. If the high has shifted, or is not there, weather in the Azores group can be very rugged.

South of latitude 38°N there may be a variable but foul current. Further to the north is the favourable Gulf Stream of between ½ and 1 knot. See chapter 17 for further details.

Shipping
Steamer traffic may be sighted at any time; some of it on the same course, or its reciprocal and some of it crossing. A good lookout should be kept night and day.

Landfall
The only two harbours offering reasonable security in the Azores are Horta on the island of Faial and Ponta Delgada on Sao Miguel. The landfall will present no problem, there being no less than six aero beacons on various of the islands.

Passage Time and Distance
Average time 16–24 days according to wind, weather and use of engine. The distance is about 1800 miles.

Charts and Sailing Directions

| | Charts | | Sailing Directions | |
	Admiralty	US	Admiralty	US
Bermuda	334	26341	70	147
Passage	2059	121	—	140
Azores	1950	51002	67	143

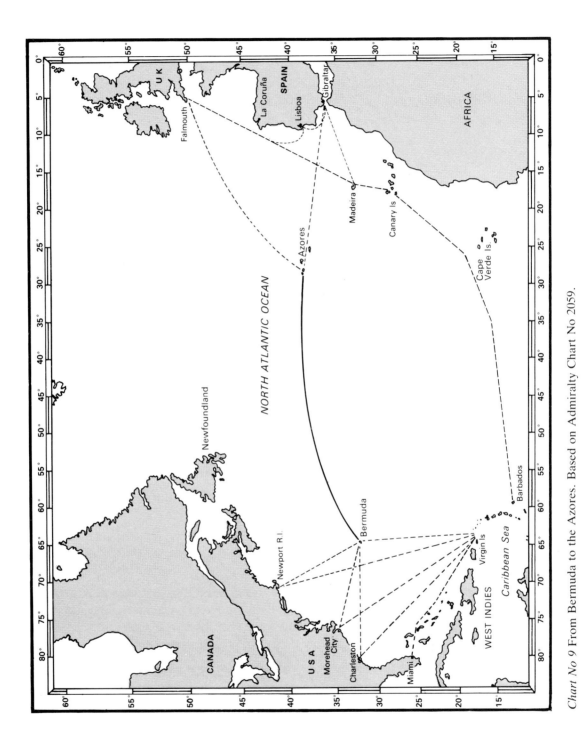

Chart No 9 From Bermuda to the Azores. Based on Admiralty Chart No 2059.

122

Gibraltar, showing the marinas with a landing aircraft-runway to their right.

Azores to Gibraltar

Route (Line 1 on Chart No 10)
Cape St Vincent lies about 850 miles due east of Sta Maria, the most southerly island of the Azores. From Cape St Vincent a direct course may be set for Gibraltar or, if preferred, a coastal cruise may be made along the coasts of S Portugal and SW Spain.

Timing
As part of a voyage from the USA to the Mediterranean, the passage will probably be in spring or early summer.

Winds and Currents
The probability is that northerly winds will predominate for most of the way. After clearing the islands and the immediate area of the Azores high you should pick up a strong steady breeze and there will almost certainly be a big beam sea to match. You should have fast, exciting sailing, with plenty of spray flying around.

The Portugal Current will be running almost exactly at right angles to your route between the islands and Cape St Vincent and will set you to the southward at about

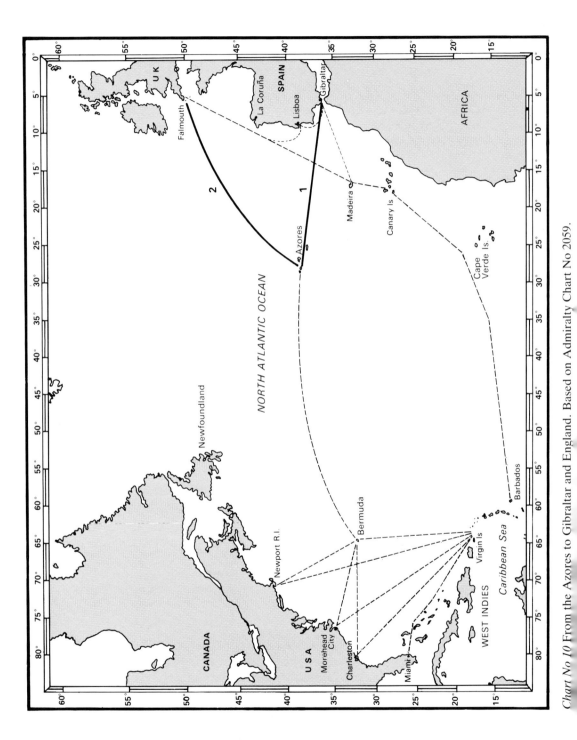

Chart No 10 From the Azores to Gibraltar and England. Based on Admiralty Chart No 2059.

12 miles per day. After Cape St Vincent the current will tend towards the Strait of Gibraltar as there is a permanent flow into the Mediterranean caused by the high rate of evaporation in that warm area. Winds may be variable.

Shipping
Watch out for north and southbound steamer traffic well before you reach the longitude of Cape St Vincent and, once you have passed under its lee, you will lose your nice steady wind but will find a lot more traffic.

Landfall
There are no navigational hazards as one approaches the Strait unless it should happen to be foggy. There is, however, a Traffic Separation Scheme in force, and this (which is shown on the official charts) should be studied and any supplementary information given in *Notices to Mariners* should be noted.

Gibraltar Strait
Weather conditions in the Strait of Gibraltar are a law unto themselves. The wind funnels through the Strait either due E or due W. If it is blowing strongly from the west it reinforces the current, over-riding any tidal stream except very close inshore, and makes it virtually impossible to sail out of Gibraltar and into the Atlantic until the wind abates. Conversely, a Levanter (the local name for a strong easterly) blowing against the current kicks up a short steep sea which makes progress into the Mediterranean difficult.

There are radio beacons on Cape St Vincent, Cape Espartel, the Rock of Gibraltar and at Casablanca. In normal clear weather this is an easy landfall with high mountains on both the Spanish and African coasts. Maintain a good plot, and watch where the steamers are going to and coming from. Fog is rare, but occurs occasionally. Avoid entering the Strait until it clears.

Time and Distance
The distance from Horta is just under 1100 miles and it should be possible to do it in from eight to ten days.

Charts and Sailing Directions

	Charts		Sailing Directions	
	Admiralty	US	Admiralty	US
Azores	1950	51002		
Passage	2059	121	67	143
Approach to Straits				
of Gibraltar	92	51160		

Azores to the English Channel

Route (Line 2 on Chart No 10)
Take every opportunity of making northing until about 45°N is reached, even if this means losing ground to the W. As the summer progresses winds tend to blow E of N in the area south of 45°N, but westerlies may be found N of this latitude.

Timing
This will depend on whether the passage is part of a voyage from America to Europe, or the return half of a cruise from England and back. In either case it is likely to fall within the period May-September.

Winds and Currents
The Azores High is a problem and may cause calms and northerly winds for a considerable area around the group. When enough northing has been made, westerlies should be found until the English Channel is approached, when the wind may come from any direction, although most likely it will be fair. The Azores Current sets SE between the islands and the tail end of the Gulf Stream (or North Atlantic Drift) sets E towards the English Channel, Ushant, and into the Bay of Biscay.

Times and Distances
Once you have made your northing, the chances are that you will have a beam wind, or at least a close reach, for most of the passage and should therefore make good progress. The distance from Horta (Faial) to Plymouth, England, is 1260 miles (but more if you have to go north to pick up the wind) and a safe estimate is 10-14 days.

English Channel to the Azores
This passage might be part of a transatlantic voyage to the USA or Canada, or it might be the outward part of a cruise from England to the Azores, and back.

Route (Line 2 on Chart No 10)
The route might be a direct one, or via Spain or even Portugal. The direct route from the English Channel is likely to be in weather that is predominantly westerly. In the event of a fair wind there would be a slight advantage in laying a great circle course. A passage via Spain and Portugal could prove profitable in mid-summer, taking advantage of the Portuguese Trades and then reaching across to the Azores in winds which might continue to be north-westerly.

Timing
This will depend on whether you make a cruise to the islands and back, or whether you are planning to sail on towards America. If the passage is to be part of a transatlantic voyage, a start might be made in May, but for a there-and-back cruise

any time within the period May-September inclusive would be possible, the ideal period being perhaps June and July.

Winds and Currents

Winds in spring are usually from N to SW with about four gale-days per month. In summer they tend to be lighter with more northerlies and a chance of nor'easterlies with, on average, three gale-days per month. When sailing the direct course, try to hold on to WSW until you have reached somewhere between 10° and 12°W. The object of this is to avoid being set towards Ushant and into the Bay of Biscay by the prevailing westerly winds and the east-going current. If the wind should be from ahead, or nearly so, the port tack should certainly be chosen.

Times and Distances

From Plymouth (England) to Horta (Faial) is 1260 miles – say 10-14 days – and from Plymouth to Ponta Delgada (S Miguel) is just over 1100 miles – say 9-13 days. A diversion to NW Spain would add 200 miles, perhaps another two days, and a call to Portugal might add from three to five.

Charts and Sailing Directions

Charts		Sailing Directions	
Admiralty	*US*	*Admiralty*	*US*
1854, 1855, 1940	51061, 51081	27, 22, 67	143, 191
1950, 2059	51062, 51082		
5124 (5)	16		
5124 (6)			
5124 (7)			
5124 (8)			

Part III

The Island Groups

1. Bermuda
2. The Azores
3. The Madeiran Archipelago
4. The Canary Islands
5. The Cape Verde Islands
6. The West Indies
7. The Bahamas

For fuller documentation on the eastern islands of the Atlantic (Azores etc), see *The Atlantic Islands: Azores, Madeira, Canaries and Cape Verde* (RCC Pilotage Foundation; Imray, Laurie, Norie and Wilson).

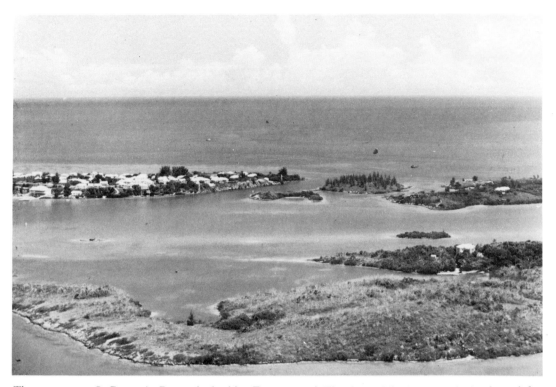

The entrance to St George's, Bermuda, looking E to seaward. The channel lies between the land, top left, and the two larger islands.

Bermuda Government

17 The Island Groups

1. BERMUDA

General Description
Bermuda is Britain's oldest colony and is self-governing. Its economy is closely linked to the American tourist trade. The islands consist of a low-lying group of small coral islets surrounded by extensive reefs; most of them are today joined by causeways.

Climate
Temperature varies between 62° in February and 82° in August. Weather is influenced by the position of the Azores high, the Gulf Stream, and the weather system on the eastern seaboard of the USA. Although not within the trade-wind zone, Bermuda's prevailing winds tend to be NE. The islands are in the area affected by hurricanes (June–November inclusive).

Approach
Reefs extend 10 miles offshore on the north of the islands. The safe approach is from a position south-east of the group. There are two hazards; first, the 200 metre soundings lie within a mile of the SE coastline in places; second, there is a magnetic anomaly giving a possible error of up to 6 degrees in excess of the normal variation for this zone.

In thick weather, those equipped with radio are advised to contact Bermuda Harbour Radio on channel 16 VHF, or 2182 kHz, for pilotage information. In clear weather and in daylight, cross the 200 metre contour, SE of St David's Head, and shape a course for the first of the fairway buoys, in Five Fathom Hole, about ¾ mile N of St David's Head. Then follow the fairway and Town Cut Channel to St George's Harbour. Do not attempt to enter at night; the outer marks may be unreliable.

Formalities
Official entry must be made at St George's. There is a good deal of paperwork to be done (see Part IV), and Q-flag must be flown when entering and until pratique has been granted. Boats may then proceed to Hamilton or elsewhere, but must obtain clearance from St George's on departure.

Visitors are allowed to remain for an initial period of three weeks. If a longer stay is desired, application must be made to the Ministry of Home Affairs (Immigration Dept). Firearms, including Very pistols and spear guns, must be declared and may be impounded until departure or placed under seal aboard. Medically prescribed drugs must be declared. There are severe penalties for the possession of illegal drugs, including marijuana.

Magnetic Variation 15°05'W (1987) increasing about 2' annually.

Depths in Metres

132

Services

There is free berthing (first-come, first-served) at the quayside at St George's. In Hamilton, berths for which fees are payable are obtainable by arrangement with one of the yacht clubs (the Royal Bermuda YC, or the R Hamilton Amateur Dinghy Club). Anchorage is free, but must be clear of any fairway. See Chart No 12.

Bermuda is a sophisticated island with all manner of shopping facilities for both the tourist and the small-boat owner. All slipping and repair services are available. Bonded stores may be obtained prior to departure.

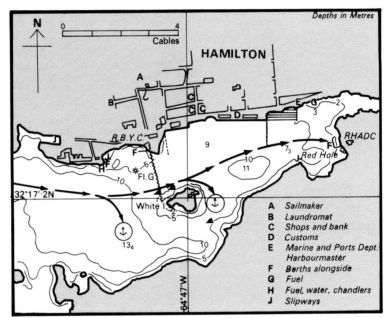

Chart No 12 Hamilton,
Bermuda. Based on
Admiralty Chart No 334

Cruising Guides

Yachtsman's Guide to the Bermuda Islands by Michael Voegeli is comprehensive and excellent. The Bermuda Department of Tourism, Front Street, Hamilton, Bermuda supplies a typed memorandum of useful information which is available gratis and should be obtained before your voyage begins.

Charts		Sailing Directions	
Admiralty	*US*	*Admiralty*	*US*
332, 334, 867	26341,	70	147
868, 1073, 1315	26342,		
	26343,		
	26344,		
	26345		

Magnetic Variation 15°10′W (1983) decreasing about 9′ annually.

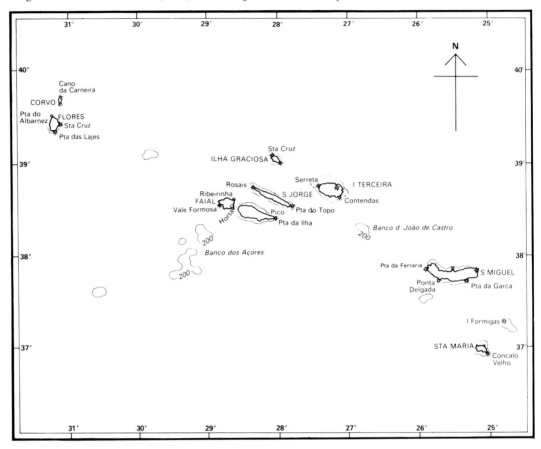

Chart No 13 The Azores. Based on Admiralty Chart No 1950.

2. THE AZORES

General Description

Compared with other island groups in the Atlantic, the Azores are thinly spread. They lie between latitudes 36°55′N and 39°45′N, and between 24°42′W and 31°16′W longitude. See Chart No 13.

The islands are of volcanic origin and there is occasionally some volcanic activity. There are three groupings: the main central one consisting of Faial, Pico, Sao Jorge, Terceira and Graciosa; the easterly one, Sao Miguel, St Maria; and the westerly one, Flores and Corvo.

The main ports, and the only two harbours which can be regarded as reasonably safe under all but extreme conditions, are Horta on Faial and Ponta Delgada on Sao Miguel (See Chart No 14). These two are useful and pleasant ports of call for transatlantic voyagers. Details of Horta are given in Part IV.

Climate

The air temperature in this part of the Atlantic varies very much according to wind direction, and the nights can be extremely cold. Your warmest possible clothes may be needed, despite the fact that the Azores may, when you reach them, be basking in a sunny anticyclone with little or no wind.

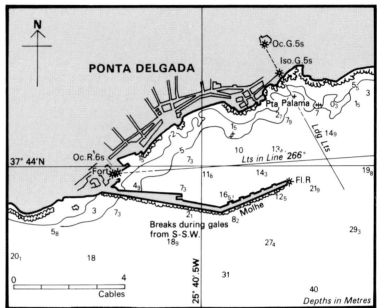

Chart No 14 Ponta Delgada, Azores. Based on Admiralty Chart No 1854.

Services

The Islands are rather primitive, but well able to supply the needs of a boat as far as food and drink are concerned. No reliance should however be placed on the possibility of obtaining yacht fittings in any of the islands in the group.

Preparations before leaving home waters should, therefore, include a careful check on all gear and on the stock of spares and replacements. A Portuguese courtesy-flag will be needed.

For all passages to or from the Azores, see chapter 16.

Charts		Sailing Directions	
Admiralty	US	Admiralty	US
366 1940	51061	67	143
1845 1946	51062		
1855 1950	51041		
	51081		
	51082		

3. THE MADEIRAN ARCHIPELAGO

General Description

Funchal is a favourite port of call for those who like to combine a bit of civilised life ashore with their sailing. For some it is the last place they visit before starting out on the trade-wind crossing of the Atlantic, and for that reason it is apt to be a point at which crew changes take place and major provisioning occurs.

Some cruising can be undertaken, both on the coast of Madeira itself and between it and Porto Santo and Ilha Deserta Grande. The whole of the south coast may be used for cruising and there are several good anchorages. The northern coast, all of which is exposed to the prevailing northerly wind, should be avoided.

Winds

The prevailing wind is NE and in most areas a good anchorage means one which provides protection from that quarter. On the south coast of Madeira itself and especially in the area of Funchal, the wind eddies round the island and although it may be blowing NE at sea it will be SW on the south coast, inshore, between Funchal and Brazen Head.

Caution

The Portuguese Man-o'war, a very unpleasant jellyfish with metre-long tentacles that sting, abounds in these waters and should be avoided by swimmers. In appearance it is like a transparent plastic bag floating on the surface and is quite obvious when seen from on deck, but less so when one is in the water. Look round before you dive in and, if handling a fishing line that has been long in the water, use gloves because the tentacles may be adhering to it. The Information Bureau in Funchal will give all details about fishing, tackle, bait and the hiring of boats.

PORTO SANTO

This island will be the first to be sighted when arriving from anywhere in Europe, its conical peak being very conspicuous. It is an official port of entry and may therefore be your first port of call. If intending to visit here it is best to do so first, because it lies up-wind of the other islands.

Arriving from the north or east, the island should be left to starboard and the anchorage approached on a westerly course after passing Ilha de Cima on which is a light. A new harbour has been built with a small marina which has showers, electricity and water but no fuel. It is also possible to anchor and the berth is said to have good shelter. It is a longish walk to town but the Port Captain's office is on the quay.

136

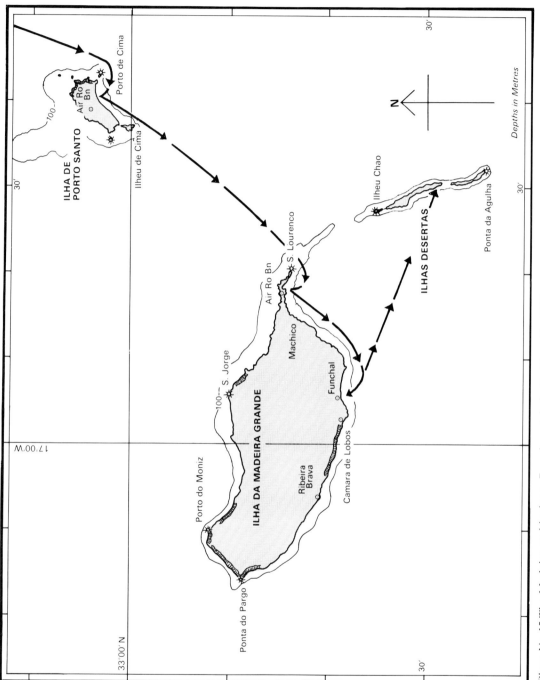

Magnetic Variation 9°30′W (1987) decreasing about 8′ annually.

Chart No 15 The Madeira archipelago. Based on Admiralty Chart No 1831.

137

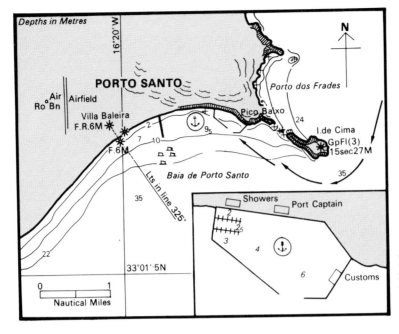

Depths in Metres

16°20' W

N

PORTO SANTO

Porto dos Frades

Air
Ro Bn

Airfield

Villa Baleira
F.R.6M

Pico Baixo

24

I. de Cima
GpFl(3)
15sec27M

2
9
5

7 10

F.6M

35

Baia de Porto Santo

Lts in line 325°

35

Showers

Port Captain

22

33°01'·5N

2
5

3

4

6

Customs

0   1
Nautical Miles

Chart No 16 Porto Santo,
Ilha de Porto Santo,
Madeira.
Based on Admiralty
Chart No 1831.

There is good fishing (trolling) over the banks to the north of the island and bottom-fishing, in 600 metres, all around the coast. Barracuda and tuna are plentiful. If fishing in shallow water off the SW coast, beware of landing a weaver, which is a small fish about the size of a big sardine. It is greenish yellow with a black dorsal spine which is highly poisonous and very painful indeed if touched. If you catch one, try to shake it off the hook but whatever happens do not touch it.

There are shopping facilities ashore; but do not count on being able to obtain fuel, and do not take on drinking water which is apt to upset some people (although the islanders bottle and export it!). There is an airport and of course an aero beacon sited in the middle of the island. It is useful as a DF aid on which to home, but is of little use for getting cross-bearings with the Madeira beacon as the two are so close to each other.

MADEIRA GRANDE

Baia da Abra
Situated at the eastern end of the south coast, two miles W of Pta do Barlavento, is Baia da Abra, a delightful little bay tucked in behind the headland known as Pta das Gaivotas. The bottom is sand at the W end, but stone towards the E; depth 11 metres. If anchoring on the stony part it is advisable to buoy the anchor as the fluke

138

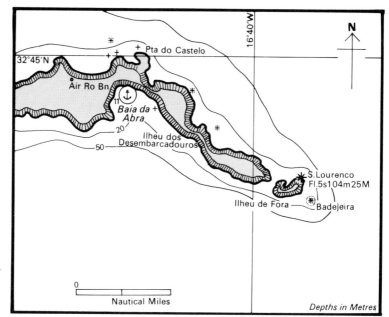

Chart No 17 Baia da Abra,
Madeira archipelago.
Based on Admiralty
Chart No 1831.

may get under a large stone. This is a quiet, deserted anchorage with no habitation ashore. The only building within sight is a small ancient chapel and there is a fossil-bed to the N of the narrow peninsula.

Ribeira Brava
Anchor east of the pier and land there by dinghy. There is good holding in sand. The town has a good market and there is a restaurant.

Funchal
For full details, see Part IV.

Camara de Lobos
This is an exceptionally busy little fishing harbour. Scenically it is very attractive and it achieved fame by having had its portrait painted by Sir Winston Churchill. While it is possible to go alongside the pier in an emergency, this place is really not for yachts.

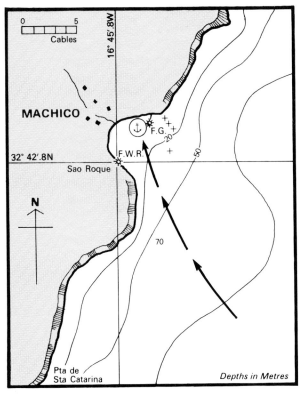

Chart No 18 Machico, Ilha da Madeira
Grande, Madeira archipelago.
Based on Admiralty Chart No 1831.

Machico

Anchor in the bay, near the main (eastern) pier in 5 metres, well sheltered from any wind except between SE and SW. By anchoring near the pier the full strength of the NE wind may be avoided. Do not leave the boat unattended, as much thieving takes place here (this is not general in the islands). If entering at night, difficulty may be found in distinguishing the entrance lights on the pierheads from the mass of town lights in the background. Machico, which was once the capital city of Madeira, is well provided with shops, hotels and restaurants, and there is a very good market for fruit, vegetables and fish. Neither fuel nor water is easily obtainable.

There is an open anchorage off Santa Cruz, 2 miles SW of Machico but there would be little point in lying there when the more sheltered anchorage at Machico is so close at hand.

140

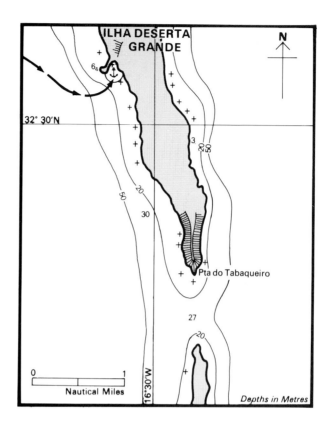

Chart No 19 Ilha Deserta Grande,
Madeira archipelago.
Based on Admiralty
Chart No 1831.

ILHA DESERTA GRANDE

Carga da Lapa (Ilha Deserta Grande)

Deserta Grande is the biggest of the three islands lying to the SE of Madeira. Except for wild goats, seals and seabirds, it is uninhabited. Shooting is prohibited. The anchorage is on the west coast at Carga da Lapa. This is shown on official charts as a small promontory with an offlying islet, but in fact the two have now joined up to form a very useful neck of land, affording shelter from the NE wind. It is normally safe to go ashore, landing on the black sand beach. Immediately south of Carga da Lapa is a cave inhabited by seals; sea birds make some noise day and night. There is a strong local movement to make the island a nature reserve – which may help to conserve the once plentiful wild tomatoes.

Charts		Sailing Directions	
Admiralty	*US*	*Admiralty*	*US*
1831	51261	1	143
1689	51263		

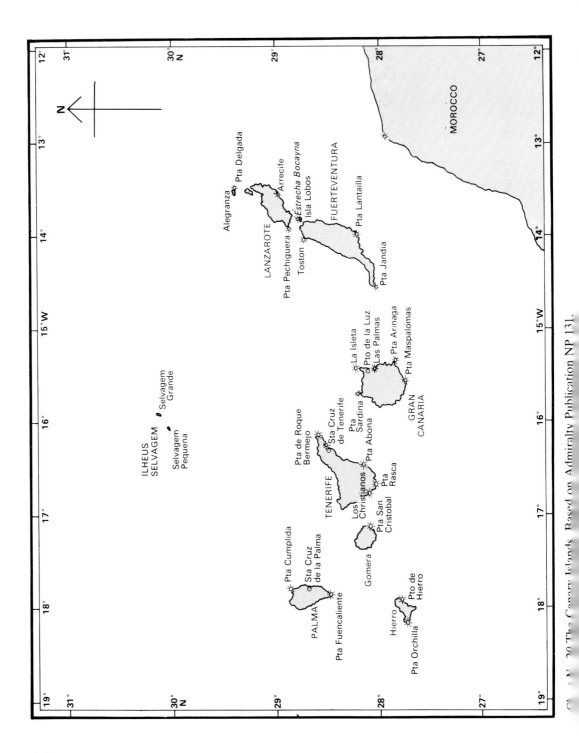

Chart 20 The Canary Islands. Based on Admiralty Publication NP 131.

142

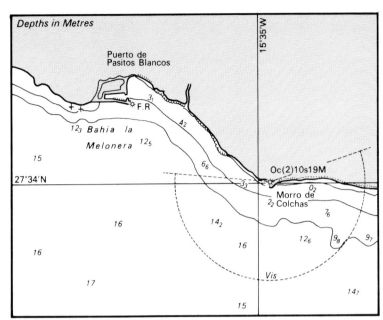

Depths in Metres

Puerto de
Pasitos Blancos

15°35'W

F.R

12_3 *Bahia la*

Melonera 12_5

15

4_2

6_6

27°34'N

Oc(2)10s19M

3_3

0_2
Morro de
2_2 Colchas

7_6

16

14_2

16

12_6

9_8

9_7

16

Vis

17

14_7

15

Chart No 21 Pasito Blanco,
Gran Canaria, Canary
Islands.

PASITO BLANCO

4. THE CANARY ISLANDS

LANZAROTE
Naos Lanzarote is likely to be the first island visited by boats coming from Europe. Go into Naos and secure at the south end of the harbour either on pontoons or at anchor. See Chart Nos 20 and 22.

GRAN CANARIA
Puerto Rico On the south-west coast, this is part of a tourist development and offers a secure berth and a wide range of services. Fuller details appear in Part IV.

Mogan Possibly better than Puerto Rico for services and is more secure against theft if the boat is to be left for any length of time.

Pasito Blanco Chart 21 shows its approximate position; it has an average depth of 3m, with berthing stern-to, a boat hoist, electricity, water and fuel. Used chiefly by those living aboard doing their own work, as security against theft is poor and skilled labour has to be brought in.

143

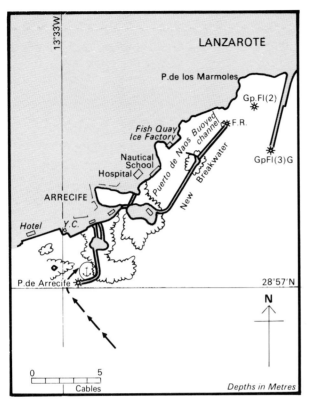

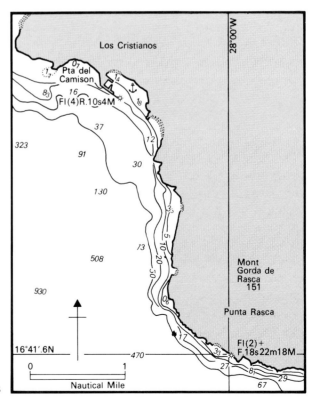

Chart No 22 Arrecife, Lanzarote, Canary Islands. Based on RCC chart.

144   *Chart No 23* Los Cristianos

La Luz   Often loosely referred to as Las Palmas (which is the city nearby). There is a yacht anchorage to the north of the marina. The best engineers in Gran Canaria are in La Luz but for ordinary provisioning (and for convenience) it is probably better to go into one of the ports on the SW coast.

TENERIFE
The capital, Santa Cruz, is also the main port serving freighters and ferries. The Club Nautico does not accept visitors. Yachts may secure in the Darsena Pesqueria, at the north end of the complex. There are no facilities, communications are bad and it is some 5km from town.

On the SW coast, Los Cristianos combines with Playa de las Americas to form a major tourist development. Los Cristianos harbour has good haul out facilities where crews may do their own work, but has limited technical services and is not well protected from the weather. Colon, at Playa de las Americas, is secure in weather terms and has good haul out facilities. See Part IV for details.

LA PALMA
Hitherto the island most favoured by experienced transatlantic sailors. Mooring facilities are now limited and the Club Nautico does not accept visitors.

Charts			*Sailing Directions*	
Admiralty		*US*	*Admiralty*	*US*
1869	1870	51380	1	143
1856	886	51260, 51341		

5. THE CAPE VERDE ISLANDS
The practical advantage of breaking the transatlantic passage in the Cape Verdes is obvious. The distance to e.g. Barbados is under 2000NM compared with 2700NM from the Canaries, and as the islands are well within the trade wind belt a direct course can usually be steered. Cape Verde is attempting to develop its tourist trade. Some provisions are available but major provisioning should be done elsewhere. Porto Grande on São Vincente is well protected (anchor in the far NE corner of Porto Grande bay) and has a boatyard with hauling facilities and diesel and electrical engineers. Portuguese is spoken, with some English and French. Officials, generally both friendly and efficient, visit a yacht on arrival and crew should not go ashore before this visit. Visas do not appear to be necessary for crew living aboard but take passport photographs. Take a 'courtesy' flag – it is obligatory. Watch out for theft.

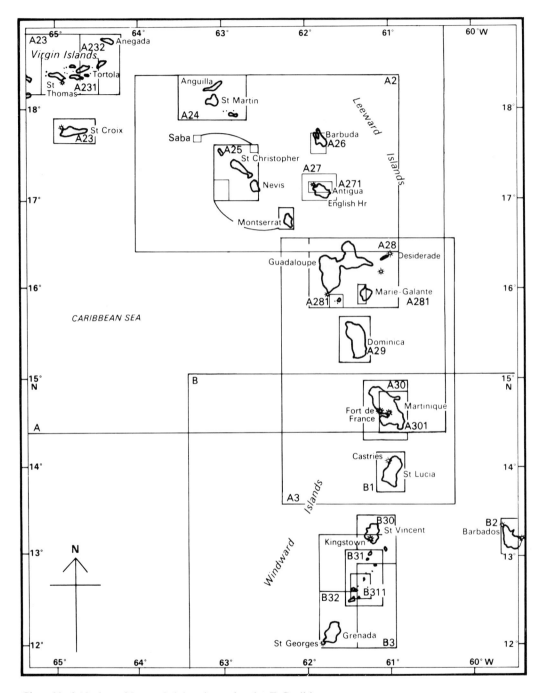

Chart No 24 Index of Imray Iolaire charts for the E Caribbean.

146

6. THE WEST INDIES (LESSER ANTILLES)

General Description

For most people these islands provide the main incentive for a round cruise of the Atlantic Ocean. Situated, as they are, in the trade-wind zone, and within the Tropic of Cancer, their waters afford the world's best sailing conditions.

Although the islands were among Columbus's earliest discoveries, recent research has revealed some very ancient artifacts to prove the existence of much earlier human occupation. The Caribs, who were mainly in possession before the Spaniards took over, are almost extinct except for a few who remain in a small reserve on the island of Dominica. Apart from them, the present-day locals are descendants of the negro slaves who were brought over from Africa to work in the plantations.

Wind and Current

During the normal cruising season, from December to the middle of May, the trade-wind is remarkably constant in strength and direction in this area: in strength, between Force 4 and 7, and in direction between N and E. For this reason the islands all afford a lee on their western coasts and in many cases there are much-frequented anchorages which are quite open to the west, yet perfectly safe.

The North Equatorial Current runs strongly from E to W between the islands.

Navigation and Pilotage

Except for Barbados, which lies to the E of the main archipelago, each island is within sight of its immediate neighbours and navigation can be mostly by eye if you are so minded. Although most of the coasts are steep-to on their west sides, there are reefs in various places, especially in the Tobago Cays in the Grenadines, around the coasts of Antigua, and in the Virgins. Except in a few places, these are not marked by any buoys or beacons; but they are well documented and careful study of both charts and Donald Street's *Cruising Guide* should keep you out of trouble. But remember always that the whole of this area was charted long ago, and errors do exist. Do not cut corners.

All along the coasts you will come upon fishermen's floats, sometimes near the approach to an anchorage or village ashore. These floats, today, may be glass, fibreglass or plastic; white or coloured. But in some cases they may be the old traditional bamboo floats, six or eight inches in diameter and six or eight feet long, and sometimes waterlogged and floating a few inches below the surface. These are a hazard when one is moving under power and a lookout should be stationed at the bow whenever they are met in quantity. Under sail they are less of a menace but can still wrap themselves around a spade or skeg rudder, or a free-turning propeller.

Tobago Cays A coral anchorage, here being shared by *Flicka II* and *Bluebird of Thorne.*

Philip Allen

They are a sound reason for not making night passages under power close inshore.

Despite the strength of the trade-wind, calm patches occur in the lee of many islands and local knowledge is needed to enable one to avoid these. Sometimes the wind is to be found offshore but sometimes it is best to go in close under the land. Do not assume that by following a charter boat you will necessarily hold the breeze; a charter skipper runs to a schedule and uses his engine whenever his speed under sail drops below that which will get him to the next anchorage by happy hour.

Sailing between island and island, you will be on the lee side of the ocean, with a trade-wind and the sea that goes with it, having a fetch of nearly 3,000 miles. Coming from under the protection of a high coastline, life will suddenly become very boisterous. If your wife is sitting on the foredeck doing her nails, or is about to come on deck bearing a tray of drinks, warn her!

Anchorages
While many of the open anchorages afford both shelter from the wind and freedom from rolling, there are others which do not. Generally speaking, a place where charter boats bring up for the night can be relied upon to provide a peaceful night's rest, because charterers just will not tolerate rolling.

148

Approach

The conventional landfall, after a trade-wind crossing of the ocean, is Barbados. If intending to visit Barbados at all it is best to make your landfall there, because it lies well to windward of all the rest of the West Indies. To call later would involve beating into the trade wind. The island is well worth a visit, especially if you need supplies of fresh food after the crossing, because the shops and market are very good, well above the standard of some of the other islands. The open anchorage in Carlisle Bay, while normally safe and comfortable to lie in, does not make for easy landing by dinghy on the beach when there is much swell. The careenage should be avoided except for watering ship or slipping, as there is a violent surge and it is difficult to avoid damage to warps and topsides. Other popular islands on which to make landfall are Martinique and Antigua.

Formalities

Except for the French, Dutch and American islands, most have been granted their independence and nearly every island that was formerly a British possession is now a separate unit, flying its own national colours. For the visiting yacht, this means a lot of different courtesy flags and a lot of formalities, entering and clearing.

In recent times, there has been a great tightening-up of entry and clearance procedures in most of the islands. When you enter, most authorities demand to see clearance papers from your last port of call. Failure to produce these may involve you in being sent back to fetch them. Make a point of obtaining them on departure, and be sure to file them all and not to part with any.

In some islands there is one entry-port only; in others there are several. All places mentioned in Part IV are official entry-ports.

Procedures vary from island to island. In some, the skipper is expected to anchor his vessel and to go ashore alone, to report; in others the boat should be moored or anchored to await the arrival of customs and/or immigration officers. In one or two places vessels are expected to go alongside. Always hoist the Q-flag at sea before entering, and if in doubt about procedure make for an official entry-port and anchor in a conspicuous place. If nobody responds within one hour, the skipper should row himself ashore, taking crew-list, ship's papers, passports and money. In Antigua they say that passports will be impounded until dues are paid. As travellers cheques cannot be cashed without a passport, stalemate could ensue.

Generally speaking the authorities on most of the islands are fair and tolerant in their treatment of yachts. They are well-accustomed to dealing with them, for the numbers are great, but the officials – quite naturally – expect to be taken seriously and do not take kindly to anyone who breaks the rules. The main concern is with immigration, drugs and firearms. The implications of this are that if a crew-member leaves the boat he must have an air-ticket to take him off the island; if any member of the crew has medicinal drugs aboard he must carry a doctor's certificate in support of them; and if there are any firearms aboard they must be declared on arrival (and possibly impounded until departure).

Services

Undoubtedly the best place for a refit is English Harbour, Antigua. The slipway is well-organised, there are good chandleries and in St Johns, the island's capital, all kinds of provisions are to be had. Communications with England, the USA and Canada are good. Services are also available in Barbados, Grenada, Martinique, St Lucia and the Virgins; and at all these places there are good supermarkets.

Currency

In most of the islands the currency is the Eastern Caribbean dollar (EC) whose value is about half that of the US dollar. The exceptions to the rule are Barbados, which has its own dollar roughly equal in value to the EC dollar but not acceptable outside Barbados (sometimes not even the bank will change it although in theory they should); next, the French islands whose currency is the French franc; and last the British and US Virgins, both of which use the US dollar, and the Dutch islands which use the guilder.

Throughout the English-speaking islands the US dollar is acceptable; but watch that you are not asked to pay in US dollars and then given the change, dollar for dollar, in EC. Traveller's cheques are exchangeable almost everywhere and certainly at banks. It is best to carry a universally known cheque such as American Express, or Barclay International. At a bank they ask for passports when cashing travellers cheques.

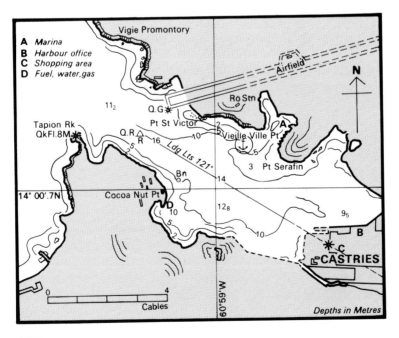

Chart No 25 Castries, St Lucia. Based on Admiralty Chart No 499.

150

Antigua Ordnance Bay, the inner anchorage of English Harbour is a land-locked 'hurricane-hole', in which boats have ridden out the worst of storms in the past.

Eric Hiscock

Charts

There are more charts for this area than can be listed here. To cover basic needs your choice is between twelve American charts, each covering a group of islands, three British Admiralty charts which cover the same area but on a smaller scale, or a selection from the Iolaire series published by Imray (whose charts have been relied on by generations of yachtsmen).

In addition you will wish to have some larger scale charts of certain places. Consult your chart agent when planning your cruise.

We list below the three British charts, and the twelve American ones, together with the respective Sailing Directions. The Iolaire series is listed on page 146.

Charts			Sailing Directions	
Admiralty	*US*		*Admiralty*	*US*
955	25481	25561	71	147
956	25482	25563		
130	25484	25570		
	25485	25601		
	25521	25607, 25613		
	25524	25611		

7. THE BAHAMAS

General Description

The Bahamas form an extensive chain of rocky islands surrounded by coral reefs and sand banks. They extend from approximately 21°N–27°30′N and from 71°W–79°30′W, covering over 5000 square miles. Columbus made his first landing in the New World at San Salvador in 1492.

Although this group lies closest to America, the least dangerous route for cruising through it is from east to west, because for most of the day the sun will be aft and the colours in the water show up best.

Navigation

The shallow waters, coral heads and sand banks, and unpredictable currents and streams all call for what is known locally as 'eyeball navigation'. It cannot be emphasised too strongly that pilotage in these waters is dangerous, and that the greatest care must be exercised. A draft of 6 feet is the absolute maximum, and 5 feet would be safer for local cruising. Official charts are often inaccurate, and official sailing directions may even be misleading in some cases; markers and beacons are few and far between, and may be out of place or missing.

Yachtsman's Guide to the Bahamas by Harry Kline gives good coverage, and *Atlantic Cruise in Wanderer III* by Eric Hiscock, although not a pilotage book, contains much useful information.

Those with most experience advise as follows.

1. Avoid night passages if possible, but if you find yourself at sea at nightfall, heave-to and await daylight.

2. Navigating from east to west, try to confine passages across shoal waters to the forenoon, with the sun at your back so that you can see the submerged coral heads. A man sitting on the spreaders is best able to do this.

3. Avoid inter-island passages from west to east, to windward with the sun in your eyes. Going in this direction, make an ocean passage.

4. Remember that tides and currents may not only be stronger than sailing directions indicate, but may flow in the opposite direction from that which is forecast. Consult local opinion whenever possible, especially among the skippers of fishing and inter-island trading craft.

5. Even Eric Hiscock was not too proud to take a pilot; but if you do so make sure of his credentials, that he knows what he is doing, and is not a smuggler or a hijacker.

Part IV

Port Information

These ports have been selected as being good places for departure, entry, or as ports-of-call. All of them have reasonable services for small craft. No attempt has been made to cover all available harbours, for which local cruising guides exist and should be consulted. The European ports featured are those which, with due caution, may be approached even in the bad weather which may occur in these waters at any time of year. They have been selected for this reason.

Local Time.   The local time, in relation to Greenwich Mean Time, is quoted for each port. In many places, including England, clocks are advanced (usually by one hour) during the summer months. The dates when this operates are decided by the government of each country and may vary from year to year. The times quoted are therefore subject to the appropriate adjustment for local 'summer' time in each place, when applicable.

Note. Co-ordinates given for each port correspond with the lines of latitude and longitude shown on the appropriate port plan. Bearings, where given, are true.

Buoyage.   The IALA A system (red to port, green to starboard) plus cardinals is in use in European waters. The IALA B system (green to port, red to starboard) plus cardinals is in use in American waters. The introduction of the new systems has not been completed.

VHF Frequencies.   On certain VHF channels European frequencies differ from those used in the USA. Channel 16 is common to both.

Definitions.   In the following pages, the word MARINA indicates the existence of custom-built berthing arrangements for yachts, although the quality of accommodation and services may vary widely.

The words YACHT HARBOUR indicate the existence of an area within which yachts may lie, or may be directed to lie.

Caution.   None of the chartlets or port plans in this book should be used for navigation: they are intended only to illustrate the text. In many ports, particularly those of Spain, Portugal and their islands, developments are being made which could render information out of date at any time. The latest official charts, pilot books, and especially Notices to Mariners, should be studied before attempting to enter any harbour for the first time.

The light characteristics shown on charts of the Atlantic islands of Spain and Portugal may not be up to date.

154

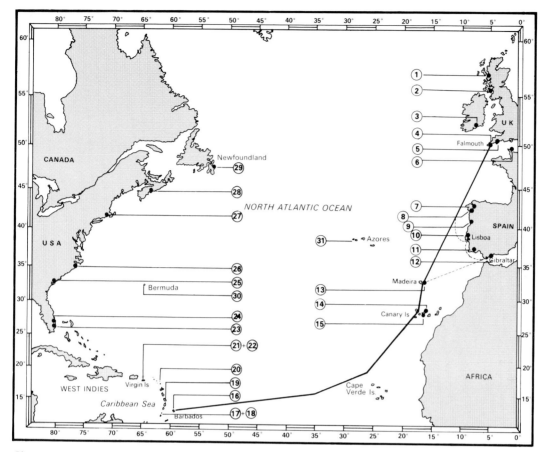

Chart No 26 The North Atlantic, showing the thirty-one ports detailed in Part IV. Based on Admiralty Chart No 2059.

. Oban, Scotland 157
. Campbeltown, Scotland 162
a. Cork Harbour, Republic of Ireland 165
b. Crosshaven, Republic of Ireland 169
. Falmouth, England 172
. Plymouth, England 176
. Cherbourg, France 180
La Coruña, Spain 183
Bayona, Spain 186
Leixões, Portugal 190
Lisboa, Portugal 193
Vilamoura, Portugal 197
Gibraltar 200
Funchal, Madeira 204
Sta. Cruz de la Palma, Canary Is. 208
Puerto Rico, Gran Canaria, Canary Is. 211

16. Bridgetown, Barbados 214
17. St George's, Grenada 219
18. Prickly Bay, Grenada 222
19. Fort de France, Martinique 225
20. English Harbour, Antigua 228
21. St Thomas, US Virgin Is. 232
22. Road Harbour, Br. Virgin Is. 235
23. Miami, Florida, USA 239
24. Fort Lauderdale, Florida, USA 241
25. Charleston, S. Carolina, USA 243
26. Morehead City, N. Carolina, USA 245
27. Newport, Rhode Island, USA 248
28. Halifax, Nova Scotia 252
29. St John's, Newfoundland 256
30. St George's Harbour, Bermuda 261
31. Horta, Faial, Azores 265

155

Spr 4m/13 ft   Nps 2.9m/9 ft 5 in
Currency: £ Sterling   Flag: British (Red Ensign)

Charts	*Admiralty*	*US*
General	2635	—
Approach	2169 & 2387	35280
Port	1790	35274, 35275

General

Oban is one of the main towns, and one of the few official entry-ports on the west coast of Scotland. It is well situated for those arriving after an Atlantic crossing.

Approach

The west coast of Scotland is a rugged coast, protected by chains of large islands. The approach route lies halfway between Barra Head and the north coast of Ireland, afterwards passing along the south side of Mull. Powerful RDF beacons at Barra Head and Eagle Island, off the west coast of Ireland to the south of your course, with a range of 200 miles, can help to fix your position when well offshore. Tory Island beacon (100 mile range) off the NW corner of Ireland can also be useful.

Make for Dubh Artach (56°08′N, 6°38′W), an isolated rock with a light lying 15 miles SW of the Isle of Mull off the entrance to the Firth of Lorne. Pass south of Dubh Artach to keep well clear of shoals and rocks which extend 5 miles off the SW end of Mull.

Proceed ENE, between Mull to the north and Colonsay and the Garvellach Islands to the south, keeping clear of isolated dangers to the NE of the Garvellachs and continue to a position about halfway between Insh Island (off Seil) and the SE coast of Mull, from where you shape course to enter Oban by one of two routes.

Arrival

Southern Entrance
Oban may be entered from the south through Kerrera Sound, a narrow passage between Kerrera and the mainland. When approached from the south it opens up in a NE direction and the light tower on Sgeirean Dubha, just inside the entrance, will be seen.

156

Magnetic variation 8°30′W (1987) decreasing about 10½′ annually.

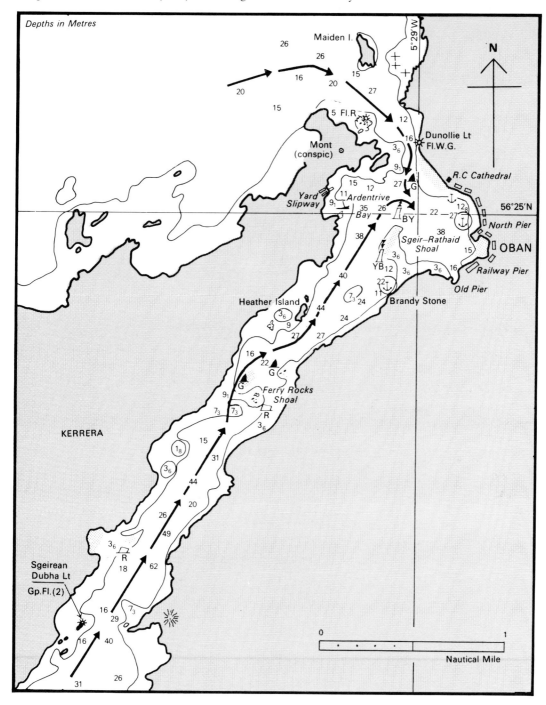

Port Plan 1 Oban, Scotland. The northern and southern entrances are shown arrowed. Based on Admiralty Chart No 1790.

Keep 2 cables off the Kerrera shore to avoid Cutter Rock (dries 2.4m) which lies 1½ cables SW of Sgeirean Dubha and pass 1 cable to the east of Sgeirean Dubha and continue as shown on the plan, passing west of the Ferry Rocks shoal light buoy, east of Heather Island and west of Sgeir Rathaid shoal. Do not turn into Oban Bay until north of this shoal when first entering.

Tidal streams in the Sound run at 1 to 2 knots. The SW stream starts about 1½ hours before H.W. Oban and the NE stream starts about 4½ hours after H.W. Oban.

Northern Entrance

From the position off Insh Island continue to the west of Kerrera, observing the dangers at Bogha Nuadh (3 miles NE of Insh Island) marked by a light-buoy, with Dubh Sgeir islands and shoal 4 cables NE of it.

Pass round the north eastern end of Kerrera to enter Oban Bay at Dunollie Light on the east side of the entrance. Leave Maiden Island at least ½ cable to port and the light beacon off the NE end of Kerrera, ½ cable to starboard. Enter the Bay, giving the Kerrera shore a wide berth but keeping west of the light-buoy marking the Corran Ledge which extends south of Dunollie Light. Beware ferry traffic entering or leaving.

The Flood Tide stream runs north, at 2 knots in the entrance.

Formalities

The Q-flag should be hoisted in the Firth of Lorne. If customs officials do not arrive after you have berthed, they should be contacted by telephone.

Berth

Berthing for yachts, fishing boats and other small craft is likely to be reallocated when construction and modification plans are completed.

1. At present (1987) the best berth for clearing Customs and easy shore going is at the pontoons off Old Pier in the SW corner of Oban Bay.

2. Alternatively the NW face of North Pier may be used, keeping clear of local ferries on the SW face.

3. The Railway Pier may provide suitable berthing at its NE end, clear of the remainder which is used by regular ferries to the Hebrides, but beware shoal water inshore to the east.

All these berths are exposed and uncomfortable in NW winds.

Anchorages

Oban Bay is deep and the holding is poor. It is necessary to go close inshore to find reasonable depths.

1. To the SE of the conspicuous Roman Catholic Cathedral, in about 6 or 7 fathoms.

2. Off (or just to the NW of) the concrete slip on the east shore to the north of North Pier. Do not obstruct ferry traffic approaching North Pier. Anchorage is prohibited between the slip and North Pier.

These anchorages are exposed to winds from NW to SW and it may be necessary to move. Landing by dinghy at concrete slip.

3. Ardentrive Bay on Kerrera. This is the favoured anchorage, and is administered by the Yard there. Go alongside the fuel pontoon, if possible and seek advice on spare moorings or anchoring position. Beware the spit extending NE from the south point of Ardentrive Bay with a wreck on it.

Services

Yacht yards and slipways
Oban Yacht Services at Ardentrive have facilities for slipping and repair work.

Fuel and water
There is normally a fuelling pontoon at Ardentrive for diesel, gasoline and water. Water may also be obtained at Berths 1 and 2. Calor gas in Oban and Ardentrive.

Chandleries, provisions and shops etc.
Oban is a busy tourist centre and is adequately provided with shops of all types, including hardware, fishing tackle, chandleries, supermarkets, banks, post office and laundry. There are also a large number of hotels on the waterfront with restaurants.

Communications
Oban is connected to the British Railways network. There are regular sea connections by ferry to the Hebridean Islands. The nearest main airport is at Glasgow.

Radio
There is a Coastguard Headquarters at Oban which constantly monitors 2182 kHz and VHF Channel 16.

Medical
There are two small hospitals at Oban and adequate medical services.

Poste Restante (General Delivery)
Mail should be addressed to PO, Oban, Scotland and clearly marked 'Hold until . . . (date)'.

Port Facilities table on next page.

159

Oban, Scotland	None	Poor	Fair	Good
Anchorage			●	
Marina		●		
Yacht harbour	●			
Slipway			●	
Yacht yard			●	
Shipwright			●	
Marine engineer			●	
Chandlery			●	
Sailmaker	●			
Rigger	●			
Compass adjuster	●			
Radio engineer				●
Water				●

	None	Poor	Fair	Good
Bunkers				●
LPG				●
Shops			●	
Market	●			
Bonded stores			●	
Banks				●
Duty-free imports			●	
Airport	●			
Post Office				●
Telegraph office				●
Chart depot			●	
Medical services				●

Spr. 3.5m/11 ft   Nps 2.9m/9 ft 5 in
Currency: £ Sterling   Flag: British (Red Ensign)

Charts	*Admiralty*	US
General	2723	35299
Approach	2798 & 2126	36103
Port	1864	36102

General
Campbeltown is the main town on the east side of the Kintyre peninsula and closest to the southern end of the peninsula. It is the only official entry-port in the area and it is well suited for those arriving after an Atlantic crossing.

Approach
The approach lies between the north coast of Ireland and the Island of Islay, the latter being the most southerly major island off the west coast of Scotland. The RDF beacons at Barra Head and Eagle Island will assist in fixing your position for the approach. The Tory Island beacon off the NW corner of Ireland will also be of assistance.

Make for Inishtrahull (55°26′N, 7°14′W), a small island lying 5½ miles NE by E of Malin Head, the most northerly point of Ireland. Proceed E by S towards Rathlin Island, which lies off the north coast of Ireland, and the Mull of Kintyre at the south end of the Kintyre peninsula. At this point you enter the stretch of water between Scotland and the north of Ireland known as the North Channel. At its narrowest point the distance between the Scottish coast and the coast of the north of Ireland is 11 miles. On both sides there are prominent features in excess of 1,200 ft and only in the poorest visibility is the land not apparent. The main aids to navigation are the light with sound signals on Altacarry Head on the north-eastern point of Rathlin Island, and the Mull of Kintyre light on the south-west point of the Kintyre peninsula.

In this area of the North Channel the tide can run at up to 5 knots in some parts, and in adverse wind and tidal conditions races can be created in some areas closest to the land.

Those not acquainted with the area are advised to pass south of Sanda Island, as there are no off-lying dangers until they are past Sanda Light. Incoming vessels should give the Mull of Kintyre a wide berth, especially when strong winds are acting against the tidal direction.

Sanda Island is situated off the south-east shore of the Mull of Kintyre. It is the largest

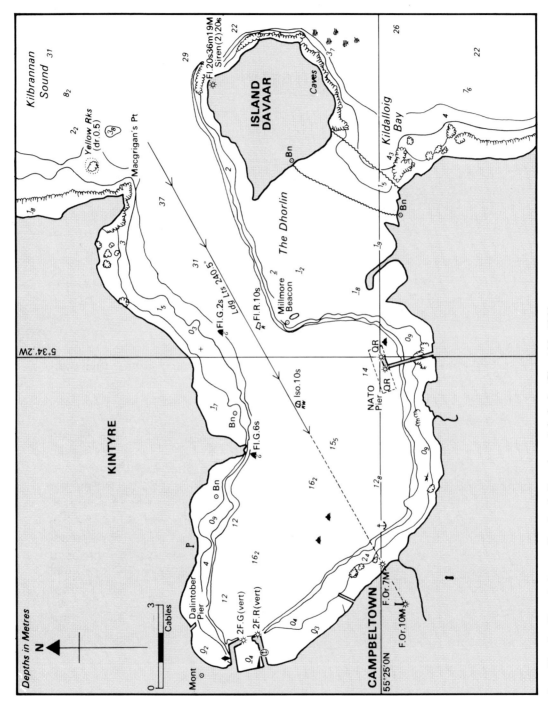

162

Port Plan 2 Campbeltown, Scotland. Based on Admiralty Chart No 1864.

of a group of islets 1½ miles off the shore with depths varying from 5 to 32 fathoms. The Patterson Rock, close to Sanda Island on its east side, is marked by a buoy.

On turning to the north to head for Campbeltown, vessels should give the Patterson Rock a wide berth, leaving it well on the port hand. A close watch should also be kept on the tidal situation in Sanda Sound as the strong south- and westerly-going ebb could draw the vessels back in towards the Sound. The shore is quite clean to the entrance to Campbeltown Loch.

Arrival

Davaar Island is situated to the south east of the entrance to Campbeltown Loch, protecting the entrance near its southern end. Entering Campbeltown Loch from the south, Davaar Island should be left to port. The island is attached to the mainland on its westerly side by a shingle spit which dries at low water and no attempt should be made to enter this way. The entrance is between Davaar Light and Macringan's Point, a distance of about 4 cables. Give Macringan's Point a good offing and pick up the leading lights bearing 240°30′N of Davaar Island. Thereafter keep to the navigation channel to avoid Millbeg Bank and Trench Flat to the north and the Dhorlin and Methe Bank to the south. Two orange leading lights on the south shore indicate the entrance channel between Millbeg Bank and Dhorlin and Methe Banks.

Formalities

The Q flag should be hoisted on approach to Campbeltown Loch. If customs officials do not arrive after you have berthed, they should be contacted by telephone at the Customs House in Campbeltown.

Berth

For clearing customs and easy shore-going, tie up inside the harbour at the new quay and see the harbourmaster. The harbour was dredged in 1983 and some steps have been taken to improve facilities for visiting yachtsmen. The life-boat, fishing boats and small craft use the western side of the main pier and there is generally quite a lot of fishing traffic. The harbour is exposed and uncomfortable in easterly and south-easterly winds.

Anchorages

It is possible to anchor near the harbour entrance for access to the main town. It is more comfortable in northerly winds to anchor to the east of the sailing club, clear of private moorings. In general, the holding is good and shelter is fine from all directions. However, strong winds gust over the hills to the SW when the wind is in that direction.

Services

Yacht yards and slipways

The yard at Campbeltown has a substantial slip and still builds vessels up to large-size fishing boats.

Fuel and water
Fuel is available from the town and water is laid on to the pier.

Chandleries, provisions and shops, etc.
Campbeltown is a busy town and is adequately provided with shops of all types, including hardware, fishing tackle, chandleries, supermarkets, banks, post office and laundry. There are also hotels and restaurants close to the harbour.

Communications
The main public transport from Campbeltown is a regular bus service. Machrihanish Airport is just over 2 miles from the harbour. This is a major NATO base with a civil airport installation at the eastern end of the runway. Frequent daily services operate to Glasgow, linking with the main commuter air services in the British Isles and with the continental services which operate from Scotland to Europe. Private aircraft may also use the airfield.

Radio
The principal Coastguard base for the area is at Greenock and keeps watch over the whole area on VHF Channel 16 and 67. Clyde Radio is the main communications link in the area on VHF Channel 26.

Medical
There is a Health Centre and Cottage Hospital at Campbeltown and an Air Ambulance Service to Glasgow.
Poste Restante (General Delivery)
Mail should be addressed to PO, Campbeltown, Scotland and clearly marked 'Hold until . . . (date).

Alternative Destinations
Troon, 53°33'N 4°41'W, has a marina, customs facilities and is only 2 miles from Prestwick International airport. For details of Troon and of the numerous other cruising facilities offered by the Clyde, consult the Sailing Directions to the Firth of Clyde available from its authors, Clyde Cruising Club Publications Ltd, S.V. 'Carrick', Clyde Street, Glasgow G1 4LN (tel: (41) 552 2183), or through chandlers.

Campbeltown, Scotland	*None*	*Poor*	*Fair*	*Good*
Anchorage				●
Marina	●			
Yacht harbour		●		
Slipway			●	
Yacht yard			●	
Shipwright				●
Marine engineer				●
Chandlery			●	
Sailmaker	●			
Rigger			●	
Compass adjuster	●			
Radio engineer			●	
Water				●

	None	*Poor*	*Fair*	*Good*
Bunkers			●	
LPG			●	
Shops				●
Market	●			
Bonded stores		●		
Banks				●
Duty-free imports	●			
Airport			●	
Post Office				●
Telegraph office			●	
Chart depot			●	
Medical services			●	

Spr 4.11m/13 ft 6 in   Nps 3.25m/10 ft 7 in
Currency: Punt (Irish pound)   Flag: Republic of Ireland

Charts	*Admiralty*	*US*
General	2424	35400
Approach	1765	—
Port	1777	35421

General

On the south coast of Ireland and 60 miles east of Fastnet Rock, Cork Harbour is a spacious natural inlet, and a busy commercial port. Crosshaven on the Owenboy river is on the west side of the entrance; it is the main yachting station and offers good shelter in all weathers. Sir Francis Drake once evaded the Spanish fleet by sailing up the Owenboy River, towards Drake's pool, it is said.

Approach

Landfall marks are an 80 ft high hammer-headed water tower about 1½m east of Roche's Point, and a high chimney with red and white horizontal bands and vertical red lights NE of Corkbeg which shows clearly east of Roche's Point.

Dangers
Pollack Rock with a least depth of 7.6m/25 ft lies 1¾ miles SE of Power Head, which is 3¼ miles to the east of the entrance to Cork harbour. It is marked by a red can buoy (Bell) moored just south of the rock. It is covered by a red sector of Roches Point Light.

 Daunt Rock with a least depth of 3m/10 ft lies 4¾ miles SSW of Roches Point and is marked by a red can buoy, moored 200 feet east of the rock. It is covered by a red sector of Roches Point light. Cork Buoy (pillar RWVS), is moored 1½ miles ESE of the rock. Two rocks, the Cow which always shows, and the Calf which dries 1m/3 ft 3 in extend 200 yards south of Roches Point.

Radio Call Cork Harbour on VHF channel 16 or its working channel 12: Royal Cork Yacht Club Channel M, daylight in season; Valencia Radio channels 16, 23, 67 and 85 for link calls.

Lights

Light, Fog Signal From a white lighthouse on Roche's Point a light is shown (98 ft). This gives red sectors covering Pollack rock, Daunt rock and Dognose bank. Also a fog signal.

166

Magnetic variation 9°00′W (1987) decreasing about 9′ annually.

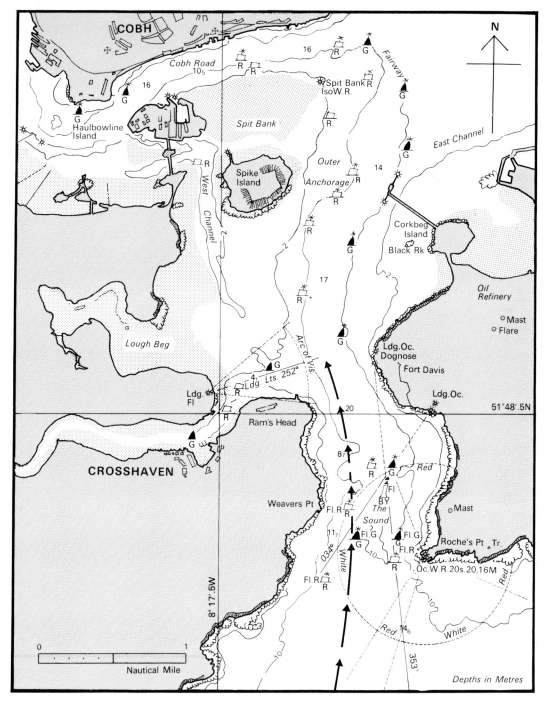

Port Plan 3a Cork Harbour, Republic of Ireland. The SW red sector of the Roche's Point light covers the Daunt Rock. The arrowed track shows the western entrance channel, leaving Harbour Rock and its associated ledges to starboard. Based on Admiralty Chart No 1777.

Leading Lights Two sets of leading lights are shown in the entrance, both being sited below Carlisle fort on the east side. See official chart and light list.

Cork Airport light, about 10 miles north of the entrance to Kinsale Harbour, can sometimes be seen from seaward.

Arrival

Formalities

Hoist Q flag on closing the land. Customs and Immigration may be contacted through the Royal Cork Yacht Club, which is at Crosshaven, or through the Police Station across the road from the Royal Cork Yacht Club.

Buoyage

Port hand buoys are red can with red lights, starboard hand buoys are green conical with green lights. The north Harbour Rock buoy is cardinal north.

Tides

Tidal Streams In the entrance the flood makes at −0540 Cobh (+0055 Dover) and the ebb at +0010 Cobh (−0540 Dover). Spring rate 1 to 1½ kn, but more over Harbour Rock and Turbot bank. It increases to 2 kn between the forts.

Entrance

The entrance to Cork Harbour is between Weaver Point on the west and Roche's Point on the east and is ¾ mile wide. There are two channels divided by Harbour Rock with least depth of 5.6m/18 ft 4 in, both of which are buoyed, and rock ledges extending 200 yards offshore on each side. Yachts must give way to commercial traffic. By day, give Ram's Head, below the western fort, a berth of at least 200 yards before altering course to port to pass close south of the G con buoy (C 1), which marks the east end of the spit dividing the west channel from the Crosshaven channel. Thence leave a red perch to port and then a red can buoy (C4) to port. The channel here is narrow at low water, so keep the buoy close aboard and the SE face of the wooden Currabinny jetty open. The Owenboy river is very shallow on the north side abreast the slipway, and cables cross the river below and above the town quay. It is essential to leave the green buoy C3, abreast the Crosshaven pier, to starboard.

Although there are leading lights and light buoys in the river, do not attempt the entrance to the river at night. Anchor just outside.

Anchorage and Berthing

No good anchorage in the lower river. A berth may usually be found at the Royal Cork Yacht Club or the Crosshaven Boat Yard marinas. A mooring may be available through the boat yard or the club dockmaster. All yellow buoyed moorings in the river between the town quay and the Royal Cork Yacht Club are available from Salve Boatyard, tel: (021) 831145. Drakes Pool, 1½ miles up the river, offers secure anchorage in delightful surroundings, but no facilities.

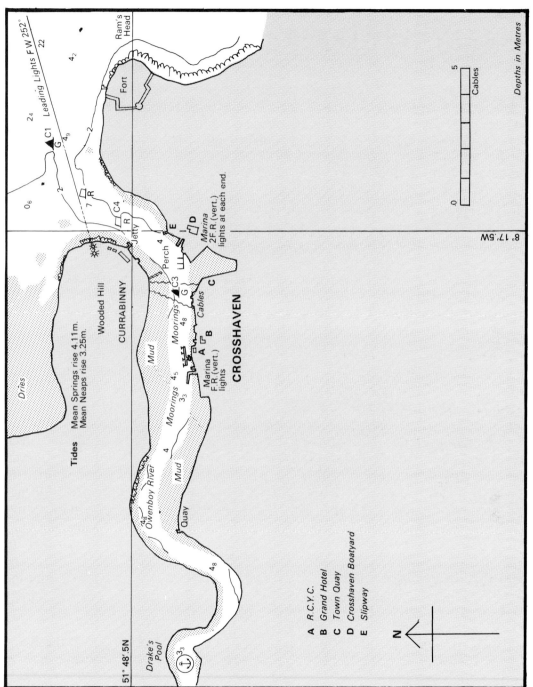

Port Plan 3b Crosshaven, home of the Royal Cork Yacht Club. The anchorage further up the Owenboy river at Drake's Pool is shown, where Sir Francis Drake once evaded a Spanish fleet. Based on Admiralty Chart No 1777.

Services

The Royal Cork Yacht Club is the oldest existing yacht club, having been founded in 1720; it has its clubhouse on the river and a marina where berths can usually be arranged; customs clearance can be arranged through the club. The Crosshaven Boat Yard has a marina, diesel, facilities for hauling out, boat lift, covered and open laying up; all repair work and rigging can be carried out. McWilliams Sailmakers repair and make first class sails. Diesel is also available in the Deep Water marina at East Ferry, on the east side of the harbour; call on channel 37.

Shops
Crosshaven offers all the facilities of the city of Cork, some 12 miles away. Shops in the village, good restaurants nearby, guest house and post office. Supermarket in Carrigaline, 4 miles away. Admiralty chart agents are Union Chandlery, Anderson's Quay, Cork (tel: (021) 271643).

Communications
Cork Airport with flights to the United Kingdom and the continent is only 10 miles distant. Car ferry to Swansea in Wales and to Roscoff in France. Train service to Dublin and to Limerick for Shannon Airport and transatlantic flights. Bus service from Crosshaven to Cork. Taxis available.

Poste Restante (General Delivery)   C/o R Cork YC, Crosshaven, Co Cork, Republic of Ireland, by pre-arrangement with the Secretary/Manager, marked 'to await arrival'. Tel: (021) 831210.

Crosshaven, Republic of Ireland	None	Poor	Fair	Good
Anchorage				●
Marina				●
Yacht harbour				●
Slipway				●
Yacht yard				●
Shipwright				●
Marine engineer				●
Chandlery (at Cork)				●
Sailmaker				●
Rigger				●
Compass adjuster				●
Radio engineer				●
Water				●

	None	Poor	Fair	Good
Bunkers				●
LPG				●
Shops				●
Market	●			
Bonded stores				●
Banks				●
Duty-free imports	●			
Airport				●
Post Office			●	
Telegraph office			●	
Chart depot			●	
Medical services				●

4 Falmouth, England   50°9'.5N 5°4'W   GMT

Spr 5.3m/17 ft 4 in   Nps 4.2m/13 ft 9 in
Currency: £ Sterling   Flag: British (Red Ensign)

Charts	*Admiralty*	*US*
General	2675	36000
Approach	1267	37041
Port	32	37042

General
Falmouth is one of the finest natural harbours in Europe, with much sheltered deep water, and several inlets and creeks. Entrance is safe under all conditions. There are all facilities for fitting out and repairs. Comparatively little commerical traffic although recently mackerel fishing has accounted for increased winter traffic. Falmouth has all the shops and facilities to be expected in a medium sized town.

Approach
After passing the Lizard the only hazard is the Manacle Rocks, clearly marked on the chart and with a buoy to seaward. An easterly wind sets up a bigger sea in the western part of Falmouth Bay than would be expected. If combined with a flood tide this can produce a race between Black Head and Manacles, 6 miles due south and on the direct course to Falmouth. In these conditions, after rounding the Lizard, head towards the Lowland Buoy in approx 50°N 5°W and thence east of the race towards Falmouth. An easterly wind may be lighter south and west of the Lizard than in Falmouth Bay, and the race may continue for some hours after the wind has dropped.

Radio   Call Falmouth Harbour on VHF channel 16.

Entrance
Apart from Black Rock in the centre, the whole entrance is clear and the shore steep-to. Inside there is adequate water for large yachts over the whole of the Roads. The entrance is safe under all conditions, even with a southerly gale and ebb tide a yacht can enter in safety though not in comfort.

171

Magnetic variation 6°05'W (1987) decreasing about 9' annually.

Port Plan 1 Falmouth, England. One of the finest natural harbours in Europe; the arrowed track shows the course to the yacht

Arrival

Formalities

Hoist Q flag at sea and on arrival wait at anchor for Customs and Immigration who will come off with little delay. Alternatively call Falmouth Customs on channel 16, give them your ETA and intended berth.

Berthing

In common with most popular harbours, all the convenient anchorages are now taken up with moorings and there is little suitable anchorage left clear. Bring up where possible and enquire for a mooring. The Royal Cornwall Yacht Club has moorings for short stay visiting yachts and the Harbour Master may have some available.

Some of the yacht yards have short stay moorings and most have them available for yachts wanting to stay for longer periods to use their facilities for fitting out etc. Landing by dinghy at yacht club hard.

Marina   This is up the river on the port hand; final approach to this marina should be made in the dredged channel between the small red can and green conical buoys, with flag topmarks on poles (Q), one hundred yards short of the marina fingers. Access to the inner berths is restricted by an underwater pipeline (well marked) which cuts across the marina, so that below ¾ tide outer berths only are accessible to keelboats.

Visitors' Yacht Haven   Pontoons for 40 visiting yachts are placed off the Customs quay between April and October.

Services

There is all that a long distance cruiser needs including several yacht yards, some capable of carrying out major refitting or repair to large yachts. Most allow the owner and crew to work on their boats both afloat and laid up, so may allow the owner to live on board during the winter but this would have to be arranged. Chandleries, riggers, sailmakers, mechanics, etc all available. Scrubbing posts at Falmouth Marina.

Water and fuel   obtainable from Falmouth Yacht Marina, at the Visitors' Yacht Haven and from a barge which plies the river all seasons.

Communications

Regular rail connections to the rest of the country. The airport at Newquay (30 miles) has daily flights to London.

Poste Restante (General Delivery)   To one of the Banks or Royal Cornwall YC by pre-arrangement; or PO, Falmouth, Cornwall.

Bonded stores   Obtainable by prior arrangement with Monsen A E (Falmouth), tel: (0326) 73581.

Falmouth, England	None	Poor	Fair	Good
Anchorage			●	
Marina			●	
Yacht harbour			●	
Slipway				●
Yacht yard				●
Shipwright				●
Marine engineer				●
Chandlery				●
Sailmaker				●
Rigger				●
Compass adjuster				●
Radio engineer				●
Water				●

	None	Poor	Fair	Good
Bunkers				●
LPG				●
Shops				●
Market	●			
Bonded stores			●	
Banks				●
Duty-free imports	●			
Airport		●		
Post Office				●
Telegraph office				●
Chart depot				●
Medical services				●

174

Spr 5.5m/18 ft   Nps 4.4m/14 ft 5 in
Currency: £ Sterling   Flag: British (Red Ensign)

Charts	*Admiralty*	*US*
General	2675	36000
Approach	1267	37043
Port	30 and 1967	37045

General

Plymouth is one of the best departure points for an Atlantic crossing with excellent facilities for the yachtsmen and good communications. Local yards and suppliers are accustomed to meeting the needs of long distance voyagers of all nationalities. Plymouth is a busy naval, commercial and fishing port but this does not conflict with the yachtsman's needs.

Approach

Plymouth can be approached safely in all weathers. The Eddystone Lighthouse is a conspicuous mark by day or night; Rame Head to the west of the entrance and the Mewstone to the east are prominent features. In clear weather, the high land of Dartmoor to the north east and the radio masts on Staddon Heights on the eastern shore of the Sound assist identification.

Radio   The Queen's Harbourmaster controls the Port and can be consulted at HM Naval Base or through his Assistant at Port Control, The Long Room, Stonehouse, Plymouth (VHF channels 16, 14, 12 and 8).

Entrance

The normal approach is to the west of the detached breakwater, and thence north east across the Sound leaving Drake's Island not less than 400 yards to port. In gales from a southerly quarter, care is needed in the breaking seas to the south west of the detached breakwater.

Bridges Channel   The marks for this narrow channel are a white post, just E of Devils Point, in line with the W side of a large light-coloured house with three prominent chimneys, bearing 332°. In thick weather keep to the normal approach.

Magnetic variation 7°35'W (1988) decreasing about 8' annually.

Depths in Metres

N

50°21'N

4°08.5W

PLYMOUTH
STONEHOUSE
DEVONPORT

River Tamar
Hamoaze

Mayflower Marina
Devils Pt
Barn Pool
Ravenness Pt
Drake's I.
The Bridge
New Grounds
Queen's Ground   Fl.(2)R
Cawsand Bay
Picklecombe Pt
Queen Anne's Battery Marina

The Hoe
Sutton Harbour
Coxside
Cattewater
Turnchapel
Jennycliffe Bay
Staddon Heights Ro.
Staddon Pt
Bovisand Bay
Ro.Masts 126

PLYMOUTH SOUND

Cobbler Channel
Mallard Shoal
Winter Shoal
Asia Pass
Melampus
Drake Channel
Western Channel
Eastern Channel
Breakwater

Dir. Fl.W.R.G.
Dir. Fl.W.R.G.
Dir. Oc. G.
Dir. F. W.R.G.
Dir. W.R.G. Fl.(2)Bl.
Dir. F.W.R.G.

Fl.R
Fl.R
Oc.(2)R
Oc.(2)G
Duke Rk
Y.B   V.Q (9)10s.

Fl.W.R 10s15,12M
+Iso4s.12M
BY

Fl.(2)W.R.G.

349°
332°

A Mashfords
B Port control- Longroom
C R.W.Y.C
D Tidal basin
E Queen Anne's Battery Marina
F RAF Mountbatten
G Millbay Dock

Cables
0   5

Arrival

Formalities

Hoist Q flag off the Eddystone and await Customs on arrival. Nobody should go ashore until pratique has been granted.

Berthing

For larger vessels Millbay Dock (VHF Channels 16, 14 and 12) is appropriate. Temporary berths can usually be obtained on the inner side of Millbay Pier where Customs can board and arrangements can be made to enter the tidal basin.

For yachts up to 65 ft overall and of any draught the Mayflower Marina (VHF Channel 37, position 50°21'.6N 4°10'W) is convenient but it is advisable to make arrangements in advance with the harbourmaster. Tidal streams run strongly in the narrows in the approach to the Marina.

Yachts up to 150 ft overall and up to 15 ft draught can also use Queen Anne's Battery Marina at the entrance to South Harbour (VHF Channel 37, 50°21'.8N 47'.8W).

For yachts up to about 45 ft overall Sutton Harbour (VHF Channels 16, 12 and 37, 50°22'N 48'W) is very convenient for the city centre and is situated in an historic area. All normal facilities required by a yachtsman are available within the harbour. Further information from the Harbour Office, tel: (0725) 664186.

The Royal Western Yacht Club of England on the foreshore to the NE of Drake's Island welcomes visitors and there are temporary moorings available off the club.

Anchorages

Quiet anchorages and good shelter, depending upon wind direction, can be found in and near the Sound; the best being Cawsand Bay to the west of the detached breakwater, Jennycliff Bay beneath the prominent Staddon Heights radio masts, and Barn Pool to the west of Drake's Island (50°21'.3N 4°10'.16W). The Tamar and Lynher Rivers afford interesting but more remote anchorages.

Services

Mashford Brothers Ltd at Cremyll (50°30'N 4°10'.3W) is the largest yacht yard with slip facilities and capacity to service yachts up to 250 tons, 37m long, 7m beam and 3.5m draft. There are numerous smaller yards, details of which are available from the RWYC. Specialised services of all kinds are available as well as many ship's chandlers, supplying all types of marine equipment, charts, stores etc. Most foreign consulates are available in the town. Water and fuel are available at Mayflower Marina, Sutton Harbour and Queen Anne's Battery Marina. Admiralty Chart Agents are Monsen's at The Parade in the Barbican adjoining Sutton Harbour.

Communications

Plymouth enjoys frequent fast trains to London (3½ hours) and good road links to the rest of the country. There is a small commercial airport with connecting services to London and the Continent. There are regular car ferries to Roscoff in France (6 hours) and Santander in Spain (23 hours).

Weather   RAF Mountbatten can supply information on Atlantic weather. A 48-hour forecast is obtainable over the telephone (0752 402534) free of charge; longer term forecast obtained for the North Atlantic on the basis of a personal briefing and negotiated fee.

Poste Restante (General Delivery)   C/o Royal Western YC, The Hoe, Plymouth, by pre-arrangement.

Plymouth, England	None	Poor	Fair	Good
Anchorage				●
Marina				●
Yacht harbour				●
Slipway				●
Yacht yard				●
Shipwright				●
Marine engineer				●
Chandlery				●
Sailmaker				●
Rigger				●
Compass adjuster				●
Radio engineer				●
Water				●

	None	Poor	Fair	Good
Bunkers				●
LPG				●
Shops				●
Market				●
Bonded stores				●
Banks				●
Duty-free imports	●			
Airport				●
Post Office				●
Telegraph office				●
Chart depot				●
Medical services				●

178

6 Cherbourg, France   49°39'N 1°37'.5W   GMT+1

Spr 6.4m/21 ft   Nps 4.8m/15 ft 9 in
Currency: franc   Flag: France

Charts	Admiralty	US
General	2675	36000
Approach	1106	37263
Port	2602	37281

General

Cherbourg is one of the major ports of northern France for both commercial shipping and yachts. It is well sheltered and offers first class services.

Approach

If landfall is made from well to the north, remember that both ebb and flood tides run fast along the northern coast of the Cotentin peninsula, so the fullest allowance should be made for the stream to avoid being swept past the entrances (and even possibly into either the Barfleur or Alderney Race).

The western entrance (Passe de l'Ouest) is straightforward but note that at night there are two sets of leading lights; the directional quick flashing pair between 140° and 142° stand out well enough but the pair on 124°, fixed green and isophase green, can be confused with other harbour and shore lights until close. The eastern entrance (Passe de l'Est) is obstructed on its east side by the drying rock plateau of the Ile Pelée, whose extremities are marked by two unlit beacon towers. At night, an approach along the division line between W and R sectors of the directional light on Fort des Flamands (at the east end of the Petite Rade) is a safe line through the Passe de l'Est.

Entering the Petite Rade near high water, bear in mind that the Jetée des Flamands, the eastern breakwater, covers at high water; its west end is marked by an R can lit buoy which must be left to port.

Radio French coastal stations do not answer an initial call on VHF channel 16 unless it is a Mayday call; call Cherbourg Harbour on VHF channel 21 or 27.

Arrival

Formalities

It is not necessary to report to customs but failure to do so implies a formal declaration that the vessel complies with all the detailed customs and health regulations. All yachts

Magnetic variation 5°30'W (1987) decreasing about 8' annually.

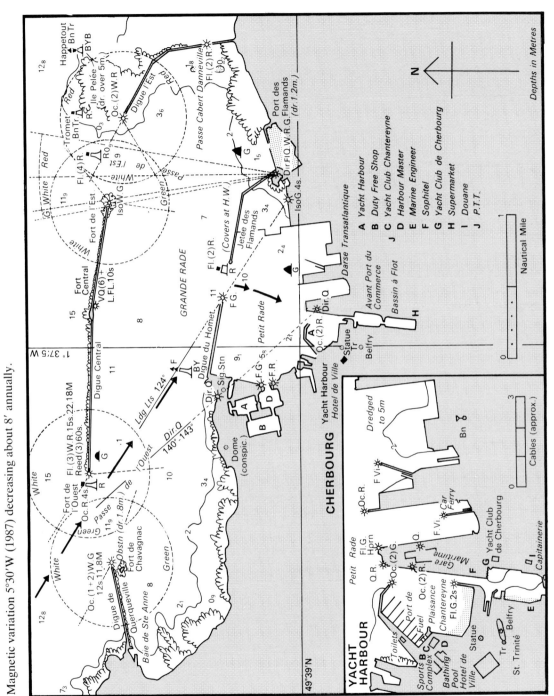

Port Plan 6 Cherbourg, France. The inset shows the yacht harbour in detail. Based on Editor's drawing.

must carry their certificate of registry; it is forbidden for one skipper to hand over to another unless the hand-over is between co-owners or immediate family. Customs often visit yachts, even under way.

Anchorage and Berthing

The small yacht anchorage, about 400m square, is just N of the yacht harbour.

The yacht harbour (Port de Plaisance Chantereyne) is just west of the conspicuous Gare Maritime and it can accommodate yachts of up to 15m LOA, drawing up to 2 metres. Larger yachts continue along the quay to the west of the Gare Maritime into the Avant-Port de Commerce (available at all tides and in any weather), and thence through a swing bridge into the Bassin à flot, whose gate opens HW −2 to HW +1. Berthing in the yacht harbour is of the pontoon and finger berth variety. Berthing can be difficult and sometimes even dangerous in strong winds from NW to NE.

Services

The yacht harbour is accessible at all times and uses VHF Ch 9. The fuelling berth is open between 0800 and 2000 and is accessible 3 hours either side of high water. Electricity (220V 10A), water on the pontoons. Showers, WCs ashore. 30 tonne travelling crane.

Cherbourg, France	None	Poor	Fair	Good
Anchorage		●		
Marina				●
Yacht harbour				●
Slipway				●
Yacht yard				●
Shipwright				●
Marine engineer				●
Chandlery				●
Sailmaker				●
Rigger				●
Compass adjuster				●
Radio engineer				●
Water				●

	None	Poor	Fair	Good
Bunkers				●
LPG				●
Shops				●
Market				●
Bonded stores				●
Banks				●
Duty-free imports	●			
Airport				●
Post Office				●
Telegraph office				●
Chart depot				●
Medical services				●

7 La Coruña, Spain   43°21′.5N   8°23′W   GMT+1

Spr 3.6m/11 ft 9 in   Nps 2.8m/9 ft 1 in
Currency: peseta   Flag: Spain

Charts	*Admiralty*	*US*
Approach	1111	37035
Entrance	1114	37506

General
La Coruña is a major city of Galicia with a significant cultural background. Although the city is mainly interested in commerce the yacht club is well geared to receiving yachts wishing to recuperate after a lengthy passage and its convenience for restocking and crew changes is excellent.

Approach
Leading lights and marks are easily seen. Entrance is easy by night or by day. Even in heavy weather there is little difficulty with the west passage, but the seas break heavily in rough weather across the northern passage, which should then be avoided. Study Admiralty Chart No. 79 (US 37506) carefully.

Arrival

Formalities
Fly Q flag if coming from foreign. The Yacht Club will arrange formalities.

Berths and Anchorages
1. It may be possible to secure to the pontoons off the new yacht club between Dique de Abrigo and Castillo de San Anton, on the promontory just to the south of the club, but this is expensive. The marina is small and usually filled with local boats. Darsena de la Marina is very oily and not recommended.
2. Near new yacht club outside the small marina and between Castillo de San Anton and Dique de Abrigo in 10m/33 ft mud. Several mooring buoys are also available in this area. No harbour dues, well sheltered but oily.
3. In small bay to NW of Punta de Oza in 6m/20 ft sand, good holding, usually clean.
4. Off east end of Playa del Burgo in 2m/6 ft 6 in sand, usually clean. Ferry every half hour to La Coruña.
5. Near fishing fleet in Ensenada de Mera on the eastern side of the bay (not shown on plan). Usually clean. Ferry to La Coruña.

Magnetic variation 7°05′W (1987) decreasing about 8′ annually.

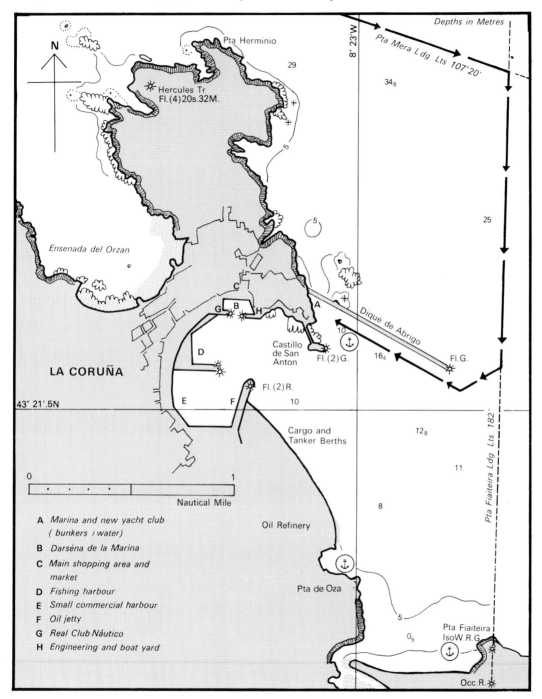

Port Plan 7 La Coruña, Spain. Darséna de la Marina is oily and not recommended for yachts. Based on Admiralty Chart No 79.

Services

Water   From hose at both old and new Yacht clubs. Showers, washing machines at the new Yacht Club.

Diesel   From pumps on quay at new yacht club; beware of depth – about 1m at LWs.

Repairs   Engineer and boat yard at the eastern side of the Darsena.

Shops

Good shopping area and excellent market about 5 mins walk to north of the new Yacht Club. Alternatively take a taxi to the hypermarket.

Poste Restante (General Delivery)   C/o Yacht Club by pre-arrangement.

International airport at Santiago de Compostela one hour.

La Coruña, Spain	None	Poor	Fair	Good
Anchorage				●
Marina		●		
Yacht harbour		●		
Slipway				●
Yacht yard				●
Shipwright				●
Marine engineer				●
Chandlery				●
Sailmaker	●			
Rigger	●			
Compass adjuster	●			
Radio engineer			●	
Water				●

	None	Poor	Fair	Good
Bunkers				●
LPG				●
Shops				●
Market				●
Bonded stores				●
Banks				●
Duty-free imports	●			
Airport				●
Post Office				●
Telegraph office				●
Chart depot				●
Medical services				●

8 Bayona, Spain 42°57′N 9°11′W GMT+1

Spr 3.1m/10 ft Nps 1.4m/4 ft 8 in
Currency: Pesetas Flag: Spain

Charts	*Admiralty*	*US*
Approach	3633	51100
Port	2548	–

General

This port is one of the most popular and useful harbours on this coast for the cruising yachtsman. The approach by the main entrance is easy by night or day. It is well protected except from strong winds with an easterly component, which are rare in summer. An excellent and helpful Yacht Club and the Parador (the hotel converted from the castle of Monte Real) are close. The town is attractive and some 16km from the city of Vigo (population 200,000), where there is a major yacht yard.

Approach from Seaward

When coming from the north inside the Islas Cies, pass Cabo Home and head for Punta Lameda below Monte Ferro, bearing about 160° and crossing the Cabo Estay leading marks. The shortest route then lies through the Canal de le Porta, between Monte Ferro and the easternmost of the three Estelas islands, Estela de Tierra. There is a 0.9m patch in the middle of this channel: keep to the west side. Alternatively, to reach the main entrance of Ensenada of Bayona, pass west of Las Serralleiras and continue south past the Carallones rocks until turning on to the Bayona leading marks Cabezo de San Juan and Panjon, 085°. In both cases go for the mole head on a bearing of not less than 160°.

If entering from the north outside the Islas Cies and in the Canal del Sur, once past the offlying dangers of Islote Boeiro, keep on 145°, crossing the Cabo Estay leading marks until turning on to the Bayona leading marks.

From the south, round Cabo Silleiro (which has rocks awash a mile offshore to the north) and head towards Las Serralleiras until turning onto the Bayona leading marks.

Arrival

Anchorage
Anchor east of the moored yachts, inside the mole. Keep clear of the fairway between the mole head and the inner pier of the fishing harbour.

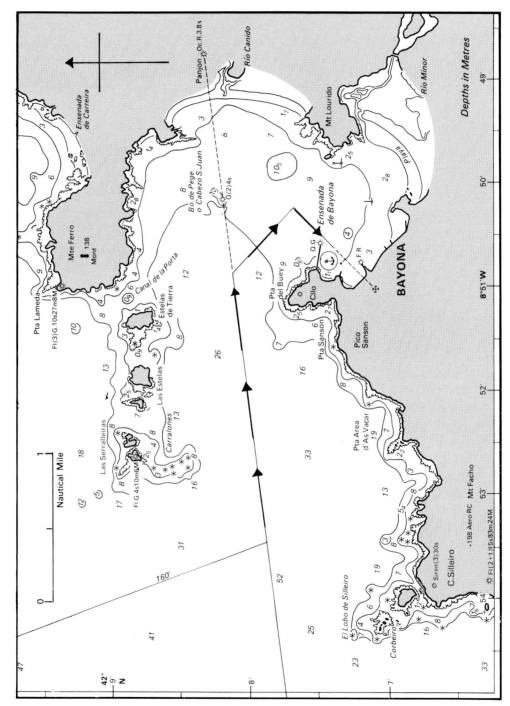

Port Plan 8 Bayona, Spain. Based on Spanish Hydrographic Office Chart No 9241.

Pick up a mooring as directed by the Yacht Club Berthing Master. This must be paid for.

Go alongside the fuel jetty on the south side of the south jetty of the Yacht Club and negotiate a berth in the marina with the berthing master. Costs of moorings and berths are the same.

Formalities
The Yacht Club handles formalities. The Berthing Master will deliver a form which must be completed and returned to the Yacht Club office.

Facilities
Diesel, petrol and water from the Yacht Club. The Yacht Club has a restaurant, bar, showers, beach, repair facilities and a travel lift.

The town has good shopping facilities including a fish market. There are many restaurants of varying quality and expense. There is no Iberia agent.

The Parador has attractive walks, a restaurant and a bar, all open to non-residents.

Any requirement that can not be satisfied in Bayona can probably be met in Vigo.

Communications
Telephone calls with operator assistance can be made in summer from a caravan 100m south of the Yacht Club. Very frequent bus service to Vigo; national and international rail service from Vigo. National airport at Vigo (European connections via Madrid) and international airport at Santiago de Compostela, reached by train or bus.

VHF: Yacht Club 16.

Bayona, Spain	None	Poor	Fair	Good		None	Poor	Fair	Good
Anchorage				●	Bunkers				●
Marina				●	LPG			●	
Yacht harbour				●	Shops				●
Slipway				●	Market (fish)				●
Yacht yard	●				Bonded stores	●			
Shipwright	●				Banks			●	
Marine engineer		●			Duty-free imports	●			
Chandlery		●			Airport	●			
Sailmaker	●				Post Office	●			●
Rigger	●				Telegraph office				●
Compass adjuster	●				Chart depot	●			
Radio engineer	●				Medical services			●	
Water				●					

Leixões, looking N.

9 Leixões, Portugal   41°11'N 8°42'W   GMT

Spr 3.0m/9 ft 10 in   Nps 1.4m/4 ft 8 in
Currency: Escudo   Flag: Portugal

Charts	*Admiralty*	*US*
General	3634	51100, 51120
Approach	3254	–
Port	3254	51109

General
Leixões with its easy entrance is by far the best port of refuge on this stretch of the coast and can be entered in any weather. It appears to be a grim oil, fishing and general commercial port but this impression is countered by the interest of its maritime activity and by the friendliness and helpfulness of the yacht club.

Approach
The oil refinery 1½ miles to the north is a good mark by day or night, reinforced ½ mile south by Leça light. On the south side, the Oporto conglomeration of buildings is an indicator of latitude. The breakwater light may be difficult to identify against the shore lights but from the south of Leixões Leça light on 353° leads through the inner moles.

Entrance
Harbour regulations state that vessels must give the northern breakwater a berth of at least 1 mile but not all fishing boats observe this. There are, however, dangers 200m on the seaward side of this breakwater. During westerly gales the swell at the entrance may be heavy, though this is lost once within the breakwater. Head for the middle of the passage between the two inner moles on about 355°.

Anchorage
The Yacht Club is by the old fishing harbour at the north corner of the main harbour. The anchorage is between the south-west wall of this harbour (here running south east) and the north wall of the breakwater (here running south west); do not anchor close to the south-west wall, which is a navy berth. Although it appears crowded, there are often free moorings available in the old fishing harbour; inquire at the Yacht Club.

Facilities
Water and diesel on the south-western wall of the old fishing harbour. Water available by hose at moorings within the harbour.

  Shipwright and engineering geared to fishing requirements, but practically any repair can be made; best plan is to ask at the Yacht Club.

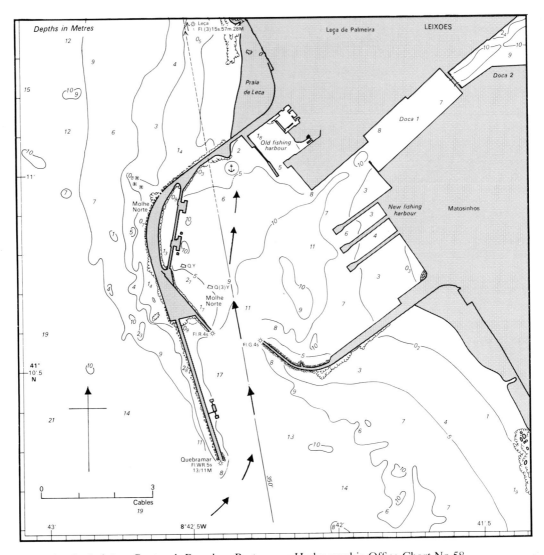

Port Plan 9   Leixões, Portugal. Based on Portuguese Hydrographic Office Chart No 58.

190

Sailmaker in Oporto.

Shops, restaurants and hotels – but not very close and better in Oporto. Market at Matosinhos, best reached by taxi.

Clube Vela Atlantico, close to the Yacht Club, provides meals and showers.

Communications

Post Office. Taxis. Buses (No 44 to Oporto from the back of the Yacht Club). National and International trains from Oporto.

The airport of Oporto has international flights.

VHF: Pilots 16, 14.

Radar Station (provides navigational control) within 18 miles of the station: 12, 16, 11, 13, 20, 68.

Port: 06, 08, 09, 11, 12, 13, 14, 16, 18, 20, 22, 68.

Posto Radionavale Leixões: 16, 11, 13, 19, 60.

Posto Central and Container Terminal: 12, 13.

Servicos Maritimos: 12, 09, 13.

Leixões, Portugal	None	Poor	Fair	Good
Anchorage				●
Marina	●			
Yacht harbour			●	
Slipway			●	
Yacht yard		●		
Shipwright			●	
Marine engineer			●	
Chandlery			●	
Sailmaker	●			
Rigger			●	
Compass adjuster				●
Radio engineer			●	
Water				●

	None	Poor	Fair	Good
Bunkers				●
LPG			●	
Shops			●	
Market			●	
Bonded stores	●			
Banks			●	
Duty-free imports	●			
Airport				●
Post Office				●
Telegraph office				●
Chart depot	●			
Medical services		●		

10 Lisboa, Portugal   38°41'.5N 9°12.5'W   GMT

Spr 3.8m/12 ft 6 in   Nps 3.0m/9 ft 10 in
Currency: Escudo   Flag:Portugal

Charts	*Admiralty*	*US*
General	3635	51140
Approach	3263	51141
Port	3264	51141

General
Lisboa stands out amongst European capitals for its arabic undertones and its history of seafaring towards both the Far East and America. It has a splendid site on the north bank of the Tejo which handles large ships in front of one of its main squares. Though its provision for yachts is not perfect, its shortcomings are compensated by the advantage of coming alongside in such an interesting place.

Approach
The Tejo is entered between Fort São Julião on the north bank and Fort Bugio to the south east. The channel has a least depth of about 8m/26 ft, and given adequate tidal range and weather entrance can be made on a passage from Cascais within a mile of São Julião – see charts. Tidal streams run at 3 knots at springs (more on the ebb after heavy rain) and in strong SW winds (unlikely in summer) there may be rollers on the bar.

Arrival
Formalities
Unless Portuguese formalities have been completed elsewhere, dock first at the Doca de Sto Amaro, which is next to the Capitania (Port Captain) and the Guarda Fiscal, and take ashore the ship's papers, all passports and 200 escudos to obtain the permit necessary for a visiting yacht.

Berthing
If there is room at the Doca de Sto Amaro stay there. Otherwise try:
a) the Doca do Terreiro do Trigo, well upstream beyond Black Horse Square, and run by the Naval Sail Training Organisation and open to foreign yachts. A depth of 2m at the entrance, slightly less at the pontoon at the north-east end, but dries out in the middle at springs. The bottom is very soft mud.

192

Magnetic variation 6°50′W (1987) decreasing about 8′ annually.

A *Torre de Belem*
B *Doca do Bom Successo*
C *Doca de Belem*
D *Doca de Santo Amaro*
E *Praca do Commercio(Black Horse Square)*
F *Doca do Terreiro do Trigo*

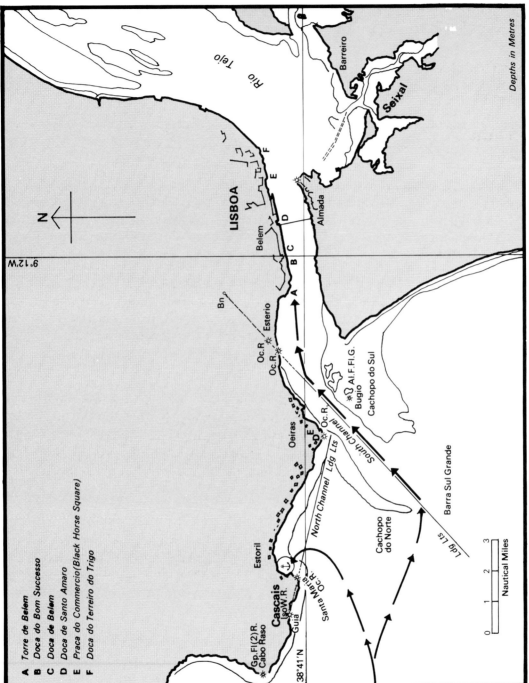

Port Plan 10 Approaches to the River Tejo, showing Cascais, which is open to the south and not safe between mid-September and May. Based on Admiralty Chart No 3263.

193

b) the Doca Bom Successo, just above the Torre de Belém or

c) Doca de Belém, normally only used by Portuguese yachts. Beware the tide setting across the entrances of all these docks. Do not anchor in any of these docks.

Services
Ask dock staff. Diesel, water and laundry can be arranged at or from all docks. Showers at Belém and Trigo. Banking hours are 0830–1200 and 1345–1430.

Charts
Instituto Hidrografico, Rua das Trinas 49 (before 1200), Garrairo, Avenida 24 Julho 2.

Shipwrights, yacht yards and chandleries
Good facilities are available in Lisboa (though two of the yards, Estaleiro Venancio at Amora and Estaleiro Jose Gouveia at Porto Brandao, are both on the south bank of the Tejo) but there are many and they change. Ask harbour staff or enquire at the Associacao Naval de Lisboa at the Doca de Belém.

Communications
Very frequent local trains along the shore to Cascais (30 minutes) via Belém and Estoril.
   Trams and buses to Belém.
   International rail and air services.

Useful addresses
British Consulate: Rua São Domingos a Lapa 37 (Tel: 66 11 91/66 11 22).
Embassy of the USA: Avenida Duque de Loule 39 (Tel: 57 01 02).
British Hospital: Rua Saraiva de Carvalho 49 (Tel: 36 31 61).

Alternative anchorages
Apart from the several anchorages in the Tejo upstream of Lisboa, Cascais, on the Atlantic side of the bar, offers good shelter except from south west to south and deserves its reputation as a holiday resort. Anchor NE of the Yacht Club, towards the bluff east of the first beach.

Lisboa, Portugal	_None_	_Poor_	_Fair_	_Good_
Anchorage		●		
Marina	●			
Yacht harbour			●	
Slipway			●	
Yacht yard				●
Shipwright				●
Marine engineer				●
Chandlery				●
Sailmaker				●
Rigger				●
Compass adjuster				●
Radio engineer				●
Water			●	

	None	_Poor_	_Fair_	_Good_
Bunkers				●
LPG				●
Shops				●
Market				●
Bonded stores				●
Banks				●
Duty-free imports				●
Airport				●
Post Office				●
Telegraph office				●
Chart depot				●
Medical services				●

Spr 3.4m/11 ft 2 in   Nps 2.6m/8 ft 6 in
Currency: Escudo   Flag: Portugal

Charts	*Admiralty*	*US*
General	89	51160
Port	—	—

General

A marina with hotels, villas, golf courses, casino etc., and with berths available for visitors.

   Although break-ins have been known, usually carried out by crews from visiting yachts, they have on the whole been few and far between. Policing is not very effective, but there are plenty of Customs guards about who instil some respect, and this is the best place to leave a yacht in Portugal.

Approach

The marina has been dredged in a lagoon just inside the coastline, and has two 500 metre moles jutting out to seaward, easily identified from seaward by two conspicuous multi-storied hotels, which limit the western end of the Quarteria resort (ex fishing village). There is to be a new lighthouse positioned on top of the control tower, 15 metres high with a range of 20 miles.

Arrival

Formalities
You must bring up at the arrival pontoon and report to Administration Office on arrival, where all formalities may be dealt with. Formalities, particularly Customs, are strict.

Berthing
On arrival you will be allocated a numbered berth by the Administration Office.

Services

Fuel at pontoon adjacent to arrival pontoon. Water, electric power and eventually telephones on all finger berths. Marine chandlery will re-fill gas cylinders. Engineers, electricians, shipwrights and sailmakers at the Marina repair department. Most makes of diesel engines have agents at Faro or Portimao.

Magnetic variation 6°30' (1987), decreasing about 8' annually.

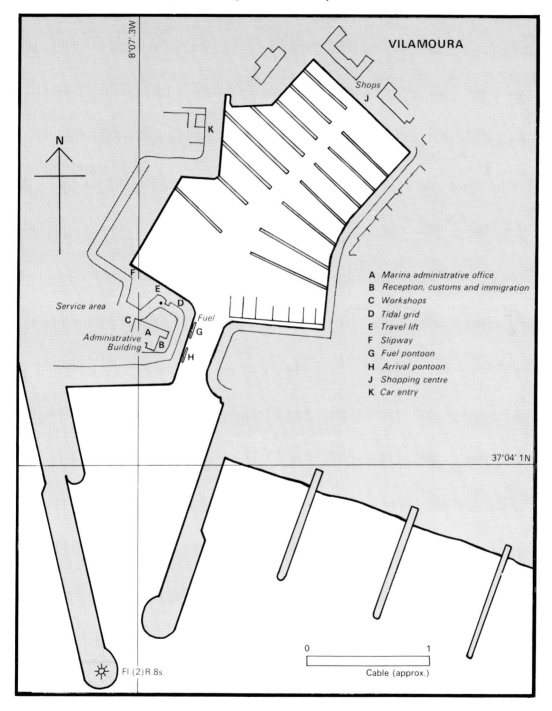

VILAMOURA

Shops

A Marina administrative office
B Reception, customs and immigration
C Workshops
D Tidal grid
E Travel lift
F Slipway
G Fuel pontoon
H Arrival pontoon
J Shopping centre
K Car entry

Service area

Fuel

Administrative
Building

8°07'·3W

37°04'·1N

N

0   1
Cable (approx.)

Fl.(2)R.8s.

Port Plan 11 Vilamoura, Portugal. A good place to leave a yacht in Portugal if need be. Based on plan by
Marina de Vilamoura.

Boatyards

Slipping by 30 ton travel lift, 5 ton mobile crane on tidal grid, on slipway or on beach in SW corner. The grid should only be used for boats drawing less than 2 metres/6 ft 6 in. Yachts can be laid up ashore but there are no undercover facilities.

Shops

Reasonable shopping at the commercial centre on the north side of the marina includes showers, boutiques, cafes, a brand new supermarket, newsagents, launderette, chemist, bank, chandlery etc. These services are increasing daily and there are plans for more shopping centres on the east side of the marina. There is also another supermarket at the Aldeia do Mar five minutes walk; and in Quarteira ten minutes walk along the beach there is a large market, ice and all essentials.

Communications

Car hire firms and taxis from either the commercial centre or the Hotel D Pedro on the east side of the marina. Direct bus service to Lisbon 4½ hours and Faro 40 minutes. Faro international airport 20 minutes by car.

Poste Restante (General Delivery)   C/o Marina by pre-arrangement. Address: Marina Vilamoura, 8125 Quarteira, Algarve, Portugal.

Vilamoura, Portugal	None	Poor	Fair	Good
Anchorage	●			
Marina				●
Yacht harbour	●			
Slipway				●
Yacht yard			●	
Shipwright				●
Marine engineer				●
Chandlery			●	
Sailmaker			●	
Rigger		●		
Compass adjuster	●			
Radio engineer	●			
Water				●

	None	Poor	Fair	Good
Bunkers				●
LPG				●
Shops			●	
Market			●	
Bonded stores	●			
Banks			●	
Duty-free imports				●
Airport				●
Post Office			●	
Telegraph office			●	
Chart depot	●			
Medical services			●	

Spr 1m/3 ft 3 in   Nps 0.7m/2 ft 4 in
Currency: £ Sterling and £ Gib   Flag: British (Red Ensign)

Charts	*Admiralty*	*US*
Approach	142	52041, 52039
Entrance	1448	52043

Approach

Gibraltar Bay has deep water everywhere, except for the offshore reefs on its western side from Pta Carnero to just south of Algeciras, and the area north of the airstrip which is gradually shelving.

Arrival

Formalities

An arriving yacht must first berth at the Customs quay. Any crew member leaving the ship's company, whether to move ashore, to another vessel, or to go abroad, must be reported by the skipper to the police and the crew-list amended accordingly. The same applies to new arrivals. Yacht departures are notified to the marina, which informs the relevant authorities.

Berthing

Temporary anchorage may be found north of the airstrip, where there are also some mooring buoys. This is noisy, inconvenient and exposed to southerly winds. Landing is not possible other than by taking the dinghy round the end of the runway and into the Waterport. To be avoided if possible.

Marina Berths

It is desirable to make advance booking in either Sheppards or Marina Bay. These two marinas are next to one another immediately south of the airstrip.

Services

Fuel oil can be obtained at the Shell jetty alongside the Customs office. Butane gas cylinders can be re-filled at 24 hours' notice at the Shell jetty; tanks over 5 years old require a test certificate. Town water is piped to marina berths.

Magnetic variation 5°20′ (1987) decreasing about 8′ annually.

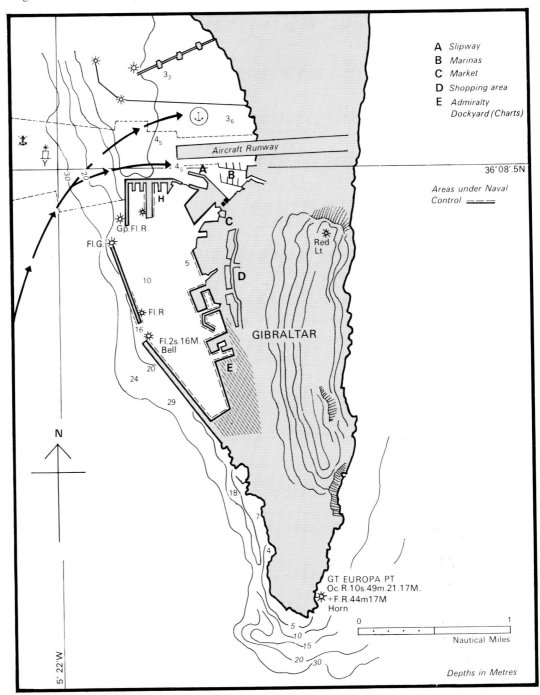

Port Plan 12 Gibraltar. A convenient point for loading bonded stores and obtaining duty-free equipment. Based on Admiralty Chart No 144.

Duty-free imports
Yacht equipment sent from abroad, addressed to the yacht and marked 'In Transit' will be admitted duty-free. Personal imports are subject to duty. Customs procedure in both cases is simple and quick.

Bonded stores
A good selection of bonded stores is available at reasonable prices, and can be delivered aboard. There is usually very little fuss by Customs. Prices are as low or lower in the free port of Ceuta where there are no Customs problems.

Boatyards and repairs
Two are available, used mainly for re-painting and antifouling work. A shipwright, engineer, rigger and sailmaker are available at the marinas. Chandlery in Irish Town and in the marinas.

Shops
Lipton's Supermarket have a branch in Marina Bay and offer a small discount if you buy in bulk and not through an agent; they will deliver to the yacht. There are several good provision shops including some which specialise in Spanish and Mediterranean foods. Gibraltar has a good range of shops covering hardware, clothing, electrical goods, photographic supplies and a great deal of tourist nonsense; Ceuta is competitive. Laundry in the town (no delivery).

Banks
Barclays International and several other banks doing international business. Currency is Sterling, £ Gib being equal to £ Sterling, but cash your Gibraltar money before leaving as it is difficult to dispose of elsewhere.

Chart depot
There is an excellent British Admiralty chart depot within the Admiralty Dockyard. A full stock of British Admiralty charts and books of all kinds is maintained but no unofficial material. Admission is by passport. Do not forget this; the dockyard is a long walk from the marinas.

Communications
Several flights daily to the UK and hourly flights to Tangiers in summer. Ferry to Tangiers.
   Trains and flights to other international destinations from Spain.

Poste Restante (General Delivery)   C/o either of the marinas (by pre-arrangement) or PO.

Gibraltar	None	Poor	Fair	Good
Anchorage		●		
Marina				●
Yacht harbour	●			
Slipway			●	
Yacht yard		●		
Shipwright				●
Marine engineer				●
Chandlery				●
Sailmaker		●		
Rigger			●	
Compass adjuster				●
Radio engineer				●
Water				●

	None	Poor	Fair	Good
Bunkers				●
LPG				●
Shops				●
Market		●		
Bonded stores				●
Banks				●
Duty-free imports				●
Airport				●
Post Office				●
Telegraph office				●
Chart depot				●
Medical services				●

13   Funchal, Madeira   32°37′.5N   16°54′.5W   GMT−1

Spr 2.37m/7 ft 9 in   Nps 1.8m/6 ft
Currency: Escudo   Flag: Portugal

Charts	*Admiralty*	*US*
Approach	1831	51261
Port	1689	51263

General
Funchal is a safe port in normal (i.e. north easterly) weather. In winds from the east or south east the anchorage can be very uncomfortable.

Approach
Funchal Bay has deep water everywhere.

Arrival

Formalities

All authorities are at the marina. Start at the marina office and work through the Capitania, the Guarda Fiscal and the Customs. Crew arrivals and/or departures while the yacht is in harbour must be dealt with and documented through the Police Office.

Clearance Before departure, advise the Capitania. If sailing direct to South America enquire from Blandy's, the shipping agents, whether a bill of health may be needed.

Berthing

Alongside in the marina, which can be crowded. The walls are oily and if you are the inside boat have polythene bags or a plank to protect your fenders.

Landing Landing is made by dinghy at the steps of the Town Quay (Cais da Cidade), or in the yacht harbour. A dinghy left at the Town Quay steps is liable to be damaged.

Services

Shipping Agents
Blandy's are most helpful and co-operative and will go to endless trouble to sort out any problem you may have.

Magnetic Variation 9°30′W (1987) decreasing about 8′ annually.

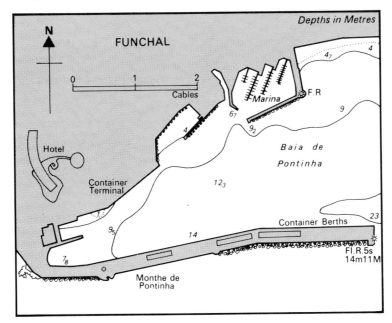

Port Plan 13 Funchal, Madeira. Holding ground is poor. Based ● Admiralty Chart 1689.

Water and Fuel
Both at the marina. LPG cylinders can be refilled at SACOR, Praca do Infante (the roundabout at the end of Main Street on the corner near the Minas Gerais supermarket).

Boatyards and Repairs
There is a small slip inside the mole at the Regional Quay, capable of handling yachts up to 10–11m, about 35 ft OA. There is a large slipway at the Madeira Engineering Co, east of the anchorage next to S Tiago Fort, where any size of yacht can be handled. Charges are high, and a firm quotation should be obtained before slipping.

Senor Franco (skipper of the pilot launch) is the best sailmaker and rigger. Contact Madeira Engineering Co for radio engineer, shipwrights, engineers and electricians.

Compass Adjustment The chief pilot will undertake this by arrangement with the harbourmaster's office. Alternatively, an owner may swing his own compass by using the following bearings:

1. Eastern end of breakwater and eastern end of harbour office are in line on a bearing of true north.

2. From a position east of the breakwater, the lampstandards are in line on a bearing of true west.

Shops
The best street generally is Rua do Aljube, north of the Cathedral, but the Minas Gerais supermarket is nearest to the anchorage and sells provisions of excellent quality. By arrangement, the manager will supply eggs laid within 24 hours of your departure.

Laundry can be arranged via Sr Franco (skipper, pilot launch) or the porter at Madeira Engineering Co.

Market Town Market (Mercado dos Lavxadores) is situated five blocks east of Town Pier. Excellent for fruit, vegetables, and fish; but buy meat from the supermarkets. Take your own plastic bags when shopping in market.

Duty Free Imports
Yacht equipment marked with the boat's name and the words 'In Transit' is theoretically admissible, but in practice there will be delay and difficulty. Small parcels fare better than large ones. GPO has its own Customs office dealing with goods by parcel post.

The best way to get hold of urgently needed items is to ask any member of the crew who may be flying out to join the boat in Funchal to bring them. Otherwise employ an agent or broker (consult Blandy's). A fee will then of course be payable.

Facilities for bonded stores are poor, but can be arranged through Blandy's or Central Supermarket.

Banks
There are several Portuguese banks with international agencies. Most convenient are Banco Espirito Santo and Commercial da Lisboa at the eastern end of the same building as Blandy's, Av do Mar.

Medical
Dr Francis J Zino MB, BS (London) MRCS (Eng) LRCP (London), Avenida do Infante 26.

Communications
The airport has direct flights to London and to Portugal.

Overseas telegrams are best sent via Marconi who have an office in Funchal.

Poste Restante (General Delivery) C/o Blandy's by pre-arrangement.

Funchal	None	Poor	Fair	Good
Anchorage	●			
Marina	●			
Yacht harbour		●		
Slipway			●	
Yacht yard			●	
Shipwright				●
Marine engineer				●
Chandlery	●			
Sailmaker				●
Rigger			●	
Compass adjuster			●	
Radio engineer			●	
Water				●

	None	Poor	Fair	Good
Bunkers				●
LPG				●
Shops				●
Market				●
Bonded stores		●		
Banks				●
Duty-free imports		●		
Airport			●	
Post Office				●
Telegraph office				●
Chart depot	●			
Medical services			●	

14	Los Cristianos	28°02.5′N 16°43′W	GMT
	Puerto de Colon Marina	28°04.5′N 16°44′W	

Spr 2.2m/7ft 3in Nps 1·7m/5ft 7in
Currency: peseta Flag: Spain

Charts	*Admiralty*	*US*
	1869	51260

General

Los Cristianos is easier to approach than Colon, some four miles to the north, and it is probably best to visit Los Cristianos first and reconnoitre Colon from there. Formerly a fishing port and still the terminal for the ferry to Gomera, Los Cristianos has been transformed as a tourist centre with high-rise apartment blocks and good shops and facilities. Colon is a new marina built as part of the larger development of Playa de las Americas; it also has good facilities and better shelter from the south.

Approach

Seen from the northwest to southwest, the three mile long line of high-rise buildings of Los Cristianos is conspicuous. At the extreme southern end is an isolated tower block. Further south there are cliffs with a small development, Palm-Mar, followed by Punta Rasca, a low-lying point with a light tower 50 m high. Steer for the isolated tower block until the harbour entrance has opened to the north. Approaching from the south after rounding Punta Rasca the entrance will be obvious.

If moving round to Colon, beware reefs which lie off the low lying coast between the two ports. The Spanish charts mark groins, there to retain the sand for bathers.

Arrival

On arrival report to the Harbourmaster's office with ship's papers. There is a charge for securing to the mole.

In the event of very bad weather the Harbourmaster is efficient in collecting yachts into the inner harbour where they are rafted together. Because of the surge it is unwise to leave yachts unattended when at anchor or moored to the mole.

In Colon, report at the reception jetty.

Anchorage

The small inner harbour of Los Cristianos is full of local boats. Visiting yachts are expected to anchor bow and stern in the bay (sand 4m but with at least one rock which

Magnetic variation 9°40′W (1987) decreasing about 7′ annually.

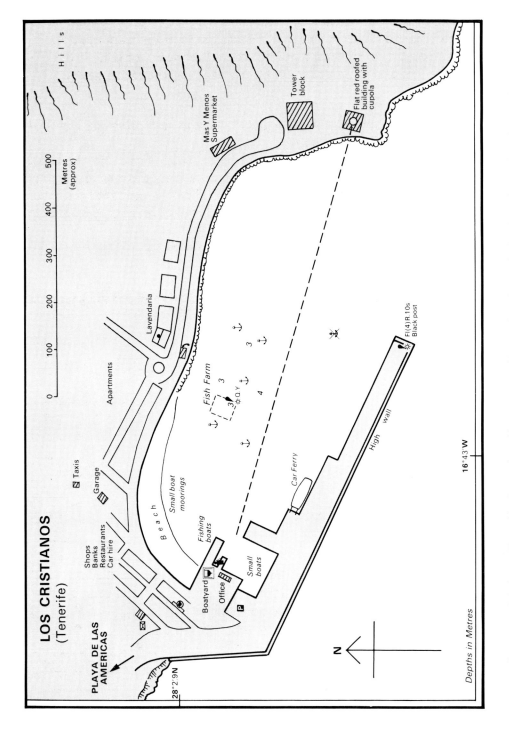

Port Plan 14 Los Cristianos, Tenerife. Reproduced by courtesy of Imray, Laurie, Norie & Wilson from *The Atlantic Islands* by the RCC Pilotage Foundation.

has fouled anchors). It is essential to anchor inshore of a line between the Harbourmaster's Office and a conspicuous low red-roofed building with a pagoda type tower at the SE end of the bay. Anchoring outside this line obstructs the manoeuvring of the ferry and can result in a heavy fine if an instruction to move is not obeyed.

Yachts may also moor or raft along the outer end of the harbour mole if there is space. If so, beware of surge from the swell and the wash of the incoming ferry.

Services

Fuel and water berth by Harbourmaster's Office. Good warps and springs are essential to counteract the heavy surge when alongside.

A Chandler/iron-monger with a fairly comprehensive stock is located in the street between Harbour office and Post Office. Engineering work can be arranged.

With the cheapest travel lift in the islands and a large DIY boat yard, the number of boats hauled out at Los Cristianos, often in preparation for 'the crossing', has recently increased dramatically.

Colon has water and electricity on the pontoons and a fuelling berth.

Communications

Car hire. Buses to Santa Cruz. The main airport of the island, which has international connections, is Tenerife Sur, about ten miles from the town.

Los Cristianos	None	Poor	Fair	Good
Anchorage			●	
Marina	●			
Yacht harbour	●			
Slipway (travel lift)				●
Yacht yard (DIY)				●
Shipwright			●	
Marine engineer			●	
Chandlery			●	
Sailmaker			●	
Rigger	●			
Compass adjuster	●			
Radio engineer	●			
Water				●

	None	Poor	Fair	Good
Bunkers				●
LPG (Camping Gaz)			●	
Shops				●
Market				●
Bonded stores	●			
Banks				●
Duty-free imports		●		
Airport				●
Post Office			●	
Telegraph office			●	
Chart depot	●			
Medical services				●

Spr 2.3m/7 ft 6 in   Nps 1.7m/5 ft 6 in
Currency: peseta   Flag: Spain

Charts	*Admiralty*	*US*
Approach	1869	51260
Port	—	—

Approach

The location of the two harbours is clear from the conspicuous apartment blocks on the hillside behind them. There are no dangers in the approach, although squalls in the lee of the land should be expected.

Anchorage

There is anchorage outside the harbours. Enter the eastern or commercial harbour and secure stern to the wall to starboard immediately beyond the shipyard to obtain maximum protection and seclusion. Pontoons are in course of installation throughout the harbour. The holding ground is good. The harbour office can be contacted on Channel 9 VHF between 0800 and 1800. Do not go into the western harbour except for fuel.

Formalities

Fly flag Q and expect a call from the authorities. The harbour master's office, to which mooring dues are payable, is at the head of the pier forming the western harbour. Berths in this harbour are normally available only to local boats.

Services

The shipyard (with a travel lift) in the east harbour will undertake work on yachts and has a good reputation. Fuel and water are available from a pontoon close to the harbour master's office in the west harbour.

The banks and the post office are situated across the gardens near the beach, where there is a small shopping centre. Here self-drive hire cars may be hired. There is a much larger shopping centre ten minutes walk inland from the beach, and day-to-day provisioning can be conveniently done. However, provisioning for an Atlantic voyage is better and more cheaply carried out at the supermarket in Arcinagin, 2 miles or so south of Puerto Rico. This may be reached by frequent and cheap bus.

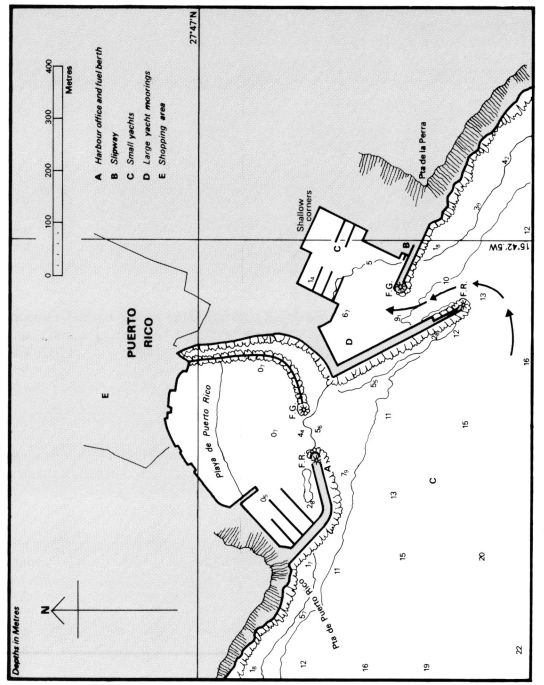

Port Plan 15 Puerto Rico, Gran Canaria. Cleaner than Puerto de la Luz (Las Palmas). Plan courtesy Imray, Laurie, Norie & Wilson Ltd.

211

Communications

The airport is about 25 miles away, but can be reached by the bus, or more easily by (expensive) hired taxi.

Yachts can be left safely in Puerto Rico in the care of Mr Ron Boot who lives in *Wellington*, flying the British flag and moored in the eastern harbour. He can be contacted by writing to him at Correos Puerto Rico, Gran Canaria, Canary Islands.

Puerto Rico, Gran Canaria	None	Poor	Fair	Good		None	Poor	Fair	Good
Anchorage		●			Bunkers				●
Marina		●			LPG				●
Yacht harbour				●	Shops			●	
Slipway				●	Market	●			
Yacht yard				●	Bonded stores	●			
Shipwright				●	Banks				●
Marine engineer				●	Duty-free imports		●		
Chandlery			●		Airport			●	
Sailmaker	●				Post Office				●
Rigger			●		Telegraph office				●
Compass adjuster	●				Chart depot		●		
Radio engineer	●				Medical services			●	
Water				●					

212

16   Bridgetown, Barbados   13°05′N   59°37′W   GMT−4

Spr 0.78m/2 ft 6 in   Nps 0.66m/2 ft
Currency: Barbados dollar   Flag: Barbados

Charts	*Admiralty*	*US*
Approach	2485	25485
Port	502	25485

Approach

Barbados differs from most West Indian islands in that it is low lying with only one high point, Mount Misery 1069 ft (329m). Transatlantic arrivals can best approach via the southern end of the island. The SE coast consists of cliffs about 50 to 60 feet high with flat country behind. Ragged Point Lighthouse stands on the cliff edge about 1 mile NW from Kitridge Point which is the most easterly headland, South Point Light stands at the most southerly end of the island. Lights on higher ground inland may be visible before Ragged Point or South Point lights are raised. Seawell airport lies about 2½ miles NE from South Point; its lights are conspicuous and there is an aero beacon which is convenient for homing. The SE coast has a reef extending from 1 to 2 miles offshore for its whole length. Keep to seaward of the coral ridge with depths of 12–18m/40–60 ft which runs from Kitridge Point to South Point.

A large bank, The Shallows, with a least depth of 60 metres/200 feet lies about 4 miles SE of South Point. This area can be very rough when a westerly swell meets an east-going current and must be avoided. Needham Point marks the southern extremity of Carlisle Bay; on it stands the Barbados Hilton Hotel and a sectored light on a red mast.

Arrival

Formalities
The formalities are particularly tedious and an attempt to buck them could be troublesome.

Arrival
Yachts must clear Customs and Immigration in Deep Water Harbour. Clearance can be obtained any day of the week but only between 0600 and 2200 hrs. On approach, yachts should call Bridge Town Harbour Signal Station (c/s 8PB) on Channel 12 for clearance to enter Deep Water Harbour or, if out of hours, to anchor at the approved holding area, within 500m of a point 750m south of the Careenage Molehead. In the latter case, yachts should enter Deep Water Harbour as soon as possible after 0600 hrs.

On entering Deep Water Harbour, fly a Q flag and keep Channel 12 open.

Magnetic variation 13°55′W (1987) increasing about 7′ annually.

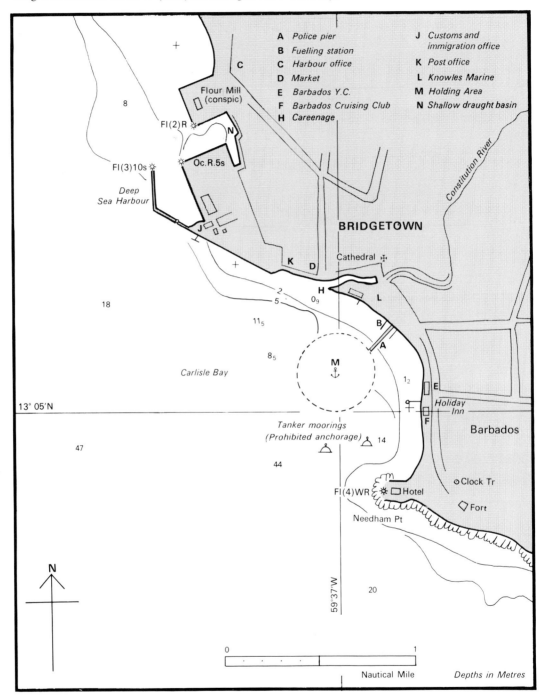

A	Police pier	J	Customs and immigration office
B	Fuelling station	K	Post office
C	Harbour office	L	Knowles Marine
D	Market	M	Holding Area
E	Barbados Y.C.	N	Shallow draught basin
F	Barbados Cruising Club		
H	Careenage		

Port Plan 16 Bridgetown, Barbados. An open anchorage on the lee side of the island. Safe, but landing by dinghy through the surf can be wet and exciting on some days. Based on Admiralty Chart No 502.

214

Besides the usual papers, the regulations say that clearance from the previous port and a health report are required.

Current charges are: Customs: BDS$25 on arrival and departure; Light dues: BDS$1 up to 50 tonnes.

Departure

To clear out, the yacht must go to Deep Water Harbour. The Port Authority's clearance has to be obtained (this includes paying harbour dues) and taken to Customs for their clearance. A copy of the crew list and all passports have to be taken to the Emigration Officer. Clearance is valid for 24 hours only and the yacht must leave Deep Water Bay directly to sea towards her next port of call. A yacht leaving on a Saturday or Sunday must obtain Port Authority clearance by 2100 hrs on the Friday.

A crew member leaving a yacht must be taken to Emigration by the master; if transferring to another yacht, both masters must be present.

Anchoring

After clearance yachts are requested to anchor in an area north of the band stand and in the vicinity of the Esso jetty.

Berthing

Alongside in the Careenage, with the permission of the Port Authority. The Careenage suffers from bad surge which can damage lines, fendoffs and even topsides unless great care is taken.

Cruising

Customs clearance is required to anchor and to cruise along the coast. Take this up preferably on arrival or through the Coast Guard on Channel 16.

Dues

Many charges are made including one for anchoring along the coast – in 1987 this was $7.20 for an indefinite period. All dues are subject to change. Inquire at the Port Authority.

Landing

At Bridgetown landing is possible on the beach north of the Holiday Inn, at the Barbados YC or south at the Barbados Cruising Club. In a westerly swell the surf can be hazardous and capsize likely. Do not use an outboard, lash all loose gear, go in a swim suit with clothes in a watertight bag. Alternatively land at the fuel jetty, the floating pontoon to the north or Knowles Marine jetty; although there may be swell there is no surf.

Services

Water Obtainable by pipeline in the Careenage which is also conveniently situated for shops in Bridgetown. If possible lie alongside a lighter to minimise the effect of surge. Water is also available in the shallow draught basin of the commercial harbour.

Fuel Can be obtained at a clearly marked jetty near to the Police Pier or in the shallow draught basin at the commercial harbour. LPG at the Texaco tank farm north of Deep Water Harbour or Knowles Marine.

Bonded Stores Available for vessels of 25 tons register and above. The discretion formerly used in favour of small yachts is no longer shown.

Ice Can be obtained from Knowles Marine, which also provides showers. Has a 24-hour watch on Channel 16 (c/s 8PKM).

Shops
All types of shops with a greater choice of merchandise than can be found in the other islands. There is a good market, but it is situated on the 'wrong' side of town, remote from the anchorage. When anchored out in Carlisle Bay it may be best for daily shopping to use the dinghy with outboard engine, leaving it in the Careenage where it should be locked.

Medical Services
A small private hospital, The Diagnostic Clinic, is situated within walking distance of Barbados YC.
    There is a large modern hospital further inland but within the city area.

Information
Both yacht clubs will be found to be very helpful when information is needed. Take local advice before employing itinerant labour.

Currency

The Barbados dollar is worth roughly half that of the US dollar. Change all your Barbados dollars before leaving the island as they are difficult to exchange elsewhere.

Communication
International air services to Europe and the Americas, and local air services to Eastern Caribbean islands. Cruise liners constantly call and anchor off Bridgetown. Taxicabs are plentiful and charges reasonable but they vanish as soon as a cruising liner drops anchor.

Poste Restante (General Delivery)   C/o Barbados YC or Barbados CC, or c/o GPO by pre-arrangement.

Bridgetown, Barbados	None	Poor	Fair	Good
Anchorage				●
Marina	●			
Yacht harbour	●			
Slipway			●	
Yacht yard			●	
Shipwright				●
Marine engineer				●
Chandlery			●	
Sailmaker	●			
Rigger	●			
Compass adjuster				●
Radio engineer				●
Water				●

	None	Poor	Fair	Good
Bunkers				●
LPG			●	
Shops				●
Market				●
Bonded stores		●		
Banks				●
Duty-free imports				●
Airport				●
Post Office				●
Telegraph office				●
Chart depot		●		
Medical services			●	

Spr 0.58m/2 ft   Nps 0.43m/1 ft 6 in
Currency EC dollar   Flag: Grenada

Charts	*Admiralty*	*US*
Approach	2821	25481
Port	2830	25481

General

Grenada is the most southerly of the Windward Group of islands. Since October 1983, when there was an abrupt change of government, restrictions on visiting yachts have been relaxed. The hurricane holes and other anchorages at the south end of the island are now available and a yacht may stay for up to 4 months. Grenada has changed to the US buoyage system i.e. 'right red returning', IALA B.

Approach

Entry is straightforward and British Admiralty chart No 2830 gives all necessary information. The fairway buoys lying west of Fort George Point mark the deep water channel, but a yacht may sail over the Three Fathom Banks provided she keeps well clear of the shallow shelf extending from the shore west of Islander Hotel.

Arrival

Formalities
Grenada Yacht Services will arrange for Customs and Immigration to grant pratique. Entry is only allowed here or at Prickly Bay.

Berthing
The alternatives are (i) to anchor at the head of the Careenage; or (ii) to enter the lagoon and find a berth in the marina, or drop anchor. The entrance to the lagoon is well marked by posts, but it is very narrow and is best negotiated under power.

Services

Most services are available here, although most people seem to prefer to visit Prickly Bay when having the boat slipped or repaired. The airport provides inter-island flights to connect with international services from Barbados and elsewhere.

Port facilities table on p. 220

Magnetic variation 12°35′W (1987) increasing about 8′ annually.

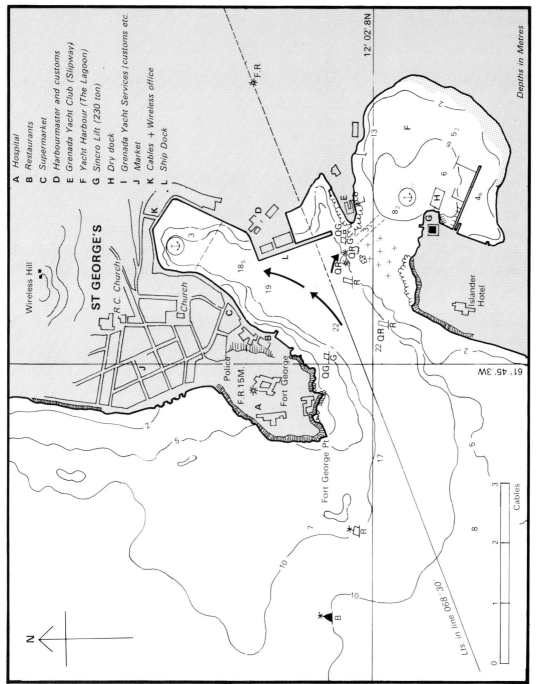

ST GEORGE'S

A Hospital
B Restaurants
C Supermarket
D Harbourmaster and customs
E Grenada Yacht Club (Slipway)
F Yacht Harbour (The Lagoon)
G Sincro Lift (230 ton)
H Dry dock
I Grenada Yacht Services / customs etc.
J Market
K Cables + Wireless office
L Ship Dock

Depths in Metres

Port Plan 17 St George's. Grenada. A safe, landlocked port affording either anchorage or a marina berth. Good shopping and picturesque surroundings. Based on Admiralty Chart No 2830.

St George's, Grenada	None	Poor	Fair	Good
Anchorage				●
Marina			●	
Yacht harbour			●	
Slipway				●
Yacht yard			●	
Shipwright				●
Marine engineer			●	
Chandlery			●	
Sailmaker	●			
Rigger	●			
Compass adjuster	●			
Radio engineer				●
Water			●	

	None	Poor	Fair	Good
Bunkers				●
LPG				●
Shops				●
Market				●
Bonded stores			●	
Banks				●
Duty-free imports		●		
Airport			●	
Post Office				●
Telegraph office				●
Chart depot	●			
Medical services			●	

220

Spr 0.58m/2 ft   Nps 0.43m/1 ft 6 in
Currency EC dollar   Flag: Grenada

Charts	*Admiralty*	*US*
Approach	2821	25481
Port	2821	25481

General

This is a popular place with all who have used it, and it offers good services combined with attractive surroundings. It is an official port of entry for Grenada.

Approach

The entrance presents no difficulty provided the shoal which lies north of Prickly Point and west of Spice Island Boatyard is avoided.

Arrival

Formalities

Fly Q flag and await customs, or ask for them. Entry to Grenada is only allowed here or at St George's.

Anchorage

Go right up into the NE corner, off the Calabash Hotel.

Services

There is no telegraph office and there are no banks here, but those apart, most of what you are likely to need will be found. Spice Island Boatyard is good for all normal repair work.

Port Plan 18 on next page

Magnetic variation 12°35'W (1987) increasing about 8' annually.

Buoys should not be relied on.
Most are lighted.

N

Nautical Miles
0   1   2

61°45'.8W

ST GEORGE'S

GRENADA

F.R15M

St. George's Harbour
The Lagoon

Ldg.F.R.

Whale Ho.

Annas Sh.

Lloyd Sh.   22

Grande Anse

Deverell Sh.   20

Point Sh.   1₄

Long Pt   12

5

9

Pte Saline
Q(9)15s

11

Airport Runway

Race Course

11

Glover I.   5

7₃

11

Mt Hartman Pt

Clarkes Court B.

Pt of Fort Jeudy

C

0

11

Hog I.

2

10

B

A

Prickly Pt

Prickly Bay

Tara I.

2   The Porpoises

7

7₃

D

Prohibited Area

A Spice Island Charters Ltd
   (Yacht port of entry, customs, small slipway.)
B Daytime anchorage only
C Restricted area
D Anchorage prohibited
   Firing Range

12° 00'N

Depths in Metres

Port Plan 18 Prickly Bay, Grenada. For slipping or repairs in Grenada most people come here rather than St Georges. Based on Admiralty

Prickly Bay, Grenada	None	Poor	Fair	Good
Anchorage				●
Marina			●	
Yacht harbour				●
Slipway			●	
Yacht yard				●
Shipwright			●	
Marine engineer			●	
Chandlery				●
Sailmaker				●
Rigger			●	
Compass adjuster	●			
Radio engineer				●
Water			●	

	None	Poor	Fair	Good
Bunkers			●	
LPG				●
Shops				●
Market				●
Bonded stores			●	
Banks	●			
Duty-free imports		●		
Airport			●	
Post Office			●	
Telegraph office	●			
Chart depot			●	
Medical services			●	

Spr 0.77m/2 ft 6 in   Nps 0.65m/2 ft
Currency: French franc   Flag: France

Charts	Admiralty	US
Approach	371	25524
Port	494	25527

Approach

Mt Pelée at the northern end of the island rises to 1350m (4500 ft). There are no unmarked hazards in Fort de France Bay. The headland west of the anchorage is Pte des Negres, on which there is an aero beacon and a light. The east coast of the island is rocky and dangerous. IALA B buoyage system plus cardinal marks have been introduced.

Arrival

Formalities
Yachtsmen are advised and indeed it is correct to fly the Q flag, although a launch will almost certainly come steaming past, and you will be hailed and told to take it down and to report to the office ashore. Ship's papers and all crew's passports will be needed and some lengthy form-filling will be called for. But it will all be conducted in a friendly and civilised way. You will be required on leaving Martinique to clear out of the same port in which you made your entry but you do not have to produce the yacht for this formality. An overland visit by the skipper with the ship's papers and passports is all that is required.

Anchorage
Mouillage des Flamands is well protected from all but SE, and forms an extensive anchorage, though always crowded. Some care is needed in choosing a berth because many of the boats are on permanent moorings, and for obvious reasons it is best not to anchor too near to them. If you anchor within the buoyed channels to the ferry quays, you will be moved. It is best not to leave a dinghy unattended too long at the small and crowded landing place, because some thieving takes place.
   The Yacht Club de la Martinique is situated in the well sheltered military and commercial port on the eastern side of the Fort St Louis peninsula; vacant berths at the Club pontoon are extremely rare. There is also a small private and very full marina at Pointe du Bout on the south side of Fort de France Bay, with a

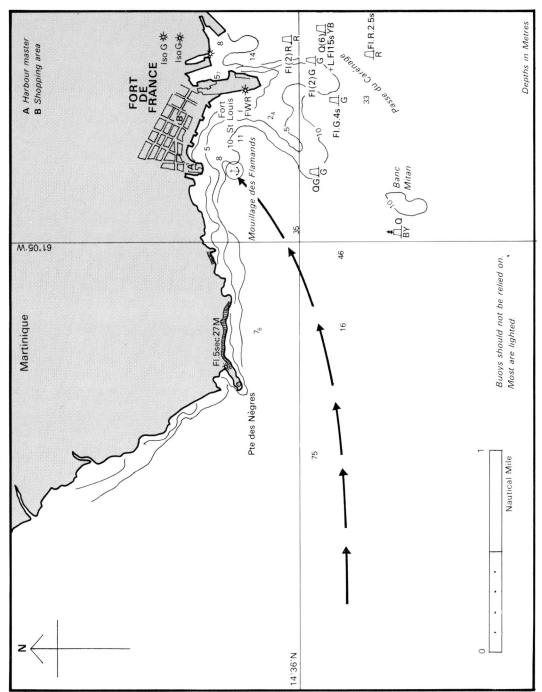

Port Plan 19 Fort de France, Martinique. Probably the most sophisticated place in the Lesser Antilles. A magnificent bay and straightforward approach to the anchorage. Good services ashore but relatively expensive. Based on Admiralty Chart No 494.

well-marked but narrow entrance, and, outside it, a cool, quiet and attractive anchorage.

Services

All services are available, but everything is relatively costly. Fuel is available at the quayside pump and water from the landing place in the Mouillage des Flamands.

Grant's slipway in the military and commercial port has a good reputation, but the draft they can handle is limited to 1.9m/6ft 3in. LPG is obtainable in the form of Camping Gaz only; and only in Camping Gaz containers. For specialized services such as rigging, compass adjusting or sail repairs, enquiries should be made through Grant's.

Shops

The market is excellent and the fruit is superb. Provision shops are handy to the Mouillage des Flamands and generally are as good as one would expect French shops to be, including the supermarket. There are simple shops on Pte du Bout, but one can use the ferry to shop in Fort de France. The Post Office can be difficult about handing over mail from Poste Restante (General Delivery). Unless the addressee attends, with his or her passport, they may refuse even to say whether they have any mail for that person.

Communications

Very cheap 'taxi collectives' work between towns.

International telephone at the Post Office in the centre of town – take an identity document and pay cash over the counter. Collect calls are not possible from telephone boxes.

Fort de France, Martinique	None	Poor	Fair	Good
Anchorage				●
Marina		●		
Yacht harbour	●			
Slipway		●		
Yacht yard			●	
Shipwright			●	
Marine engineer			●	
Chandlery			●	
Sailmaker			●	
Rigger			●	
Compass adjuster			●	
Radio engineer			●	
Water				●

	None	Poor	Fair	Good
Bunkers				●
LPG				●
Shops				●
Market				●
Bonded stores			●	
Banks				●
Duty-free imports	●			
Airport				●
Post Office				●
Telegraph office				●
Chart depot	●			
Medical services			●	

Sps 0.61m/2 ft   Nps 0.46m/1 ft 6 in
Currency: EC dollar   Flag: Antigua

Charts	*Admiralty*	*US*
Approach	2064	25570
Port	2064	25570

Approach

The entrance lies towards the eastern end of the south coast of Antigua. When coming from the north (unless conditions make it preferable to get under the lee of the island) it will be best to sail round the E. coast, to avoid a long turn to windward on the south coast. From the south the approach is straightforward although the entrance is not always easy to see from far out at sea. Seen from the south, the coastline is green at its western end. Inland there are high rolling hills and some conspicuous radio masts. The point where the tree covered land ends and the cliffs begin is the entrance to English Harbour.

Barclay Point, which is part of Middle Ground Peninsula, appears as a dark, wooded bluff with a small rocky headland in the middle of it. It marks the western side of the entrance. The sandstone cliffs and the high land behind them known as Shirley Heights terminate at their western end with a short section of somewhat lower cliffs with unusually shaped vertical clefts. These are easily recognisable and they mark Charlotte Point which is the landward end of the western side of the entrance. From Charlotte Point a shallow reef extends for about half a cable (100 metres) in a north-westerly direction. Admiralty Chart No 2064 gives all necessary information for entering.

Note that in Antigua, the VHF calling Channel is 68, not 16, which is reserved for vessels actually at sea.

Arrival

Formalities
Arrive flying the Q flag. Drop anchor in Freeman Bay or secure at a yellow buoy if one is vacant, and await arrival of port officer. If nobody has come within an hour, the skipper should go ashore to get things moving, or call Antigua Port Authority on Channel 16, VHF.

The transfer of crew from one yacht to another is not permitted unless the yacht to which he is moving is due to depart at once. New crew arrivals must be registered at the Police Station. Outward clearance is normally given on the day of departure only.

Magnetic variation 12°50′W (1987) increasing about 7′ annually.

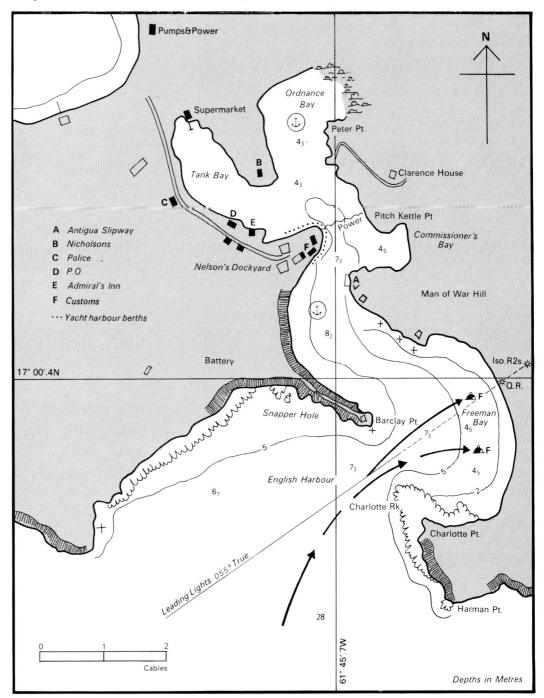

Port Plan 20 English Harbour, Antigua. Considered by many to be the centre of the West Indies' sailing scene. Easy entrance, now with leading marks to help, and all services once you are inside. There is a safe 'hurricane hole' anchorage. Based on Admiralty Chart No 2064.

Anchorage

Between Barclay Point and Nelson's Dockyard, or in Ordnance Bay, N of the Dockyard. Freeman Bay is the quarantine anchorage and may be occupied by boats requesting pratique.

Yacht Harbour

Yachts may lie to their own anchor and stern-to at the Dockyard, for which higher berthing fees are payable. There are showers and toilets in the Dockyard and DIY laundry facilities.

Services

Antigua Slipway Ltd All normal services are available at this well managed yard. Slipping and anti-fouling are handled quickly and efficiently but forward booking is essential, and all work while the yacht is on the slip must be carried out by the company. There is a good chandlery.

Crabb's Marina In Parham harbour. DIY is allowed and it is a good pace to leave a yacht ashore.

Nicholsons The original yacht charter company in Antigua, they also now operate a travel agency, supermarket and chandlery at the old Powder Magazine.

Marine & General Services In Temple Street, St John's, they are official agents for Admiralty charts and have a large stock covering the Caribbean, Atlantic and South Pacific.

Water, LPG and Bunkers

Water supplies are sometimes subject to restrictions but are normally available at the Dockyard Quay by arrangement with the Harbour Office, and from Antigua Slipway Ltd. Normally, diesel and other fuel from Antigua Slipway Ltd. LPG from Pumps & Power, just past Falmouth Harbour.

Shops

In the Dockyard area is a bank, Post Office and the Carib Marine chandlery. Laundresses and fruit sellers offer their services on the quayside. There is also a souvenir shop where clothes and other articles (aimed at the tourist trade) are on sale. A short walk inland there is a fruit and vegetable shop and a poultry farm where new laid eggs may be bought. At St John's, the capital on the W side of the island, there is a good choice of shops some of which will deliver to English Harbour. There is also a market adjacent to the bus terminal. Cheap travel to St John's is by frequent bus. Apart from the Supermarket in Nicholsons, there is another in Tanks Bay with its own jetty.

Bonded Stores   While it is possible to ship bonded stores, the duty on spirits is so low in Antigua that it is scarcely worth the extra trouble. (This point should be checked in case of law change.)

Duty-free Imports   Yacht equipment is allowed in duty free if marked with the yacht's name 'in transit'. Normally the owner is required to collect personally from St John's, but an agent can be appointed. Nicholsons will advise.

Communications

There is an international airport with direct flights to America and England daily; also inter-island services. Taxis, available on the Dockyard quay, are expensive. Self drive hire cars are available but a local driving licence is mandatory. International licences are not recognised.

Nicholson & Sons have a radio station operating from English Harbour and in contact with their charter fleet and other radio-equipped yachts on 2527 k/c. Also VHF. They have a scheduled transmission at 0900 local time each morning at which, in addition to other traffic, there is a weather forecast. Telephone and telex service from Cable and Wireless in the dockyard.

Medical Services

Doctors are in private practice at fees comparable with USA. By English standards they are high. Hospital service is primitive but, in an emergency adequate. It is unbelievably cheap.

Poste Restante (General delivery)   C/o Nicholsons.

English Harbour, Antigua	None	Poor	Fair	Good		None	Poor	Fair	Good
Anchorage				●	Bunkers				●
Marina	●				LPG				●
Yacht harbour				●	Shops			●	
Slipway				●	Market			●	
Yacht yard				●	Bonded stores			●	
Shipwright				●	Banks				●
Marine engineer				●	Duty-free imports				●
Chandlery				●	Airport				●
Sailmaker				●	Post Office				●
Rigger				●	Telegraph office				●
Compass adjuster			●		Chart depot				●
Radio engineer			●		Medical services			●	
Water				●					

Tidal rise and fall is negligible
Currency: US dollar   Flag: USA

Charts	*Admiralty*	*US*
Approach	130, 2452	25641
Port	2183	25649

Approach

The Virgin Islands stand on a bank of coral sand with varying depths over it. The bank is steep-to south and east of the islands, but it extends for as much as 10 to 20 miles from the northern coasts.

The approaches to St Thomas are likely to be made from all four points of the compass: from Puerto Rico in the west, America or Bermuda in the north, the British Virgins in the east, or St Croix in the south. The only one which could involve any navigational challenge is that from the north, which involves a landfall at the end of a thousand-mile passage.

Provided your longitude is not in doubt, and the echo sounder is used, there should be no great difficulty in fixing the boat's position and finding the Virgin Passage between St Thomas and the island of Culebra. Culebrita light should be visible if you are on course, shortly after soundings of 200m/660 ft are reached. There are two rather low-powered aero beacons which may be of help: Saint Croix and Roosevelt Roads, Puerto Rico.

Arrival

The buoyed channel leading to Charlotte Amalie is quite straightforward, and the landlocked harbour offers a choice of marinas, together with every kind of service for small boats. Beware of flying boats landing when approaching this area. The anchorage is open to swell from the south, and dinghy landings are unsafe.

Formalities

Fly Q flag on arrival. All crew members, including US nationals arriving from foreign ports, must report to customs and immigration officialdom.

Services

All services are available and, because this is virtually a free port, many things are cheaper than elsewhere in the Caribbean.

Magnetic variation 11°45' (1987) increasing about 8' annually.

A Customs (arrival)
B Customs (departure)
C Fuel, Water
D Ferry Quay
E Seaplane Dock

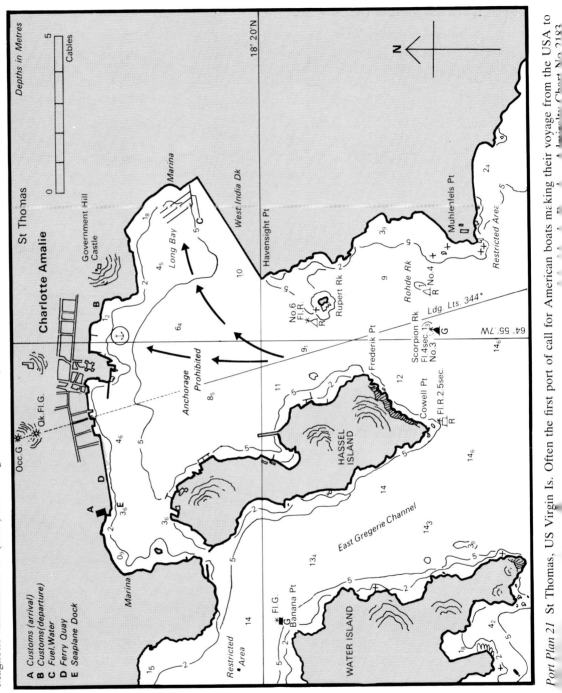

Port Plan 21 St Thomas, US Virgin Is. Often the first port of call for American boats making their voyage from the USA to

Warning

Some experienced authorities advise against going into the town at night.

St Thomas, US Virgin Is	None	Poor	Fair	Good
Anchorage			●	
Marina				●
Yacht harbour				●
Slipway				●
Yacht yard				●
Shipwright				●
Marine engineer				●
Chandlery				●
Sailmaker				●
Rigger				●
Compass adjuster				●
Radio engineer				●
Water				●

	None	Poor	Fair	Good
Bunkers				●
LPG				●
Shops				●
Market				●
Bonded stores	Free port			
Banks				●
Duty-free imports	Free port			
Airport				●
Post Office				●
Telegraph office				●
Chart depot			●	
Medical services				●

Tidal rise and fall negligible
Currency: US dollar   Flag: Br Virgin Is

Charts	*Admiralty*	*US*
Approach	130	25609
Port	2020	25611

General

Roadtown is the capital of Tortola and centre of the bare-boat charter business in the British Virgin Islands. Entry-port for BVI. Being a chartering centre, it is well supplied with all services.
IALA B buoyage system used.

Currency Although the island is essentially British, the official currency is the US Dollar. British and American credit cards are accepted, and there is a branch of Barclays International, as well as American banks.

Approach

Via Sir Francis Drake channel. The entrance is buoyed but do not rely implicitly on the buoys being on station. Careful bearings and a keen lookout are needed. A course of 315° True will take you up the middle of the fairway to Tortola Yacht Services. The only danger of note, when entering, is Harbour Rock which lies about 100 yards east of the Customs House.

Arrival

Anchor temporarily off the customs jetty.

Formalities
Fly Q flag on arrival. Skipper should go ashore to report to customs and immigration, taking ship's papers, crew-list, passports and clearance from last port of call. There is a good deal of form-filling to be done. Officials are polite but very thorough. A cruising permit must be sought if you intend cruising in the BVI. Stamping of passports is done at immigration office nearby.

Berthing
Two marinas, the Moorings and Village Quay, are situated in Wickam's Cay at the north-west end of the harbour. Alternatively, anchor in Bauger Bay or off the Customs

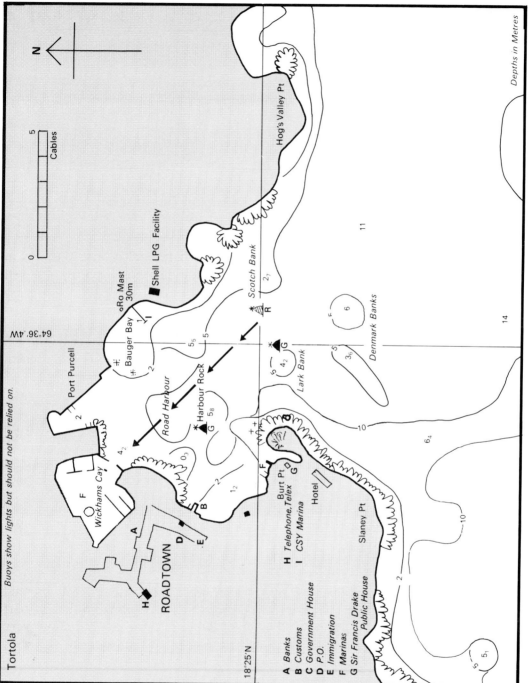

Magnetic variation 11°55′W (1987) increasing about 8′ annually.

Buoys show lights but should not be relied on.

64°36′.4W

N ←

0 5
Cables

18°25′N

Port Purcell

Bauger Bay

°Ro Mast
30m

■ Shell LPG Facility

+ +

2

5₅
5

Road Harbour

★ Harbour Rock
G 5₈

Wickhams Cay

F ○

4₂

0₃

2

1₂

B

A

D
E

H

ROADTOWN

Scotch Bank

2₇

R ⚓

G ✕

5₅

4₂

Lark Bank

Denmark Banks

F

6

3₆

5

11

14

★ G

F

10

Burt Pt

G

Hotel

Slaney Pt

Sir Francis Drake
Public House

10

6₄

2

5₁
5

Hog's Valley Pt

A Banks
B Customs
C Government House
D P.O.
E Immigration
F Marinas
G Sir Francis Drake
   Public House
H Telephone,Telex
I CSY Marina

Depths in Metres

Port Plan 22 Road Harbour, British Virgin Is. The centre for a great deal of bare-boat chartering. Study your official charts and local cruising guides carefully when sailing in these waters and keep a good lookout in case buoys or beacons may be missing or out of position. Based on Admiralty Chart No 2020.

office. There is a good deal of movement whether you anchor or go into a marina berth in this area. In the marina, use plenty of fend-offs and beware of fouling your spreaders with those next to you; and warn new arrivals who may berth next to you.

Communications

Inter-island flights connect with flights to America and England, via Puerto Rico and Antigua respectively.

Services

Water at the marinas. Best at CSY·marina in Bauger Bay – this is a private marina so ask first.

Fuel at marinas – best may be the Shell station at Fort Burt marina, 2.3m.

LPG at the Shell facility, behind CSY marina.

Poste Restante   C/o Post Office, Roadtown.

Road Harbour, Tortola	None	Poor	Fair	Good
Anchorage				●
Marina			●	
Yacht harbour				●
Slipway			●	
Yacht yard			●	
Shipwright			●	
Marine engineer			●	
Chandlery			●	
Sailmaker			●	
Rigger			●	
Compass adjuster		●		
Radio engineer			●	
Water				●

	None	Poor	Fair	Good
Bunkers				●
LPG			●	
Shops				●
Market				●
Bonded stores				●
Banks			●	
Duty-free imports				●
Airport			●	
Post Office				●
Telegraph office				●
Chart depot	●			
Medical services			●	

Notes on US Ports

Radio

As most US yachts are equipped with radio transmitters it is customary for them to advise their approach to any harbour by calling up the local Coast Guard. This procedure is strongly recommended to any stranger who does not know the full details of the port he is approaching. Frequencies used on US VHF channels are not identical with those used in Europe. Take advice.

Summary Tables

No Tables have been included for Miami, Fort Lauderdale, Charleston, or Morehead City. All these ports are situated on the Intracoastal Waterway where good services of all kinds may be found.

Sailing Directions

The whole of the coast from Cape Henry to Key West is covered in the National Ocean Survey Coast Pilot No 4. The Intracoastal Waterway is fully dealt with in the Waterway Guide and also in Chapter 12 of the US Coast Pilot No 4.

Documents

In addition to the ship's papers, it is necessary to have a clearance certificate from the last port of call and all passports should have a visa for travel to the USA. A cruising licence should be applied for on arrival at the first port of call.

Buoyage
IALA B system used.

Spr 1.54m/5 ft   Nps 0.61m/2 ft
Currency: US dollar   Flag: USA

Charts	*Admiralty*	*US*
Approach	2866	11466
Port	3684	11468

Approach

The fairway, Outer Bar Cut, begins at a point which is just over 2 miles east of Fisher Island, and at the edge of the 10 fathom line. Leading lights are in line on a bearing of 250° True.

After passing No 5 (porthand) buoy, line up the Bar Cut marks on a back bearing of 115° True (course 295°). This line leads via Government Cut straight along Main Channel which is bordered on the north by the McArthur Causeway and to the south successively by Fisher Island, Lummus Island, and Dodge Island. To the west of Dodge Island is the City Yacht Basin – one of the many marinas. It may be approached either around the west end of Dodge Island, or by leaving Main Channel east of the Island end taking the buoyed Dodge Island Channel which leads south and west. This is slightly further, but it avoids the bridge which crosses the Waterway west of the Island.

Radio   Call the Coast Guard on VHF channel 16.

Arrival

Formalities
Q-flag should be flown on making the entrance and nobody should go ashore until pratique has been granted. Customs will normally be in attendance at the main marinas or will arrive promptly in response to a request. In addition to the ship's papers, it is necessary to have a clearance certificate from the last port of call and all passports should have a visa for travel to the USA.

Services
Every kind of service is available throughout the whole complex area, comprising Miami, Fort Lauderdale and Port Everglades. There is such profusion that it is impossible to list specific services and their locations. Much information is given in *The Waterway Guide*, but in case of need the Coast Guard or marina personnel will be able to locate any technical help which may be needed.

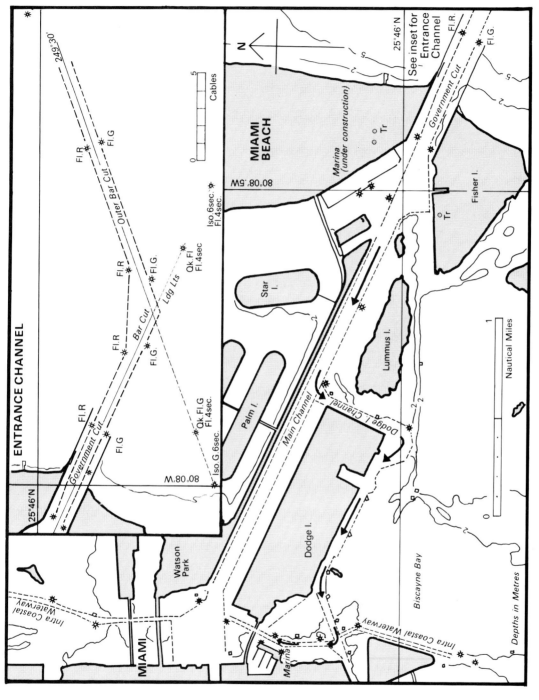

Port Plan 23 Miami. Being the nearest port to the Bahamas it may be used for departure, taking advantage of the Gulf Stream when making towards the islands. A narrow, well lit entrance to an entirely man-made harbour with all possible services and high prices. Based on US Chart No 11468.

239

Spr 1.29m/4 ft   Nps 0.37m/2 ft 5 in
Currency: US dollar   Flag: USA

Charts	*Admiralty*	*US*
Approach	2866	11466
Entrance	3684	11470

Approach

The outer fairway buoy, marked '1', lies about 1½ mile due east of the harbour entrance. Due west of this buoy and ½ mile inshore of it, is the first port-hand mark '3', to the north of which is the starboard-hand mark '2'. The fairway lies between these two buoys, and the leading marks are in line on a bearing of 270° True. The front leading mark carries a fixed G light at a height of 85 ft, and the rear mark carries a fixed G light at a height of 135 ft.

Between the pair of fairway buoys numbered 2 and 3 and the North and South Jetties at the entrance, there are submerged breakwaters lying immediately north and south of the fairway (Outer Bar Cut). A light is shown from the lighthouse at the root of the North Jetty.

Arrival

Formalities
Fly Q flag when entering port from foreign. If not immediately visited by Customs, on berthing the skipper only should go ashore to telephone or should ask the marina to advise Customs. In addition to the ship's papers, it is necessary to have a clearance certificate from the last port of call and all foreign passports should have a visa for travel to the USA.

Berthing and services
If equipped with VHF, seek directions from the Coast Guard before making harbour; otherwise try to arrive during daylight and proceed to one of the many marinas and report to Customs by telephone. The Coast Guard monitors VHF Channel 6. Pier 66 Marina and Lauderdale Marina are both situated immediately beyond the bridge north of the turning basin in Port Everglades. Bahia Mar is a short way further north along the Intracoastal Waterway. And there are many more. None of them is cheap. Services are excellent, but consult the *Waterway Guide* or your marina office for any particular requirement.

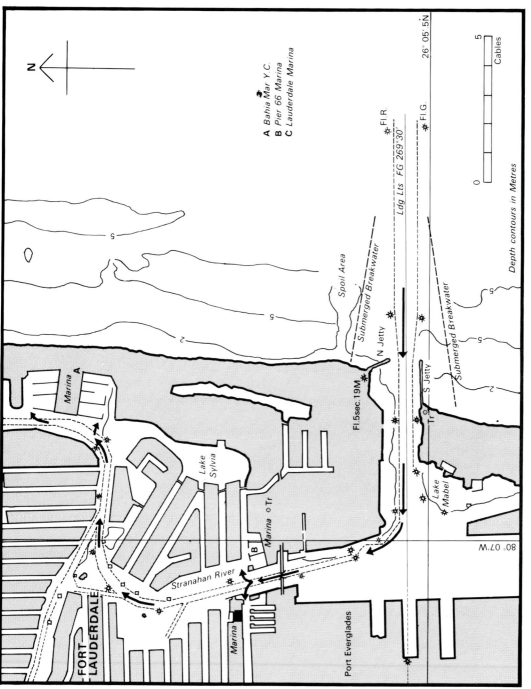

Port Plan 24 Fort Lauderdale. More likely than Miami to be used for those arriving from the Bahamas and not wishing to buck the Gulf Stream. Like Miami it is a man-made port with a buoyed entrance channel. Inside, sophisticated and expensive services. Based on US Chart No 11470.

241

Spr. 1.84m/6 ft   Nps. 1.23m/4 ft
Currency: US dollar   Flag: USA

Charts	*Admiralty*	*US*
Approach	2865	11521
Entrance	2806	11524

Approach

There is a lighthouse at the entrance. The entrance channel, known as Fort Sumpter Range, lies between two converging breakwaters. The outer end is marked by a light buoy. Only the seaward ends of the breakwaters are above water. There are leading marks for each part of the entrance. See US chart 11524 for details of these and other marks.

Arrival

Berthing
Temporary anchorage may be found off the Coast Guard base. Upstream is the Municipal Marina and beyond it the Ashley Marina. The tides run strongly especially on the ebb.

Formalities
Fly Q flag on entering from foreign. If equipped with radio seek advice from Coast Guard before arrival and follow directions for berthing.

Services

Charleston is a big commercial harbour but is not primarily a yachting centre. Services are not of the standard to be found in good US yacht harbours. The town is of great historical interest and beauty.

Magnetic variation 5°15′ (1987) increasing about 8′ annually.

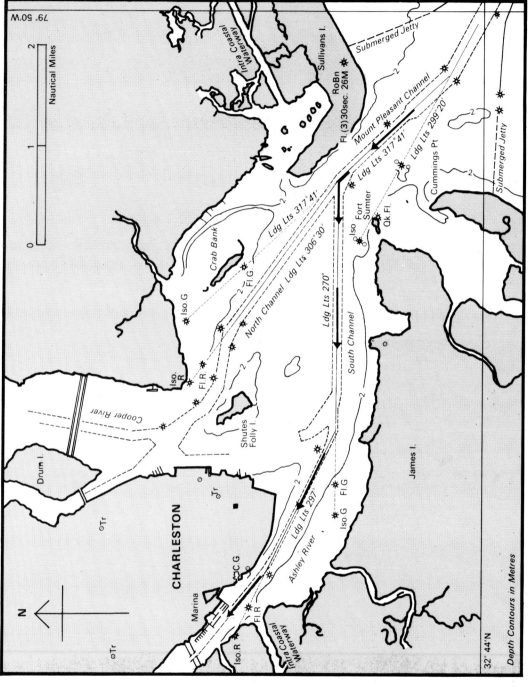

Port Plan 25 Charleston. Not primarily a yachting port although there is a marina. The town is however of great interest. Based on US Chart No 11524.

243

Spr 1.47m/4 ft 10 in   Nps 0.86m/2 ft 10 in
Currency: US dollar   Flag: USA

Charts	*Admiralty*	*US*
Approach	2864	11543, 11544
Entrance	2864	11547

Approach

Beaufort Inlet lies west of Cape Lookout, and the principal danger when making the approach is from the Lookout Shoals. There are radio beacons on Diamond Shoals, Frying Pan Shoals and on Cape Lookout, and it should therefore be possible to fix your position accurately when making landfall.

Beaufort Inlet Channel is maintained to a depth of about 40 feet and is buoyed from the 7 fathom line inwards, a distance of nearly three miles from the coast. The leading marks are lined up on a bearing of 011° True. This course should be held until the light on the west end of Shackleford Pt is abeam, when course would be altered on 340° True. This course takes you up Fort Macon Reach, until Fort Macon is approximately abeam to port, where you should pass between two lit marks, picking up the leading lights for Morehead City Channel on a back bearing of 127° True. Follow the lit marks up Morehead City Channel.

Tidal streams in the area of the Beaufort Channel may attain 2 to 3 knots. A northerly or southerly wind will cause troublesome seas when opposed to the tidal stream. In the vicinity of the State Ports Authority Terminal the stream can run at from 4 to 5 knots at springs.

Radio   Call the Coast Guard on VHF channel 16.

Arrival

Formalities

Q flag should be flown when making the entrance and nobody should go ashore until the Customs have granted pratique. In addition to the ship's papers, it is necessary to have a clearance certificate from the last port of call and all foreign passports should have a visa for travel to the USA.

Magnetic variation 8°15′W (1987) increasing about 7′ annually.

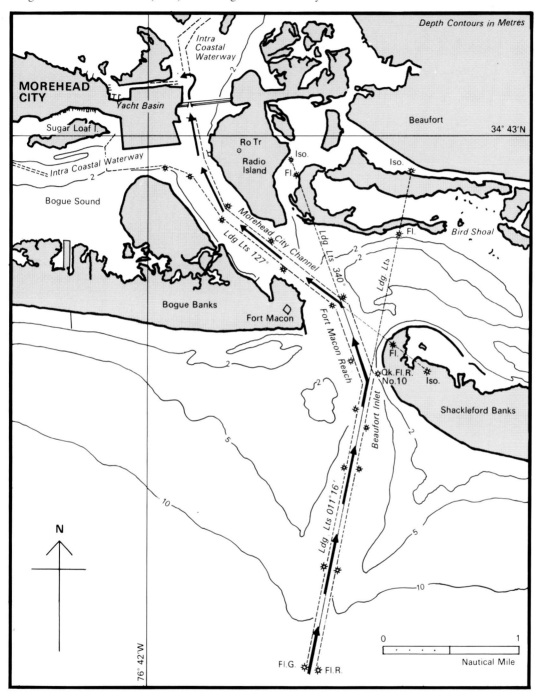

Port Plan 26 Morehead City. Beaufort Inlet provides good services for those arriving from, or starting out on, an ocean passage. The buoyed channel through the off-lying shoals is maintained to a depth of 40 feet. Tidal streams run strongly. Based on US Chart No 11547.

Berthing

Facilities for small craft exist along the southern waterfront of Morehead City and there is a yacht harbour off the NW side of the State Ports Authority Terminal. The latter basin is approached via two bridges, an opening bascule bridge (railroad) and a fixed bridge, clearance 65 ft (highway).

Services

There are services for yachts along the Intracoastal Waterway to the west of the city.

Spr 1.28m/4 ft 2 in   Nps 0.91m/3 ft
Currency: US dollar   Flag: US

Charts	*Admiralty*	*US*
Approach	2492, 2489, 2456, 2890, 3096	13218, 13246
Entrance	2892	13221, 13223

Approach

Newport, Rhode Island is an official port of entry, and an important yachting centre. It is situated off the main entrance channel to Narragansett Bay. The landfall coast is low lying with shoal waters and low islands to the south of Cape Cod. The area is subject to fog. It can be difficult to identify your landfall.

For these reasons it is advisable to make the first landfall at Nantucket Shoals Lanby and thus keep clear of Nantucket Shoals, and establish your exact position before closing the land. Nantucket Shoals Lanby has a fog horn, Racon and a DF beacon (50 miles). It is 50 miles from the nearest land which is unlikely to be sighted until much closer in and careful navigation is advisable, with an awareness of tidal current, to enable the land to be identified when sighted.

Alternatively, if approaching from the north-east, make Race Point on Cape Cod at 42°04′N 70°15′W and pass through Cape Cod Bay to the Cape Cod Canal. The latter has no locks, and there are traffic signals; if green, the canal is open but beware two-way traffic which is sometimes allowed; if red or amber, proceed about ¾ mile into the canal on the south side and enter the East Boat Basin. Traffic control monitors channel 16 (VHF). A railway bridge at the west end is kept raised (open position) except when trains pass. Tidal currents can be strong (5 knots). Power is mandatory. Proceed with great caution if visibility is poor. The canal leads into a dredged channel at the NE end of Buzzard's Bay.

A middle approach route, through Nantucket Sound and Vineyard Sound, is not recommended except possibly in really favourable conditions and perfect visibility.

In the final approach, by any of these routes, make the Brenton Reef Light structure 1½ miles off the entrance to Narragansett Bay. It shows a light at a height of 87 ft from a tower on a red square structure standing on four black legs. It has a fog horn and a low-powered DF beacon (10 miles). Point Judith Light, 6 miles to the south west, and Block Island south-east light, 18 miles SSW, and Buzzard's Light, 16 miles to the east, all with DF beacons and fog horns, can assist in fixing

Magnetic variation 14°45'W (1987) increasing about 1' annually.

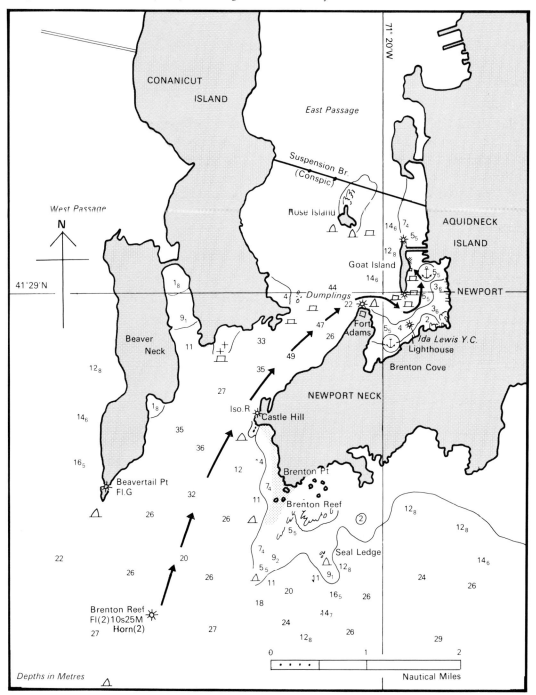

Port Plan 27 Newport, Rhode Island. A name as well known to yachtsmen on both sides of the Atlantic as Cowes, Isle of Wight. Arrival-port for many famous races, it offers a welcome to all small-boat sailors. Every kind of service is available, except bonded stores. Based on Admiralty Chart No 2892.

your position on the final approach. Beware the shoal water to the south of Brenton Point in the final approach.

Radio Call the Coast Guard on VHF channel 16.

Arrival

Formalities
Q flag should be hoisted when three miles off the coast. Arrival must be reported by the skipper within 24 hours and formal entry made within 48 hours. No one may board or leave the yacht (except to report arrival) until customs give permission. Customs authorities may be telephoned from any marina; normal office hours are 0800-1700, excluding Saturdays, Sundays and holidays. Fees are charged for customs services, and a standard overtime charge is made for services outside normal office hours.

Entrance
Enter between Beavertail Point and Brenton Point as shown on plan. Make round Fort Adams and enter Newport Harbour between Fort Adams and Goat Island.

Berths
There are many marinas with berths alongside fixed stagings or floating pontoons. Goat Island marina is the largest and easiest to identify and approach, but is furthest from the town. It is situated about half-way up the island on its east side. Other marinas are situated along the waterfront of the town on the east shore of the harbour.

Anchorages
In Brenton Cove, at the south-western arm of the harbour, clear of the yacht moorings off the Ida Lewis Yacht Club and south of a line of buoys running across the entrance marking submarine cables.

Services

Yacht Yards and Slipways
There are a number of yards on the waterfront of the town.
  The usual full facilities are available, including sailmakers, engineers, electricians etc. with slipways or hoists. Compass adjusters and radio engineers can be called in from outside Newport. Marinas will advise.

Fuel and Water
Most marinas have fuelling berths for diesel and gasoline (petrol). Water and ice are readily available at marinas. LPG bottles can be refilled.

Chandleries and Shops

Newport is well provided with chandleries (many are situated at marinas), supermarkets, hardware shops, clothing stores etc., as well as a launderette, banks and post offices. There is also a launderette at Goat Island marina.

Bonded Stores   No facilities for yachts to take on bonded stores. All imported merchandise, whether for a yacht in transit or for personal use, is subject to duty.

Medical

Medical services are readily available in Newport but hospital treatment and doctors' services can be costly in America and visitors are advised to take out medical insurance before leaving their own country.

Communications

The main communication route, by plane, bus or train, is to Providence, Rhode Island and thence to Boston or New York for international connections.

Radio   There is a coastguard station at Castle Hill on Newport Neck which maintains a 24 hour watch on 2182 kHz and 156.8 MHz (Channel 16).

Poste Restante (General Delivery)   C/o Goat Island Marina or the Post Office by pre-arrangement.

Newport, Rhode Island	None	Poor	Fair	Good
Anchorage				●
Marina				●
Yacht harbour				●
Slipway				●
Yacht yard				●
Shipwright				●
Marine engineer				●
Chandlery				●
Sailmaker				●
Rigger			●	
Compass adjuster			●	
Radio engineer			●	
Water				●

	None	Poor	Fair	Good
Bunkers				●
LPG				●
Shops				●
Market	●			
Bonded stores	●			
Banks				●
Duty-free imports			●	
Airport			●	
Post Office				●
Telegraph office				●
Chart depot				●
Medical services				●

28 Halifax, Nova Scotia   44°38′N 63°34′W   GMT−4

Spr 2.5m/8 ft   Nps 1.64m/5 ft 4 in
Currency: Canadian dollar   Flag: Canada

Charts	*Admiralty*	*Canadian*
Approach	1651, 729	4013, 8007, 4320, 4385
Entrance	2410, 311	4312, 4316

General

Halifax is the capital of the Canadian province of Nova Scotia. It is an official port of entry, a large commercial port and a naval base. Northwest Arm, a long narrow bay branching off just inside the main entrance and before the city and waterfront is reached, is almost entirely devoted to small boat and yacht activity and is the recommended anchorage.

Approach

Sable Island is an off-lying danger which must be given a wide berth. The coastline of Nova Scotia is somewhat rugged and hilly, with many inlets and with off-lying rocks and small islands extending to about five miles offshore in places. It is well buoyed, but subject to fog during summer months, particularly with onshore winds. In clear weather the land will be visible and may be identifiable well before any dangers are closed but, in poor visibility, exercise great caution when closing the coast.

If approaching from a position west of 63°30′W, care must be taken when off Pennant Point and Sambro Island as this is an area of shoal water and isolated rocks, many of which dry or are awash, and in bad weather the sea breaks on these and on the shoal banks. It is well buoyed but these may be missed in thick weather. Sambro Island has a powerful DF beacon (125 miles) which can be of great value in establishing your approach position.

The final approach to Halifax is made between Chebucto Head (100 feet high of whitish granite with a light shown at a height of 162 feet from a white tower close to the north of it), and Devils Island (a low island with a light (53 ft) on it, which lies off Hartlen Point on the north-east side of the approach). Between these points lie Portuguese Shoal and Rock Head shoal, both marked by buoys; and there are numerous other buoys and leading lights for big ships, on the final approach. To identify these an up-to-date chart and/or a list of lights or almanac is essential.

The cleanest shore and deepest water lie on the west side inwards from Chebucto Head.

Magnetic variation 20°25′W (1987) decreasing about 5′ annually.

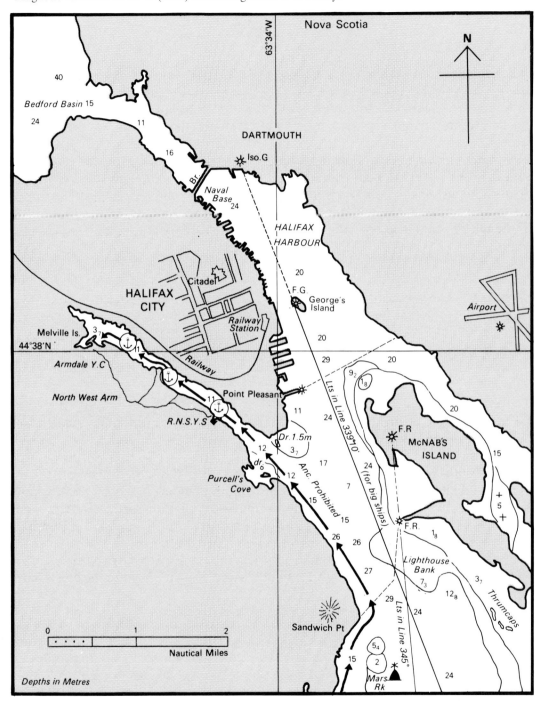

Port Plan 28 Halifax, Nova Scotia. A big commercial and naval port, but with two yacht clubs, which have slipways and repair facilities for members and at times for visitors. Care is needed in making your approach but there is safe anchorage where shown on the plan. Based on Admiralty Chart No 311.

Radio   Call the Coast Guard on VHF channel 16. In fog they may talk you in.

Arrival

Formalities

Q flag should be hoisted in the outer approaches. It will probably be necessary to go ashore (to one of the yacht clubs) to telephone the customs and immigration authorities. Canadian customs officials work strictly to office hours (0900-1700) and are entitled to charge a heavy fee if they are summoned to clear a vessel outside these hours.

A yacht arriving at a Canadian port outside these hours, or between 1200 Saturday and 0900 Monday (and possibly on public holidays too) need not be cleared by customs until normal office hours, provided the crew and the yacht do not leave port until cleared. It may be advisable to inform customs on your arrival (if the telephone is manned) and agree a time for clearance during the next working period.

Entrance

Enter between Sandwich Point and Macnab's Island. Keep in the deep and clear water on the west side and make up NW to enter Northwest Arm between Purcell's Cove and Point Pleasant. If, as frequently happens, it is foggy keep out of the way of shipping by passing the buoys close to but out of the shipping lane.

Anchorage

There are many groups of yacht moorings in Northwest Arm and care should be taken if entering at night or in thick weather. Anchorage is prohibited until about half a mile inside Northwest Arm.

The Royal Nova Scotia Yacht Squadron Clubhouse is ½ mile up Northwest Arm on the south-west shore, with moorings off it. Visitors can anchor off, or go alongside floating pontoons or stone quay, if there is room. Armdale Yacht Club is on Melville Island on the south side at the head of the Northwest Arm, with moorings off it and pontoon berths and jetties round the island's shore. Beware a rocky shoal patch 200 feet off the western end of the island.

It is also possible to moor alongside a jetty near the centre of the city approximately ½ mile east of the citadel. This is only for limited periods but it is near to the banks, chart agents and customs.

Services

Repairs and Slipways

The two yacht clubs have facilities for slipping boats and repair work for their members, and will advise visitors about alternative yards if they cannot offer the necessary service. Fuel and water are available at the yacht clubs.

Chandleries and Shops

Halifax is a large city with all the usual stores and provisions, with post office, banks, launderettes and chart agent. There are also shops, supermarkets, sub-post offices, bank branches, launderettes etc in the suburbs near the head of Northwest Arm, but the immediate area of the anchorages is almost devoid of shopping facilities. Local advice should be sought as to the best area to visit to meet your requirements.

Yacht Clubs

The Royal Nova Scotia Yacht Squadron and the Armdale Yacht Club have eating and bar facilities, also showers and changing rooms, and they may offer the use of these at their discretion to visitors.

Communications

Halifax is served by many airlines and shipping lines to international destinations. The new airport is some 25 miles north of the city. Halifax is also served by the Canadian national railway system. The main station is near the southern end of the docks. A local bus route serves the area of the anchorages.

Radio Canadian Coast Guards at Chebucto Head operate a vessel traffic management system on VHF for all vessels over 65 feet. They may be called up as 'Halifax Traffic' on 156.8 MHz (Channel 16) or 2182 kHz.

Poste Restante (General Delivery) C/o either of the two yacht clubs by pre-arrangements.

Halifax, Novia Scotia	None	Poor	Fair	Good
Anchorage				●
Marina		●		
Yacht harbour				●
Slipway			●	
Yacht yard			●	
Shipwright			●	
Marine engineer			●	
Chandlery				●
Sailmaker				●
Rigger			●	
Compass adjuster			●	
Radio engineer			●	
Water			●	

	None	Poor	Fair	Good
Bunkers			●	
LPG			●	
Shops				●
Market	●			
Bonded stores	●			
Banks				●
Duty-free imports	●			
Airport				●
Post Office				●
Telegraph office				●
Chart depot				●
Medical services				●

Spr 1.22m/4 ft   Nps 0.85m/2 ft 9 in
Currency: Canadian dollar   Flag: Canada

Charts	*Admiralty*	*Canadian*
Approach	232A	8014
Entrance	2902, 298	4574, 4588

General
St John's is the capital and principal port of Newfoundland and is an official port of entry. The harbour is landlocked and sheltered but is purely commercial with no special provision made for small boats. However, it makes an acceptable arrival or departure port as it is the nearest port to northern Europe.

Decca and Loran A have been discontinued and Loran C introduced.

Approach
The approach is straightforward with no offlying dangers, except Vestal Rock (12 ft/3.7 m), 450 ft/137 m east of Fort Amherst light, and those caused by icebergs carried south by the Labrador Current (see Chapter 2).

The approaches to Newfoundland are in one of the foggiest areas in the world. The immediate approaches (within 2–3 miles offshore, inside Cape Spear) are often clear even when there is thick fog elsewhere.

The coast has many hills between 500 ft and 800 ft and the shore line is generally very steep, rising to about 200 ft, with a somewhat barren appearance and few signs of habitation; the shore is generally steep-to and clear of underwater rocks. The 20 fathom line runs between 400 yards off or less, and not more than ½ mile off. In thick weather the coast can be approached using the depth sounder, but the identification of the exact landfall can be difficult. The bluff coastline can result in squally winds or wind shadows when close inshore.

There are DF beacons on Cape Race and Cape St Francis with a range of 100 miles which can be of great help. Sugarloaf Head 3 miles north of St John's is conspicuous, 500 ft high with sheer cliff faces. It appears wedge-shaped when seen from NNE, but from ENE to SE it appears as a truncated cone. Cape Spear, 3½ miles SE of St John's is a promontory 200 ft high, projecting north-eastwards from the coast and a light is shown at a height of 223 ft from a lighthouse 45 ft high on its eastern face, with a fog horn.

The entrance to St John's is very narrow (350 yards) between North Head and South Head, two high headlands. It is not easily identified from a distance, but becomes clear as the land is closed. North Head is a steep headland of 235 ft rising

Magnetic variation 23°25′W (1987) decreasing about 11′ annually.

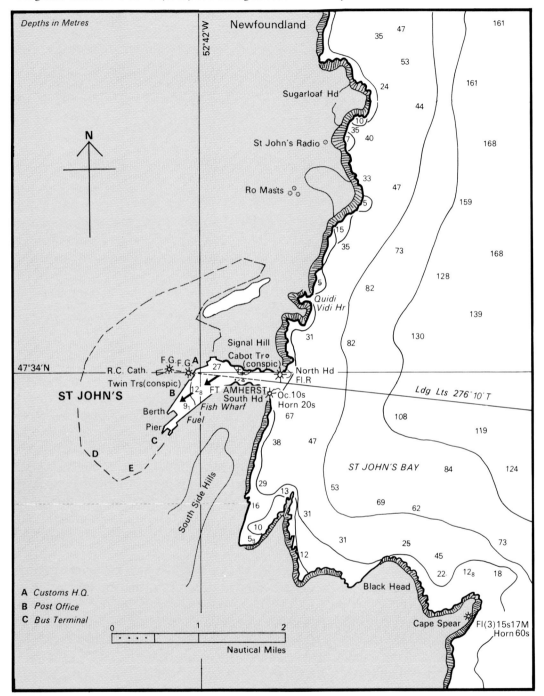

Port Plan 29 St John's, Newfoundland. A safe landlocked harbour but not geared to the needs of small yachts. Useful for arrival or departure because it is the nearest port to Europe, although neither fuel nor water are easy to obtain by small boat standards. Based on Admiralty Chart No 2902.

256

to 500 ft immediately to its north-west as Signal Hill, with the conspicuous Cabot Tower on its summit. A light is shown at a height of 78 ft from a very small, white 'pepper pot' structure on the southern shore of North Head.

South Head may be identified by Fort Amherst Light, shown at a height of 132 ft from a small (25 ft) tower attached to a white building built on bare reddish rock just below the vegetation line. A fog signal is also sounded from this building.

In thick weather care must be taken not to mistake the entrance to Quidi Vidi harbour, 1 mile north of St John's for that of St John's; the former has no lighthouses or fog horns.

Radio　Call the Coast Guard on VHF channel 16.

Arrival

Formalities
Q flag should be hoisted before entering. The customs officers in St John's are on duty from 0800–2400 including holidays. A yacht arriving between 2400 and 0800 need take no action and will be contacted by an official when the office re-opens. No one may disembark until the yacht is cleared. If clearance is essential between 2400 and 0800, a substantial fee will be charged (minimum $54).

Entrance
Enter between North Head and South Head, making to pass about 100 yards south of North Head, on a course of 276°T. There are two leading lights with daymarks which lead in through the channel on a bearing of 276°10′T, but they are difficult to identify. The twin towers of the Roman Catholic Cathedral are conspicuous because their tops break the skyline behind St John's; the rear light and daymark is just to the north of these towers and almost level with their bases. It is better to use power in the entrance channel to maintain the correct course.

If the leading line cannot be identified, continue to steer 276°T after passing 100 yards clear of North Head, and this should take a vessel between the buoys and lights which mark rocks and shoals off the north and south sides of the channel, and which are sufficiently obvious not to require explanation.

Berthing
At the western end of the channel the harbour opens up to the south-west, and is entirely surrounded by wharves. The recommended berth is alongside at the south-western end of the long straight wharf which forms the western side of the harbour. This area is used by small craft. The fenders and wharf face can be oily, and it is best to secure alongside another small craft. The Harbourmaster may redirect a yacht to an alternative berth.

Anchoring off is only allowed under the direction of the Harbourmaster. Good holding in mud.

Services

Boatyards and Slipways
There are no yards specialising in yachts at St John's. There are a few small-boat yards for building and servicing fishing boats and similar small craft, who might offer some service in an emergency. There is a small boatyard equipped with a mobile lift at the port of Harbour Grace on the west side of Conception Bay, about 40 miles by sea from St John's. Enquire about their facilities before sailing there.

Repairs and Chandlery
Several firms provide services: United Sail Works (tel: 754-2131), D. F. Barnes (marine engineers, tel: 579-5041), Capt. Wilf Blackmore (compass adjuster, tel: 579-0567), Windshift Marine (agents and small chandlery, tel: 753-3892), Cambells Ships Supplies (chart agent, provisions and bonded stores, tel: 726-6932), IMP Group (main agents for fishing boat stores and chandlery, tel: 722-4221). There are also radar and radio technicians.

Duty Free Imports
Equipment to be fitted or used on a foreign registered yacht may be imported duty free through St John's Customs office.

Fuel and Water
No provision is made for taking on small quantities of fuel and water. A heavy connection charge is made for supplying water from the main wharf, the same as for large ships taking on water by the ton. It is better to fill with jerricans from some convenient tap, or to seek the help of the personnel at one of the fish wharves on the south eastern side of the harbour, where you may also get ice.

   The fuel wharves are also on the south eastern side of the harbour, and are mainly equipped to supply fuel by the ton but some do have small pumps for supplying small boats. LPG bottles are not available for exchange or re-charging.

Chandleries and Shops
The recommended berth is close to the main shopping area which includes large stores of all types, banks, post office, launderette and chandlery.

   Some useful small hardware/chandlery shops, grocers etc may be found in the area to the south-west of the berth, away from the main shopping area. Large shopping centres/supermarkets are situated on the south western outskirts of the town.

Medical
There are hospitals in St John's with good medical services.

Yacht Clubs
The Royal Newfoundland Yacht Club is situated at Long Pond, Manuels,

Conception Bay. This is about 40 miles by sea from St John's, round Cape St Francis, and about 15 miles by road, and St John's remains the nearest town. Local advice should be sought if intending to visit. There is also the Newfoundland Cruising Club which may be contacted through the Secretary.

Communications

St John's airport, Torbay, has direct international flights to Europe as well as national flights.

There is a daily bus service to Port-aux-Basques (14 hours) for the ferry to Cape Breton Island.

Radio St John's Radio broadcasts weather forecasts and ice reports as well as providing radio communications. They may be called up on 2182 kHz or VHF Channel 16. The Coast Guard administers a Vessel Traffic Management system from the harbour and Signal Hill, to direct shipping traffic. They may be called up as 'St John's Traffic' on VHF Channel 11.

Poste Restante

Address mail to Poste Restante, General Delivery, Main Postal Station 'C', 354 Water Street, St John's, Newfoundland, Canada, A1C 5Y1.

St John's, Newfoundland	None	Poor	Fair	Good
Anchorage		●		
Marina	●			
Yacht harbour	●			
Slipway		●		
Yacht yard		●		
Shipwright		●		
Marine engineer			●	
Chandlery			●	
Sailmaker				●
Rigger			●	
Compass adjuster			●	
Radio engineer				●
Water		●		

	None	Poor	Fair	Good
Bunkers		●		
LPG	●			
Shops				●
Market	●			
Bonded stores				●
Banks				●
Duty-free imports				●
Airport			●	
Post Office				●
Telegraph office				●
Chart depot				●
Medical services				●

Spr 1.22m/4 ft   Nps 0.61m/2 ft
Currency: Bermudian dollar   Flag: British (Red Ensign)

Charts	*Admiralty*	*US*
Approach	334	26341
Harbour	1315	26343

Approach

The Bermuda Islands are encircled by coral reefs which cover a wide area to the north of the islands. Soundings are of little value as the 200 metre/100 fathom line is so close to the reefs that virtually no warning is given.

Approach should be made from a position east of the meridian of St David's Head (64°38'.7W) and on a True course of more than 226°.

Bermuda adopted the IALA B buoyage system in 1985.

Magnetic Anomaly

There is a local magnetic anomaly of up to 6° either side of the standard variation. Great care must, therefore, be taken to check the vessel's position by visual means when approaching the entrance channel. For this reason (and the fact that all the approach channels are narrow) it is not advisable for a stranger to attempt to enter at night.

Arrival

St George's is the official port of entry and must be used for both entry and outward clearance.

Formalities

Hoist Q flag and, if equipped with VHF radio, call up Bermuda Harbour on channel 16 and they will arrange for Customs to meet you at Market Wharf, St George's. They do not visit yachts lying at anchor in the harbour.

There is a good deal of paperwork, but the officers are helpful and courteous. Regulations are strict, and strictly applied, but in no way unreasonable. The possession of cannabis or other drugs is a crime punishable with a heavy fine or imprisonment. Firearms must be declared and will be impounded or sealed by Customs who will return them immediately prior to the boat's departure.

Clearance Twenty-four hours' notice of intended departure should be given to Customs.

Magnetic variation 15°05′W (1987), increasing about 2′ annually.

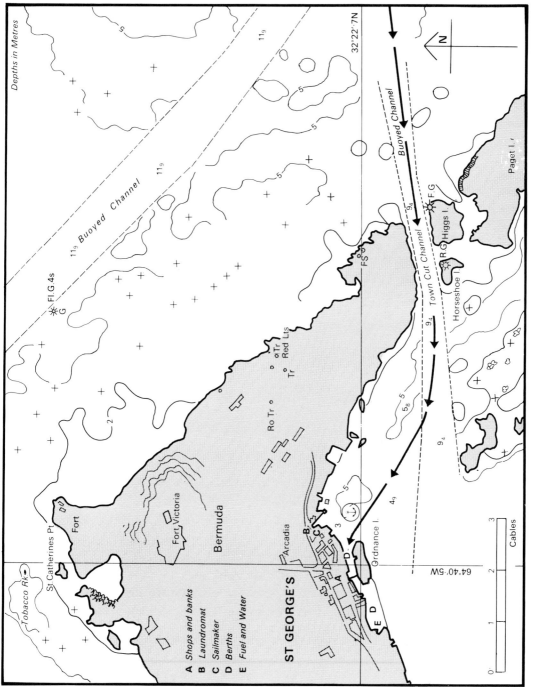

Port Plan 30 St George's, Bermuda. The only port of entry, which must be used on arrival and departure. Approach via the narrow Town Cut Channel and do not attempt the entrance in the dark. Based on Admiralty Chart No 1315.

Anchorage

Boats may be anchored in most places, provided they lie clear of the fairway or any recognised small-boat channel, and do not foul permanent moorings.

Berthing

The space is limited. Market Wharf is crowded in summer. There is space west of the bridge near the fuel station, and the marina usually has room for about six. There are toilets and showers at the marina and electric outlets (115v 60 cycle). Berthing fees are of course payable at the marina. The yacht club is nearby and has showers and a bar.

Services

Repairs

Meyer's, next to the marina, have a slipway and good shipwrights and engineers. The sailmakers are Ocean Sails.

LPG

Propane is in general use in Bermuda. Butane, apart from Camping Gaz, is not obtainable. Kerosene and alcohol spirits may both be bought.

Shops

There are normal shopping facilities in St George's for provisions, but for a wider selection one must go to Hamilton. There is a laundromat, on a cash-and-carry basis.

Medical

Doctors, dentists and an excellent hospital.

Duty Free Imports

Yacht equipment addressed to the boat and marked 'In Transit' may be imported free of duty; all other imports are subject to tax.

Bonded Stores

Bonded stores are available by arrangement immediately prior to clearing outwards.

Communications

International telephone, telegraph and postal services. Air services daily to USA, Canada and Europe. Frequent passenger, cargo and cruise ships call at both Hamilton and St George's.

There are government bus and ferry services. Taxis are privately operated (controlled fares), and mopeds may be hired at reasonable prices, but no other motor vehicles.

Poste Restante (General Delivery) C/o GPO.

St George's, Bermuda	None	Poor	Fair	Good
Anchorage				●
Marina			●	
Yacht harbour	●			
Slipway				●
Yacht yard				●
Shipwright				●
Marine engineer				●
Chandlery				●
Sailmaker				●
Rigger				●
Compass adjuster	●			
Radio engineer				●
Water				●

	None	Poor	Fair	Good
Bunkers				●
LPG			●	
Shops				●
Market	●			
Bonded stores				●
Banks				●
Duty-free imports		●		
Airport				●
Post Office				●
Telegraph office	●			
Chart depot	●			
Medical services				●

Spr 1.6m/5 ft 3 in   Nps 1.26m/4 ft 2 in
Currency: Portuguese escudo   Flag: Portugal

Charts	*Admiralty*	*US*
Approach	1855	51061
Harbour	1940	51062

Approach

Deep water surrounds the Azores islands, and visibility in summer is generally good. There are aero-beacons on Flores, Graciosa, Terceira, Sao Miguel and Santa Maria; as well as at Horta itself. No difficulty should, therefore, arise in fixing your position from whatever direction you make your approach.

Horta lies on the SE corner of the island of Faial, with the Canal do Faial separating it from Pico. At its narrowest point the Canal is about 2½ miles wide. If coming in from the north, avoid the eastern side of the Canal do Faial which is subject to rollers, and on which is situated the unlit pair of islets known as Ilheus da Madalena.

Lights   A light, height 480 ft (146m) is exhibited at Ponta da Ribeirinha on the NE corner of Faial. There is a light, height 69 ft (21m), on the end of the mole at Horta. On the western side of Pico there is a light, height 49 ft (15m), sited just south of the town of Madalena. This light is obscured by Ilheus Madalena between bearings 120° and 130°, and 138° and 140°.

Tides   In the Canal do Faial, the flood and ebb set respectively NNE and SSW, at between 1 and 2 knots.

Arrival

Fly the Q flag if not arriving from Portugal, and once round the pier head enter the marina, which is the only place a yacht may come-to. Berth at arrival jetty to clear formalities (the offices of the Capitania, Guarda Fiscal and Customs are adjacent and have to be seen whether or not you come from Portugal) and collect berthing instructions. The marina has good shelter from all winds but occasionally some swell. Water and electricity (220V) laid on.

Services

Shipboard
Facilities are limited but straightforward engineering (Benesandos), radio and

Magnetic variation 15°05′W (1987) decreasing about 1′ annually.

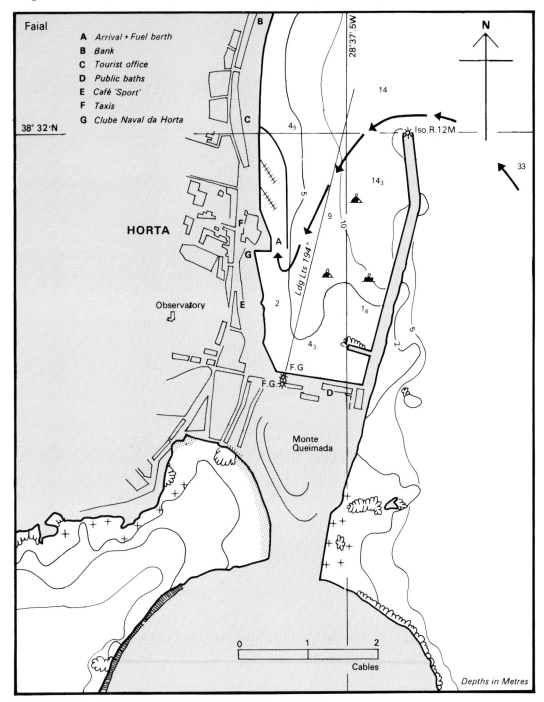

Port Plan 31 Horta, Faial, Azores. This, along with Ponta Delgada, S. Miguel, is the best port of call in the Azores. There are no problems in making the approach but it may be wise not to enter at night because anchoring is inadvisable due to a foul bottom. Based on Admiralty Chart No 1940.

sailmaking (Silverman, author of *Cruising Guide to the Azores*) work can be done. If stuck, consult Peter Azevedo, proprietor of the Café Sport, or his son José, for advice on this or any subject to do with the island.

Shopping
Good market for fresh fruit and vegetables most of the year. Good cheese which keeps well in its wax coating. Reasonable shopping (one supermarket).

Fuel
Diesel at the marina. LPG: bottles refilled (not replaced). Allow 24 hours (though personal delivery to and collection from the filling station speeds things up).

Banking hours   0830–1200 and 1345–1430.

Communications
Inter-island steamer and sea connections with Portugal.
  Bi-weekly air service to Portugal and regular services to San Miguel and Terceira, which also have international airports.

Poste Restante   By arrangement, c/o Peter Azevedo, Café Sport.

Inter-island cruising
There are no restrictions on inter-island cruising but check in and out with each Capitania.

Horta Faial, Azores	None	Poor	Fair	Good
Anchorage		●		
Marina	●			
Yacht harbour	●			
Slipway	●			
Yacht yard	●			
Shipwright	●			
Marine engineer	●			
Chandlery	●			
Sailmaker	●			
Rigger	●			
Compass adjuster	●			
Radio engineer		●		
Water			●	

	None	Poor	Fair	Good
Bunkers			●	
LPG		●		
Shops			●	
Market			●	
Bonded stores	●			
Banks			●	
Duty-free imports	●			
Airport			●	
Post Office			●	
Telegraph office			●	
Chart depot	●			
Medical services			●	

266

Bibliography

Weight and bulk will limit what you can take with you. The lists which follow are divided under two headings: (1) Essential books and other documents; (2) Local cruising guides, background reading, and the names of publishers.

Users of special navigational systems should consult the makers about appropriate charts or tables. See the key to the publishers' initials at the end of this bibliography.

1. Essential books and other documents

(a) *Seamanship and navigation*

Title	*Author*	*Publisher*
Cruising Under Sail 3rd Edition	Eric C Hiscock	AC
Celestial Navigation for Yachtsmen	Mary Blewitt	SM
Practical Pilotage	J Howard-Williams	AC
Navigation Primer for Yachtsmen	F S Howell	ILNW
Deep Sea Sailing	Erroll Bruce	NB (UK), McK (USA)

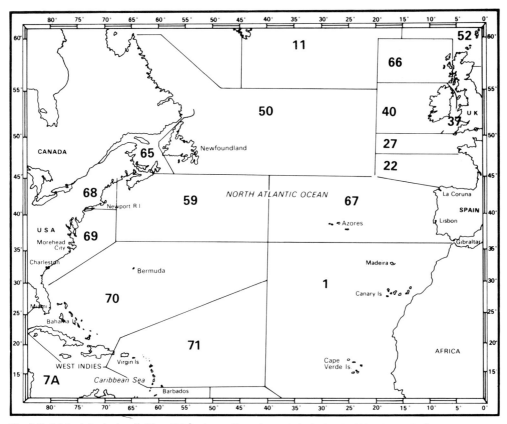

Fig 8 British Admiralty Sailing Directions. Based on Admiralty Publication NP131.

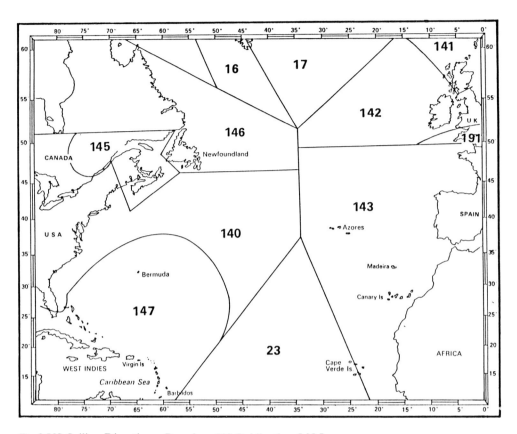

Fig 9 US Sailing Directions. Based on US Publication I-N-L.

Title	Author	Publisher
(b) *Standard reference material*		
Ocean Passages for the World	Admiralty	HD
*Sailing Directions, Vols 1, 22, 27, 40, 50, 52, 65, 66, 67, 68, 69, 70, 71	Admiralty	HD
*Sailing Directions, Vols. 23, 140, 141 143, 144, 145, 146, 191	DMA	DMA
*Sight Reduction Tables AP3270, Vols 2 and 3	US Navy	HMSO (Eng)
*Sight Reduction Tables 249 Vols 2 and 3	US Navy	DMA (USA)
*Admiralty List of Lights, Vols A, D, J, H	Admiralty	HD
*Lists of Lights including Fog Signals. Vols 111A, 113, 114	DMA	DMA
World Cruising Routes	Jimmy Cornell	AC

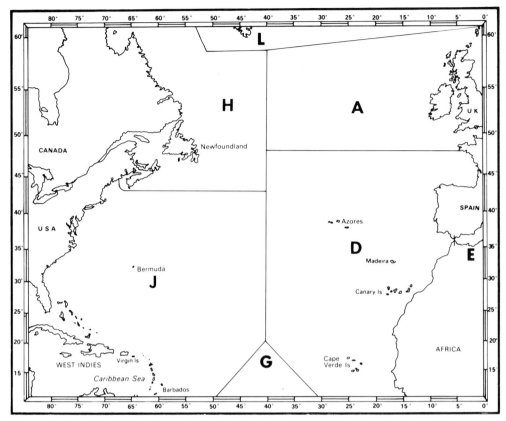

Fig 10 British Admiralty List of Lights. Based on Admiralty Publication NP131.

Title	Author	Publisher
*Admiralty Lists of Radio Signals Vols 1, 2, 3, 5	Admiralty	HD
*Radio Navigational Aids – Atlantic and Mediterranean, Vol 117A	DMA	DMA
*Routeing Charts	Admiralty	HD
*Pilot Charts	DMA	DMA
Baker's Position Line Chart	ILNW	ILNW
(c) *Seasonal publications*		
Admiralty Nautical Almanac	Admiralty	HD
Reed's Nautical Almanac		
European Edition	O M Watts	TR
Reed's Nautical Almanac, US Edn	O M Watts	TR
*Notice to Mariners	Admiralty	HD
*Notice to Mariners	DMA	DMA

Note Consecutive items asterisked *and dealing with the same subject*, are English and American alternatives; only one of which need be obtained.

2. Local Cruising Guides, Background reading, List of Publishers

It is impossible to give a full list of all the books and other useful information, but the following will be found helpful. In both England and the USA, nautical bookshops and yacht chandlers will be able to supply most of the books mentioned and may also be able to offer an even wider choice.

Title	Author	Publisher
Europe		
Cruising Association Handbook	CA	CA
Norwegian Cruising Guide	Mark Brackenbury	SM
Frisian Pilot	Mark Brackenbury	SM
Scottish West Coast Pilot	Mark Brackenbury	SM
Sailing Directions for West and North-east Coasts of Scotland, Orkney and Shetland Islands. (Seven sections.)	CCC	CCC
Atlantic Spain and Portugal	RCCPF	ILNW
Yachtsman's Pilot Antwerp-Boulogne	W T Wilson	ILNW
Normandy and Channel Islands Pilot	Mark Brackenbury	AC
North Brittany Pilot	RCC Pilotage Foundation	AC
Brittany and Channel Islands Cruising Guide	David Jefferson	SM
French Pilot	Malcolm Robson	McM
Channel Islands Pilot	Malcolm Robson	McM
Shell Pilot to South Coast Harbours	K Adlard Coles	FF
Pilot Packs	Brian Goulder	AC
Channel Harbours and Anchorages	K Adlard Coles	NB
South England Pilot	Robin Brandon	ILNW
Sailing Directions for S & W Coasts of Ireland		ICC
Sailing Directions for N & E Coasts of Ireland		ICC
North Biscay Pilot	RCC Pilotage Foundation	AC
South Biscay Pilot	Robin Brandon	AC
East Spain Pilot	Robin Brandon	ILNW
Sea Guides to the Mediterranean	H M Denham	
The Adriatic		JM
The Aegean		JM
The Ionian Islands		JM
Southern Turkey		JM
The Tyrrhenian Sea		JM
Greek Waters Pilot	R Heikell	ILNW

Title	Author	Publisher
America, Canada and Nova Scotia		
Cruising Nova Scotia	Clark, Penner & Rogers	CB
Cruising Guide to the New England Coast	Duncan & Ware	DM
Waterway Guide Charts		
Cape Cod – Canada		
New York – Norfolk		
Norfolk – Key West		
Waterway Guide		
Maine – New York Harbor		MA
New York – The Florida Line		MA
Florida, Alabama, Mississippi, Louisiana & Texas		MA
Cruising Guide to the Florida Keys	Capt Frank Papy	
The Intracoastal Waterway	Jan & Bill Moeller	
Tide & Pilot Book for N. American Waters		REW
The West Indies and Bermuda		
Cruising Guide to the Windward Is	Stevens	TI
Yachtsman's Guide to the Windward Is	J M Wilensky	WC
Yachtsman's Guide to the Greater Antilles	Harry Kline	TI
Cruising Guide to the Eastern Caribbean, Vols 1–4	Don Street	WWN
Cruising Guide to the Caribbean and Bahamas	Hart and Stone	DM
Yachtsman's Guide to the Bahamas	Harry Kline	TI
Bahama Islands	Rigg and Harry Kline	
Cruising Guide to the Abacos and Northern Bahamas	J M Wilensky	WC
Yachtsman's Guide to the Bermuda Is	Michael Voegli	
Sailor's Guide to the Windward Isles	Chris Doyle	

The Ocean Cruising Yacht, in two volumes by Donald M Street Jnr, is a valuable work, full of useful information. *Atlantic Cruise in Wanderer III*, by Eric Hiscock

(OUP) although a cruising log and not a technical book, contains many pieces of importance to those visiting American waters for the first time and it covers a full cruise from England via Spain and Portugal, to the West Indies and the USA; and then back to England via Bermuda and the Azores. *Special note for users of LPG.* Write to Consumer Services Manager Calor Gas Ltd, Calor House, Windsor Road, Slough SL1 2EQ, England, for a free copy of their *Notes for Blue Water Yachtsmen.*

Publishers
The following list contains the names of the main publishers whose books have been quoted here, together with a key to the abbreviations in the foregoing pages:

AC	Adlard Coles, Grafton Books, London, UK.
BB	Bowker and Bertram, London, UK.
CA	The Cruising Association, London, UK.
CB	Charles Bartlett, New York, USA.
CCC	Clyde Cruising Club Publications Ltd., Glasgow, Scotland.
CP	Channel Press, Aylesbury, UK.
DM	Dodd Mead & Co, New York, USA.
DMA	Defense Mapping Agency, Washington, USA.
FF	Faber and Faber, London, UK.
HD	The Hydrographic Department of the Navy, Taunton, UK.
HMSO	Her Majesty's Stationery Office, London, UK.
ICC	The Irish Cruising Club, Irish Republic.
ILNW	Imray, Laurie, Norie and Wilson, St Ives, UK.
JM	John Murray, London, UK.
McK	David McKay Inc, New York, USA.
McM	Macmillan Press, London, UK.
MA	Marine Annuals Inc., New York, USA.
NB	Nautical Books, Huntingdon, UK.
REW	Robert Eldridge White, New York, USA.
SM	Stanford Maritime, George Phillips, London, UK.
TI	Tropic Isle Publishers, Florida, USA.
TR	Thomas Reed Publications, London, UK.
WC	Westcott Cove, Connecticut, USA.
WWN	W W Norton, New York, USA.

Index

Abra, Baia de, Madeira, 138
Admiralty *List of Lights*, 268
Admiralty *List of Radio Signals*, 14, 83, 92, 93, 269
Admiralty Nautical Almanac, 269
Aero beacon, 20
Alcohol cooking fuel, 40
Alderney Race, 87
Almanac, 14, 269
Alternators, 27, 43
Amateur radio, 54
America, *see* USA
Anchors and anchor chains, 38
Andrews, Dr R. A., xvii
Anomaly, magnetic (Bermuda), 131, 260
Antenna, 52
Antigua, 147, 149, 150, 227–30
Antilles, Lesser, 147–151
Ardentrive Bay, Oban, 159
Arrecife, Lanzarote, 144
Astro navigation, 12
Atlantic gale, 29
Atlantic roundabout, 5, 8
Atlantic strategy, 5
Auto-steering, 60
Awnings, 63
Azevedo, Peter, 266
Azores, 5, 90, 134–5
  current, 7
Azores to English Channel, 126
Azores to Gibralter, 123

Bahamas, 5, 112, 152
  Yachtsman's Guide, 112, 113
Baker's Position-line Charts, 18, 269
Barbados, 104, 146, 147, 149, 150
Barometer, barograph, 14
Barra Head, Hebrides, 84, 156
Barton, Humphrey, 59
Batteries, 27, 29, 45, 46
Bayona, 102, 185
BBC, Overseas Service, 14
  weather forecasts, 84
Bermuda, 5, 11, 115–120, 131–33, 260
Bermuda to Azores, 121
Berths, sleeping, 3, 42
Bilge pumps, 35
Bill of Health, Bill of Sale, 22
Biscay, Bay of, 98, 102, 126

Bishop Rock, Scillies, 85
Blewitt, Mary, 12
Bluebird of Thorne, watchkeeping system, 26
  USA to Bermuda, 115
Boat and her gear, 34
Books, 8, 23
Books, essential for navigator, 14, 23, 267
Brenton Reef and Light, USA, 247, 248
Bridge-deck, cockpit, 35
Bridgetown, Barbados, 213–216
Bruce, Commander Erroll, xvii, 25, 267
Bulldog grips, 43, 45
Buoyage systems, 31
Butane gas, 41

Cabin heater, 80, 92
Calculator, 12, 21
Camara de Lobos, Madeira, 140
Camden, Maine, 92
Campbeltown, Scotland, 161
Canada, 88, 93, 96
Canary Current, 7
Canary Islands, 98, 103, 143, 145
Cancer, Tropic of, 147
Canvas dodgers, 29
Cape Cod, Mass, 77, 95–7, 243, 247
Cape Espartel, Morocco, 125
Cape Finisterre, 98
Cape Hatteras, USA, 118
Cape Race, Newfoundland, 88, 90, 91, 255
Cape Sable, Nova Scotia, 78
Cape St Francis, Newfoundland, 95
Cape St Vincent, 102, 123, 125
Cape Spear, Newfoundland, 95
Cape Verde Islands, xiii, 5, 98, 104, 145
Careenage, Barbados, 213–215
Carga da Lapa, Ilha Deserta Grande (Madeira), 140
Caribbean, 6
Caribs, 147
Carlisle Bay, Barbados, 148, 213–215
Casablanca, 102, 125
Cascais, Portugal, 102
Castletown, Ireland, 85
Castries, St Lucia, 150
Chafe, 27, 37, 38, 70
Chain, anchor, 38
Chain-wheel, windlass, 38
Charleston, S. Carolina, 111, 115, 242, 243

Charts, general, 8, 18
　list for this book, ix
　table, 12, 13
Cheques (checks), traveller's, 23
Cherbourg, 86, 87, 179–81
Chronometer, 12, 13
'Chum', use on anchor chain, 38, 39
Clearance papers, 22
Clothes, 29, 30
　stowage, 43
Coast Guard, US, 5, 8, 77, 94
Coast Pilot No 4, US, 93
Cockpit, 29
Cockroaches, 32
Cold wall, Gulf Stream, 8, 78, 91
Collision avoidance, 70
Columbus, Christopher, 98, 147, 151
Communications, radio, 52–4
Compass deviation, 19
Computer, 12
Cook, choosing a, 48
Cooking apparatus, 41
　fuel, 40, 41
Cork Harbour, 167, 170
Corrosion in engine, 46
Coruña, La, 53, 102, 182–4
Courtesy flag, 32, 135, 149
CQR anchors, 38
Cranberry Island, Nova Scotia, 96
Crew, 3, 47–50
　discipline, 49
　list and manifest, 22
　recruitment, 47
　replacements, 48, 49
　training, 49
Crosshaven, Ireland, 84, 166–70
Cruising Club of America, xii, xvi
Cruising Guides, 270
Cruising licence, USA, 22, 94, 237
Cruising permit, British Virgin Islands, 234
Cruising Under Sail, xvii, 12, 19
Currency, 23
Currents, general, 6, 7, 8
　West Indies, general, 151
Customs formalities, Europe, 83
Cyalume sticks, 67

Danforth anchors, 38
Daunt Rock, Ireland, 166
Dead reckoning, 18, 24
Decks, insulation, 39
　water-tightness, 35
Deep Sea Sailing, xvii

Defect book, 23
Defense Mapping Agency, US, 15
Dental check, 71
Deserta Grande, Ilha, Madeira, 141
Deviation of compass, 19, 46
Diagram, plotting, 18
Diet, spartan, King, 58
Dinghy, 46
Direction finding and beacons, 20, 31, 58
Distress, radio, 54
Docking plan, 28
Documentation, French, 83
　US, 22
Dogs, 83
Dollars, 151
Dominica, 147
Dorade ventilators, 39
Double sideband, radio, 52
Doubloon, yacht, 115
Down wind sailing and rig, 59
Drake, Sir Francis, 166
Drake Channel, Tortola, 234
Drake's Pool, Owenboy River, Ireland, 168–9
Drinking water, 40
Drugs, 30, 31, 94, 131
Dubh Artach, Scotland, 156

Echo-sounder, 20, 31, 55
Eddystone Light House, 175
Eggs, 57
Electric mains and equipment, 46, 54
Electronics, 55
Eleuthera, Bahamas, 111
Emergency tiller, 46
Engine and electrics, 44, 45
Engine spares, 43, 44
English Channel, 85, 86, 87, 98
English Channel to Azores, 126
English coast, arrival off, 85
English Harbour, Antigua, 54, 150, 227–30
Ensign warrant, 22
EPIRB Emergency Radio Beacon, 54
Error, compass, 19, 21
Error, sextant, 15
　watch, 13
Eyeball navigation, 152

Facsimile weather maps, 54
Faial, Ilha, Azores, 264–6
Falmouth, 44, 85, 86, 171–4
Fans, ventilation, 39
Finisterre, Cape, 98, 100, 101
Firearms, 73, 131
Fire blanket, 70

Fires and firefighting, 69, 70
First aid, 66, 72
Fisherman anchor, 38, 84
Fishing, 30
Flannan Isles, Scotland, 84
Floats, fishermen's, 147
Florida Strait, 110, 112, 113
Florida, Miami and Fort Lauderdale, 5, 238–41
Fog, 6, 77, 78, 88, 91, 95
Food, provisioning, 56–8
  stowage, 42
Forestays with running sails, 61
Formalities
  entering Europe, 83
  entering the USA, 94
Formula, provisioning, 57
Fort Collins, Colorado (WWV), 14
Fort de France, Martinique, 224–6
Fort Lauderdale, Florida, 110, 240–41
French coast, arrival off, 85–7
Fuel, cooking, 40, 41
Funchal, Madeira, 102, 103, 203–6

Gale, 28, 29
Galley lay-out, 41
Gas, cooking, 41
Genoa jib, 36, 37
Gibbs Hill Light, Bermuda, 118, 119
Gibraltar, 100, 102, 104, 105, 123, 199–202
Gibraltar Strait, 125
Gloucester, Mass, 92
Gnomonic charts, 19, 79, 89
Gran Canaria, 142, 143
Grand Banks, 6, 77, 88, 91
  fishing fleets, 95
Great circle sailing, 19
  Atlantic routes, 77, 78, 88, 90
Grenada, 218–23
Grenadines, West Indies, 147
Ground tackle, 37, 38
Gulf Stream, 5, 6, 8

Halifax, 90, 92, 96, 251–4
Halyards, 36, 62
Hamilton, Bermuda, 11, 131–33, 262
Hanks, sail, 37
Harness, 64
Heads, 4, 44
Heavy weather, 28, 29
Herreshoff anchors, 38, 84
Hiscock, Eric, xi, xii, xvii, 12, 19, 109, 151, 152, 267, 271

Horse latitudes, 121
Horta, Faial, Azores, 92, 121, 134, 264–6
Hull of boat, 34
Hurricanes, 5, 10, 98, 117

Ice, 6, 77, 88, 92
  Patrol, US, 77, 88
Illness, 71
Index error, sextant, 17
Insulation, deck, 39
Insurance, 22, 23
Intermediate passages, 110
Intermediate route, Atlantic, 81
Intracoastal Waterway, 92, 237, 271
Iolaire watchkeeping system, 25
Irish coast, arrival off, 84, 85
Island Groups, The, 129

Jib, 37

Kerosene, 40, 41
Kerrera Island and Sound, Scotland, 156–9
Ketch, 37, 64, 68
King, Commander, W. D., 58
Kinsale, Ireland, 85
Knock-downs, 29

Labrador Current, 5, 6, 8
La Coruña, 53, 182–4
La Luz (Las Palmas), 103, 145
Landfalls, general advice, 20
  Canada and N. America, 94
  Europe, 83
  preparation, 31, 32
Lanzarote, Canary Islands, 143, 144
Las Palmas, 145
Law, the, 30
Lee-boards, berths, 42
Leixöes, 189
Levanter, Gibraltar, 100, 125
Licence, cruising, US, 94
  driving, 230
  firearms, 73
  radio, 54
Lifebuoys, 65
Lifejackets, 65
Lifelines, 63, 64
Liferafts, 65
Lifting gear for man overboard, 65
Lightning, 21
Lights, Admiralty List, 268
Liquid petroleum gas (LPG), 40, 41
Lisboa, 102, 192

Lizard Point, 85, 171
Loch Boisdale, Scotland, 84
Log book, 14, 23, 24
Los Christianos, Tenerife, 145, 207–9

Machico, Madeira, 140
McLeod, Major J. K., xvii, xviii, 11
McMullen, Captain C. W., R.N., xvi
Madeira, 102, 103, 105, 136–41
Magnetic anomaly, Bermuda, 131, 260
Mains, electric, 45
Mainsail, 37
Maintenance, 27
Man overboard, 66–9
Marblehead, Mass, 92
Martinique, Diamond Rock, 105
    Fort de France, 224–6
    landfall, 104
Maspalomas, Gran Canaria, 143
Mast, 35, 36
    guard rails, 64
Mayday, *see* Distress
Mechanics of cruising, 22
Medical insurance, 33
Mediterranean, 7, 9, 98, 100
Meridian altitude, 18, 19
Miami, 109, 238–9
Millbay Dock, Plymouth, 177
Mizen Head, Ireland, 84, 85
Money, 23
Morehead City, N. Carolina, 111, 244–6
Moscow time signals, 14
Mosquito netting, 39

Nantucket Light Vessel and Shoal, 77, 95, 96, 247
Naos, Lanzarote, 143
Navigation, Bahamas, general, 151, 152
    general, 12
    systems (Decca, Loran, etc.), 55
    West Indies, general, 147
Navigator, 13
Newfoundland, 95, 255–9
Newport, Rhode Island, 81, 92, 96, 111, 247–50
North Atlantic Current, general, 7, 80, 90
North Atlantic Chart showing ports, 155
North-east trade wind, 6, 103
North Equatorial Current, 6, 104, 109, 147
North Rona, Scotland, 84
Notice to Mariners, 15
Nova Scotia, 96, 251–4

Oban, xiii, 154–8
Ocean cruising, philosophy, 3

Ocean cruising strategy, 5
Ocean passages
    eastward, 77
    westward, 88
Oil-rigs, 87
OSTAR, 11
Ottawa time signals, 14

Palma, La, Canary Islands, 145
Papers, ship's, 22
Pasito Blanco, Gran Canaria, 143
Passports, 22
Pentland Firth, 84
Perpendicularity, sextant, 15, 16
Pests, 32
Pilot charts, 8, 9, 268
Pilotage Foundation RRC, v
Piracy, 72, 73
Planets, 20
Plotting diagrams, 18
Plymouth, 175–8
Ponta Delgada, Azores, 120, 135
Porto Santo, Madeira, 102, 136–8
Portugal Current, 7, 8
Portuguese Man-o'war, 136
Portuguese Trades, 100, 126
Position line, 17, 18
Prickly Bay, Grenada, 221–3
Primus stove, 41
Providence Channel, Bahamas, 109, 111, 112
Provisioning, 56, 58
    formula, 56
    for trade wind passage, 105, 106
    test run, 56
Puerto Rico, Gran Canaria, 143
Pulpits, 64
Pumps, bilge, 35

Q flag, 32, 84
Quartz watches, 13

Radar, 55, 70, 71
Radio, and electronics, general, 52
    direction finding, 20, 31, 32, 83
    distress, 54, 72
    navigational aids, 269
    Signals, Admiralty List, 14, 83, 92, 93, 269
Rats, 32
Receivers, radio, 52
Recruitment of crew, 47, 48
Reed's Nautical Almanac, 6, 14, 31, 83, 85, 93, 269
Registry, certificate of, 22
Repairs, 27
Replacements, 43

Rhumb line, 19
Rhythmic rolling, 42, 59, 106
Ribiera Brava, Madeira, 139
Rig, downwind, 59
Rigging, check of, 27
  standing and running, 36
Riverdale, Lord, 26
Road Harbour, Tortola, 234–6
Robinson, W. A., 71
Roches Point, Ireland, 166
Rocket packs, 65
Roller reefing and furling, 63
Roundabout, the Atlantic, 5, 8
Round Island, Scilly, 84, 85
Routeing charts, 8, 9, 93, 268
Royal Cruising Club, v
Rugby time signals, 14
Running sail rig, 60, 61

Sable Island, 78, 88, 90, 95, 251
Safety, 63
Sailing directions, 8, 237
Sails, 36, 37
  stowage, 43
St David's Head, Bermuda, 118, 119
St George's, Bermuda, 118, 131, 260–63
  Grenada, 218–20
St Johns, Newfoundland, 92, 95, 255–9
St Kilda, Scotland, 84
St Lucia, 150
St Thomas, Virgin Islands, 111
Sambro Island, Nova Scotia, 96
Samuel Pepys watchkeeping system, 25
San Miguel, Azores, 134, 135
Santa Cruz de la Palma, Canary Islands, 105, 145
Santa Cruz de Tenerife, 103, 145
Santa Cruz, Madeira, 139
Satellite navigation (Satnav), 21, 55
Scaterie Island, Nova Scotia, 96
Scottish coast, arrival off, 84
Seacock, 34
Seasickness, 71
Sea Letter, US (ship's papers), 22
Security, 72
Self-steering, 59
Self-sufficiency, 3
Selvagem Islands, Madeira, 102
Sewage disposal, US, 94
Sextant, adjustment, 15, 16
  general, 12, 15, 17
  purchase, 15
  stowage, 13

Ship's papers, 22
Ship's stamp, 22
Ship's time, 33
Side error, sextant, 16
Sights, astro, 12
Sight reduction tables, 12, 268
Single side band, radio, 52
Skin fittings, 34
Skipper, qualities, etc., 50, 51
Slides, sail, 37
Slipping for anti-foul, 27
Somerset, Robert, 25
Spain, west coast, 101
Spares, 43
Spars for running sails, 59, 60
Special equipment, 59, 62
Spinnaker, 37
Standing rigging, 35, 36
Stars, 20, 21
Stern gland, 35
Stores list, 22
Storm jib, 37
Stornoway, Scotland, 84
Stowage, 43
Street, Donald, 147
Strongbacks for doors, etc., 29
Stugeron, 71
Sula Sgeir, Scotland, 84

Tallulah watchkeeping system, 26
Tank, water, 40
Tarifa, Spain, 102
Tenerife, Canary Islands, 145
Teredo worm, 32
Thermometers, 14, 80, 92
Thieves, 72
Tides and tidal streams, 31
  European coasts, 83, 85, 86
Tiller, emergency, 46
Time checks and signals, 14
Timing of, sights, 13
  voyages, when to go, 9, 10, 11
Tobago Cays, West Indies, 147, 148
Toggles, rigging, 36
Toolbox, 44
Tortola, Virgin Islands, 234–6
Tory Island, Ireland, 156
Track, sail, 37, 60, 62
Trade wind, 6, 103
  route, etc., 98
Traffic separation lanes, 85, 86, 125
Transmitters, radio, 52, 53
Traveller's cheques, 23, 149

Trysail, 37, 62
Turnbuckles, 27
Two-way radio, 53

US Coast Guard 5, 8, 77, 94
US ports, general 229
USA to Bermuda, 115
Ushant, France, 102

Vane self-steering, 59
Ventilation, 39
Verde, Cape Islands, xiii, 5, 98, 104
VHF, 53, 94
Vilamoura, Portugal, 98, 100, 196–8
Virgin Islands, 145, 231–6
    to USA, 112

Watches, time-keeping, etc., 13
Watchkeeping systems, 24–6
    trade wind passage, 106

Water, allowances, 40
    collection of, 40
    tanks, 40
Waterway guide, intracoastal, 93, 237, 238, 240, 271
Weather, 5
Weatherfax, weather radio facsimile, 54
Weaver (fish) 138
West Indies, 5, 147–50
    to Bermuda, 119
Westerlies, 5
Westward in high latitudes, 88
Whale hazard, 71
'Where to be and when', 9
Whistle, man overboard, 66
Winds and weather, 5, 91
Winds, general, 5
Wind-sail (scoop), 39
Work-book, navigator's, 14, 23
WWV time signal, 14